D1534711

# Probable Fictions
# ALICE MUNRO'S
## Narrative Acts

*Edited by*
LOUIS K. MACKENDRICK

*ECW PRESS*

CANADIAN CATALOGUING IN PUBLICATION DATA

Main entry under title:
Probable fictions: Alice Munro's narrative acts

ISBN 0-920802-72-9

1. Munro, Alice – 1931 – Criticism and interpretation.
I. MacKendrick, Louis King, 1941–

PS8576.U57Z8 1983   C813'.54   C83-098973-0   PR9199.3.M8Z8 1983

This book has been published with the help of a grant from the Canadian Federation for the Humanities, using funds provided by the Social Sciences and Humanities Research Council of Canada. Additional grants were made available from the Ontario Arts Council and The Canada Council.

*Probable Fictions* was typeset by Compeer and printed by Hignell.

The cover drawing, "Valerie," is by Martine Gingras; the cover was designed by The Dragon's Eye Press.

Published by ECW PRESS, Stong College, York University, Downsview, Ontario.

# CONTENTS

Abbreviations used in the following essays:

DHS    *Dance of the Happy Shades*

LGW    *Lives of Girls and Women*

SIB    *Something I've Been Meaning to Tell You*

WDY    *Who Do You Think You Are?*

# Probable Fictions:
## Alice Munro's Narrative Acts

### LOUIS K. MACKENDRICK

IN HIS INTRODUCTION to *The Canadian Novel: Here and Now*, John Moss has observed that the quality of "heightened realism"[1] in the writing of Alice Munro "invites analysis of content rather than of form or style," and that it is what he nominates her major themes which "attract critical inquiry far more than does her subtle genius with language and narrative technique."[2] It may be suggested that much critical inattention has until recently been the almost invariable fate of Canadian writing which follows the conventions of realism. The present collection of essays attempts to redress the oversight in part by examining some aspects of form, language, style, genre, and narrative technique in Munro's fiction. Considered as a whole, the thrust of these essays begins to reveal some creative ranges visible behind the familiar foothills of realism, crossed and often deeply patterned as they are with thematic trails that obscure some marvels in plain sight.

To some extent, "probable fictions" acknowledges the credibility and reality of Munro's stories, an exactitude of human feeling and situation which many readers have attested. From a more objective point of view, the term means to imply the literary gestures which she deploys with consistent mastery, the hallmarks of wholly fictional worlds which are realized through the most elegant channels of language, and which are not to be confused with actuality. These worlds are made, rather than rendered, made, not begotten, created rather than re-created. The literary dimensions of her fictions, not their approximations of life-as-it-is, are the collective focus of this collection. Munro's stories retain probability and authenticity, while they also delight the attentive reader with their fictionality: their realities are constructs of rare skill and masterful invention, a facsimile at

I

best. However "real" or "true to life" the residual impression of her writing remains, Munro's probable fictions firmly show that Art is necessarily grafted on from some other reality.

These essays are variously stylistic, generic, or structural in emphasis. Most of the contributors discuss the body of Munro's writing, before the publication of *The Moons of Jupiter*, clarifying consistencies as well as developments in her practice of fiction. A real distinction between her subjects and the manner of their presentation appears at times — as do some intriguing interrelations between story and form. Two "themes" may become apparent: the provocative elaboration and mystery beyond the seemingly "real" represented in some stories (often strongly signalled in linguistic texture), and the surprising freedoms taken with linear narrative. The notion of reflexivity, too, is a not unrelated consideration. Nuances of Munro's technique and specifics of her style — "Lovely tricks, honest tricks" ("Material," *SIB*, p. 43) — are frequently understood as the significant foreground of critical attention. The accent is upon the art of the creative acts and processes, immediate and exact and demonstrable, which sustain Munro's fictions.

The writer herself gives considerable attention to broadly technical aspects of her writing in the interview with which this collection begins. Under J.R. (Tim) Struthers' experienced inquiry, Munro — with characteristic honesty about her work — recognizes writers and writing important to her during her career, and identifies herself as a reader. She comments on her use of voice in fiction, on her "changing points" in detail, and discusses the ordering and connections of her books of stories. The particulars of this extensive and original conversation form a rich prolegomena for the essays which follow.

At the risk of simplifying any of these reasoned and often widely ranging essays, their individual concerns may be generally suggested. The first three are considerations of Munro's narrative perspective. Robert Thacker traces the growth of her distinctive technique of "retrospective narration" from her first published stories — particularly "Good-by, Myra," later revised as "Day of the Butterfly" — in persuasive detail. The ultimate evolution of a first-person narrator in dual person, observer and participant in present and past, is followed up to and through *Dance of the Happy Shades*. Gail Osachoff provides a study of Munro's first-person narratives as forms of the memoir, confession, or meditation, again reminding us of the centrality of voice in these fictions. These careful discriminations in perspective enforce the degrees of confidentiality and intimacy in such auto-biographical modes. John Orange discusses Munro's uses of the narrator and of time, and the changes in point of view between her first two books. He points out the note of dislocation struck in several of these essays; the complication of perspective complements the nature of the apprehension of reality in the later books, and the theme, as well, of the mysteries and illusions of experience.

The next two essays are essentially structural studies. Lorna Irvine presents the idea of change, and its analogues, as both theme and structural practice in Munro's stories, an "insistent illustration of flux" that often extends to female identity itself. This leads naturally to the idea of ambivalent, indeterminate ego boundaries, and Irvine also makes some convincing extrapolations about women's fiction. Catherine Ross writes of the ceremonial and even mythic substructures, the ritualized events, that are often beneath the realistic surfaces of Munro's writing; she sees patterns of order realized in higher or lower worlds beyond, and mediated by, such instances of the apparently ordinary.

Two succeeding essays concentrate on some ramifications of Munro's precision in language, expanding their topic centrifugally. Michael Taylor begins by looking at the texture of individual words in some stories and goes further into some notable illuminations, vivid significations, and elaborations of surfaces. He demonstrates the release of words from convention into a new recognition of reality, into associations of eccentricity and non-conformity and even into a distrust of language itself. Lorraine McMullen presents linguistic paradox in Munro as a principle that considerably extends its nominal function into a more comprehensive perspective. She moves from a consideration of incidental paradox deeper into Munro's eccentrics and irony, beyond conventional humour into the principle of human polarity.

The final two essays concentrate on dislocation and disarrangement as a significant practice in Munro's fiction. Gerald Noonan approaches her "structure of style" by proposing the increasing complexity of the purely factual level of the stories and the sometime subversion of linear narrative expectations. He shows how Munro's structures themselves sometimes epitomize

3

art's ultimate unreliability in reproducing real life which is, in her work, fundamentally paradoxical. Lawrence Mathews focuses on *Who Do You Think You Are?*, showing how in that collection art seems not to speak to life: the essential falsity of aesthetic patterns imposed on life is strongly put forward as an active principle in the resolutions of these narratives and their apparent story lines.

I wish to commend the critical imagination, amiability, and forbearance of the contributors to this collection. Some of these essays represent the clever elaboration of some intensely held but inchoate proposals of the editor; some are liberal, and serendipitous, developments and evolutions of these; some almost preternaturally, fortuitously, and independently answered to the general idea of Munro's technical foundations — a subject whose time has quite evidently come. I would be remiss in not acknowledging the encouragement of J. R. (Tim) Struthers, and I owe much to the guiding facetiae and sententiae of Jack David; he initially proposed the present volume and subsequently moderated the editor's communiqués — from the other country, of course, where he lives.

NOTES

[1] *The Canadian Novel: Here and Now: A Critical Anthology* (Toronto: NC, 1978), p. 8.
[2] Moss, p. 9.

# The Real Material:
## An Interview with Alice Munro

### J. R. (TIM) STRUTHERS

J.R. (TIM) STRUTHERS: My impression of *Dance of the Happy Shades* was formed, to a large extent I think, by the photograph that appears on the cover of the paperback edition.

ALICE MUNRO: That means you didn't read it when it came out in hard cover, eh? It was out for quite a while before the paperback appeared. Have you seen the hard cover?

TS: Yes, I have.

AM: Very geometric.

TS: I was wondering if you'd look at that photograph, now, and tell me what you see in it.

AM: Oh. I see an effective, rather arty, book-cover photograph. You mean, do I see it in any relation to my writing?

TS: Well, the images that are there, with the light and the shade and that solitary person holding...a cat?

AM: I thought she was knitting when I first saw it, but I think she is holding a cat. I think you're right. She's barefoot, isn't she. I suppose the idea is of loneliness, perhaps mild eccentricity, bit of an overgrown sunlit world outside. I'm very interested in photography, but photographs are too explicit to relate to stories as far as I can see. For a cover I don't think I would ever choose anything quite as explicit as a photograph or a painting, though I know some of those covers that have been chosen for my books have been very effective.

TS: Would you say that the photographic styles of Walker Evans, on the one hand, and Diane Arbus, on the other hand, suggest to you certain assumptions about life, about the nature of reality?

AM: Oh yes, I think they do. But that's the sort of question that I just can't say anything about because I haven't figured out what the assumptions are. I look at the pictures.

5

TS: Do you think one style is more fictional than the other?

AM: I suppose some people might say Arbus' work was more fictional. But that might simply be that, as far as I know, she deliberately chose material that was more obviously grotesque and extreme. My favourite Arbus photographs are probably not the ones that are best known. There's one I like *very*, very much of the sort of middle-class suburban backyard and two ordinary, youngish, suburban people stretched out on lawn chairs. Do you know that one?

TS: No, I don't know that one.

AM: They're not grotesques at all, and around the yard is just a very dark border of trees. It's just a very simple photograph, with a powerful effect that can't be analyzed, really. So I have more response to that than I have to the more famous pictures of the sad-looking twins and the grotesques.

Evans' photographs I don't really know as well. I think of the ones in *Let Us Now Praise Famous Men*, which wouldn't seem to me particularly fictional, if you mean "Is he imposing very much of his point of view on what he sees?" And it looks as if he isn't; that is, the fictionalizing or the imposing is very skilful and very artless-seeming. I have the feeling, there, that I'm just looking at pictures someone has taken of what these people are like, and that nobody is telling me anything in particular about them and their lives.

TS: Do you, sometimes, distrust fictionalizing?

AM: Yes. The idea I have in my own work is to.... Well, what I most admire is where the fictionalizing is as unobtrusive as possible, where there has been as strong an attempt, as honest an attempt, as one can make to get at what is really there. But I'm not so naïve as to suppose that even this, of course, is not trickery. One is always doing it.

TS: You mention *Let Us Now Praise Famous Men*. In the past you've discussed the affinity that you feel with Southern writing and the sense of identity that you have in regard to the relationship between rural Ontario — I suppose at an earlier time than this — and the South that writers like James Agee and others were writing about. What of Agee's work did you read? Did you read *Let Us Now Praise Famous Men* first?

AM: I read *A Death in the Family* first and was *enormously* moved. That probably comes close to what I mean by the art which doesn't appear artful, though it is not at *all* a naturalistic

6

book. The technique just seems to me transparent. It was one of the most powerful books in personal terms, in the way of thinking "I want to be able to write like that," that I ever read. I like particularly, oh, the long scenes where nothing much seems to be happening. Remember when she's waiting to get news about her husband's death, and she has the water on to boil, and there's stuff about the water. And then there's another thing about the curtains moving. Things like that seem to me wonderful. And the chapter I think I read to your group at Western about the men watering the lawns in the evening. And then the boy's walk with his father. There's a very...careful, I suppose, lack of pointing up in those scenes, lack of making something special happen, which is what I mean when I'm talking about not fictionalizing, dispensing as much as possible with this "Here I've got to make something happen," which is usually the point where you most manipulate reality instead of letting it dictate by itself what is going to happen in the writing. By reality I don't mean the reality I see. I mean the reality you feel. This is what he does in that book.

And then after that I read *Let Us Now Praise Famous Men*, which also has things in it which were as important to me as anything I've read. The description of a meal he eats with the tenant farmer's family. The texture of the biscuits and the home-made jam. The smells of everything. The description of the interior of the sharecropper's house is to me one of the most important things I've ever read.

TS: When did you read these?

AM: After I was an adult.

TS: Late '50s?

AM: Yeah. *A Death in the Family* was only published after he died, and I think he died in 1955. It would be shortly after that, I think. I had already been writing when I read them. They weren't the *early* things that influenced me but were certainly the strongest later influences.

TS: In 1949, you arrived here in London to study for two years at the University of Western Ontario. That was the same year that Eudora Welty's *The Golden Apples* was published. Nowadays, many books get tremendous media coverage. I'd be interested to know how, at the end of the '40s and the beginning of the '50s you learned about new books.

AM: I learned nothing at university about new books, though I

7

did stumble on some books. I worked in the library, and I stumbled on books, but they weren't new. I read all of Thomas Mann when I was here. He may have been taught in some courses, certainly not in anything I was taking. I didn't discover anything through my courses. So the most important work I did here was reading in the library. Then that just went on. After I was married and was having children, I was led from one title to another. It's very hard to even remember how.

Oh, I remember. My husband worked at Eaton's, and for some reason Eaton's thought it important to get a subscription to *The New York Times* because it had news on what New York department stores were advertising. He would be able to filch the book reviews and bring them home to me, and sometimes he'd bring four and five at a time, and I would just go crazy. That's where I first heard of Patrick White. Eudora Welty I think I discovered in some more roundabout way. Carson McCullers I just found in the library, and the title *The Ballad of the Sad Café* made me know I had to read it. And then from Carson McCullers I discovered probably a lot of other people.

Also, I was reading, then, two little pocketbook periodicals which you'd find on drugstore newsstands. This was before there were a lot of pocketbooks around. One was called *Discovery*, and the other was called *New World Writing*. And they would publish excerpts from novels-in-progress. That's where I discovered Flannery O'Connor. And they would publish short stories by people I hadn't heard of before, some of whom haven't become important names, some of whom have, but they were all very exciting to me. And of course as soon as I discovered them I started firing off manuscripts to them, none of which they accepted. I think *New World Writing* for the '50s was publishing some of the most interesting writing you could find anywhere, and it was just a gold mine for me.

TS:   Hugh Hood mentioned to me that you were both greatly taken with Walker Percy's novel *The Moviegoer*.

AM:   *Yes.* I *loved* that. Yes. I don't know how I discovered that. I don't know what it was about it. It wasn't technique there as it so much was in Agee. It was the subject that he was tackling in a head-on sort of way.

TS:   You mentioned a couple of digests that you read in the '50s. Something that interests me is your sense of the fashions of fiction-writing at certain periods.

AM: Well, when you've been writing for a while, you can't help but be aware of this. You may flatter yourself that you're not influenced by fashions, but I certainly am. That is, I don't adopt a fashion in order to get published somewhere or in order to win critical acclaim. It's just that there is a current way of saying things which seems effective, and so one begins to experiment with that way and to use it. And then later on, it seems possible to say things in another way. And these are actually fashions.

TS: Could you identify a number of the fashions — magazine fashions, perhaps — that...

AM: Oh, I wouldn't get that definite. I don't mean this thing ...you know the way you used to be advised to read about the market [laughter] and then write stories for the market. I don't mean at all that kind of thing because I was never interested in it. But, for instance, when I read over my stories of the '50s...and I've never been an innovator or an experimental writer. I'm not very clever that way. I'm never ahead of what's being done at the time. So in those stories in *Dance of the Happy Shades* there's an awful lot of meaningful final sentences. There's an awful lot of very, very important words in each last little paragraph. And that's something that I felt was necessary at the time for the stories to work. It must have been a prevalent fashion. That's the idea I got that it was necessary. But it wasn't something any market was demanding or any critic was demanding. It was the way I felt that you made a story most effective. And now, I would go back, if I could rewrite most of those stories, and I would chop out a lot of those words and final sentences. And I would just let each story stand without bothering to do the summing up, because that's really what it amounts to.

TS: I remember when you read "Postcard" at Western in the mid-'70s.

AM: I know I often chopped...

TS: You dropped the last paragraph when you read the story.

AM: And if I ever do a final edition of all those things, I'll drop the last paragraphs. God knows if I'm right or not. That is just the way I feel now. Isn't it true that Henry James went through and made a lot of his early stuff more difficult and obscure later on? And I believe that Frank O'Connor continued writing stories over and over even after they'd been published. I haven't seen the different versions, but the point I'm making is just that it's not even that you are necessarily improving the story. You are telling

9

it the way you see it now. And you have no idea what improvement means. You're just telling it the way it seems to work now. And I could go on and on doing my stuff over and over that way. I wouldn't do any of the stories in *Dance* quite the same. And that's why the rewriting after a while gets to be such a strange thing. I rewrite stories now, and my editors don't like them as well as earlier versions. And sometimes they may be right. There's a point after which you're not sure what you're doing with the rewrites.

TS:  Do the people at *The New Yorker* prefer a certain kind of story among your stories?

AM:  No. Not at all. In fact, this is one of the great myths everybody has about *The New Yorker*, that there is a *New Yorker* story. I've only sold them one story that I think qualifies as anything like a *New Yorker* story. And it wasn't written to be a *New Yorker* story. That's the form the material demanded, and it turned out that way.

TS:  Which was it?

AM:  It's called "Prue." It's a *short* story, and it's a neater story than I usually write. But this doesn't mean it was a formula story. I wanted to write it, and I wanted to write it that way. But I think people reading that might say, "Aha, a *New Yorker* story!" But with all the other stories, it has certainly been my experience.... A couple of times I've written a story and thought, "That reads like a *New Yorker* story," and both times they've turned it down.

TS:  Which stories were they?

AM:  "Working for a Living" and "Hard-Luck Stories." *They* don't want stories that read like *New Yorker* stories. That's the point. I think probably that's true about all this writing for markets business. I think that was bad advice even to give to the commercial writer because I think the market always wants something a little different from what it did last time.

TS:  If you had the opportunity to prepare an anthology of your favourite short stories, what would you choose?

AM:  Oh, oh, I'd *have* to think that over and write out a list.

TS:  Would you do that for me and we can include it later?

AM:  Yes. Maybe I would. Because that's a fairly important question and right now off the top of my head I'd be saying "Well, some of his, and some of hers," and so on, but I might miss some of the ones. I know one thing that would be in it: Tillie Olsen's

"Tell Me a Riddle." You see, there are people like that who have never become very well known writers, who have written just maybe a few marvellous stories. One tends not to think of them when you're on the spot with a question like this.

TS: Let's add the list later.

AM: OK.

TS: But that's an interesting point about how publishing a collection of stories or several collections of stories can bring a writer to the attention of a broader public, and that excellent individual stories, which don't get collected, can get lost.

AM: Or get collected in the O. Henry collection or something like that. But even there they're only read by people with a particular interest in the short story. Is Tillie Olsen a familiar name to you?

TS: Yes.

AM: Is she? So she is reaching now, though actually her body of work is very small.

TS: She also writes non-fiction, doesn't she?

AM: Yep.

TS: I think it's the non-fiction that I've heard about.

AM: Well, here's the list. I'd start off with "Tell Me a Riddle." Other stories I like a lot are "The Country Husband" and "The Day the Pig Fell into the Well" by John Cheever, "The Finder" by Elizabeth Spencer, "A Rose in the Heart" by Edna O'Brien, "Pigeon Feathers" by John Updike, "Flowering Judas" by Katherine Anne Porter, "And Here Tecumseh Fell" by Hannah Green, "The Springs of Affection" by Maeve Brennan, Nabokov's "Spring in Fialta" and "Mademoiselle O," and Welty's "A Worn Path." I find I really can't pick favourites.

I like nearly all the stories of Mary Lavin, Frank O'Connor, Mavis Gallant, Flannery O'Connor, Grace Paley, Elizabeth Cullinan, and William Maxwell, as well as nearly all the stories of the writers listed above. I like the stories of Clark Blaise, Beth Harvor, Audrey Thomas, John Metcalf, Hugh Hood, Shirley Faessler. I love the early stories of Reynolds Price. There are many, many good short stories being written at this time.

TS: You've said on different occasions that Eudora Welty is probably the writer whom you feel closest to.

AM: Course that changes. When I started talking about Agee, I thought he was just as important. However, Eudora Welty.... *The Golden Apples*, specifically, had a hypnotic effect on me. I kept going back to it and reading it over and over. But that, however, was as a reader. I didn't think of writing like this. It was just something that I had to immerse myself in, over and over again, as happens with a few books in one's life.

TS: At one time you mentioned to me that you felt that Welty's later work wasn't as successful.

AM: It is not for me. But I don't think this is a generally shared critical opinion. I have a feeling that this may happen. Usually, people who *loved Dance of the Happy Shades* don't like my later work as well. I think you may participate so intensely in that first created world of the writer that later on, if you see the same world being created, and it may be done as well, your participation in it can't be the same. I feel that way about *Losing Battles,* Eudora Welty's big novel — that it's probably done just as well, and she's doing perhaps the same thing, but to me it doesn't mean as much. I think these are very personal judgements and probably not good critical judgements.

TS: Is that a problem, that she's doing a similar thing?

AM: Well, I wouldn't say it was a problem. It seems to me such an enormous triumph that one can do it *once* so well. And she may be doing it over and over again just as well. You see, I disagree with this picture of writing that you progress from one book to the next and that you do different things, you open up new areas of your own consciousness and for your readers, and that it's supposed to be a kind of step-ladder. It seems to me just an enormously chancy thing every time. And if you are lucky once, you should thank God for it. Even when I think some of a writer's books are definitely inferior, I feel those books probably *have* to exist for the good book. Where I can think of a writer who has written half a dozen books and one book I like tremendously and I don't like the others, I think, that's fine, I want those other books to exist so the good book can exist. It may be that you do have to go back over and over again and mine the same material and look at it in different ways, or in the same way, and sometimes you get to it and sometimes you don't.

TS: Is the development that takes place, there, a matter of the deepening of your appreciation for the content or a development in technique?

AM: You mean the development in the writer that one would hope for? Well, the technique changes and you may get....But this is what I was saying before. I don't think you ever know that because your technique has changed it's actually more effective or more appropriate. You think it is, but this is something the writer can't judge. The technique probably has to change to keep you interested in working. Otherwise you would become mechanical, and you'd be doing the things you already knew how to do well. And this is something you do see happening. So that's the reason, I think, for changes in technique, not that there's necessarily a development but that it maybe assists you to fresh perception. What I think is important is the fresh perception, which, again, you may delude yourself that you are getting, but you wouldn't keep on working unless you thought you were getting it.

TS: When I think about the books that influenced Clark Blaise, his favourite books, they seem to come often from many parts of the world, from many different traditions of writing; and when I think of the books that influenced Hugh Hood, I think of a very strongly literary, almost academic, kind of tradition. In your case, almost all of these favourite books seem to belong to a more popular tradition, and particularly an *American* tradition. How would you account for the fact that it was these books that reached you?

AM: Well, I think maybe a difference that you're pinning down is that I'm mentioning books that reached me on a more than emotional, almost mystical level, a very important level, and I'm not mentioning books that influenced me intellectually, gave me ideas about writing, because they didn't. This doesn't mean that I didn't read....I think I have read fairly widely — not as widely as Hugh, of course. But I've read perhaps more widely than you'd think.

I don't *think* about writing at all. I *think* very little about writing. I have practically no coherent....I have no ideas or theories about it that I can ever put together. I mean I might on the spot, on a platform, put together something because that's what people expect you to do. But I don't, in private, operate that way *at all*.

So I would probably mention just a few books that had mattered in this very important way because I had not been thinking about being a writer and I hadn't been thinking about what kind of writer I would be or what kind of writing I would do. And I still don't. I tackle the next story. And it's always a bloody miracle if I can pull it off. But I never know how. I never think out how. I might think very specific things about the story.

I don't proceed from any thinking about writing, which may have something to do with the books that influenced me. But I don't even know what kind of books you're talking about. I think the sort of standard books that everybody reads when they're young were exciting to me. But I separate those from the books that influenced me, that made me feel that there was something in life to be got at that maybe I could get at through writing.

TS:  Someone commented that you are Canada's most Proustian writer.

AM:  Well, I was reading Proust all the time I was writing *Lives of Girls and Women* — [laughter] reading him mostly for encouragement because I used to worry about going into too much detail about things, then I would go and read several pages of Proust, and you know how long he will take to describe.... There's an enormous reassurance there that anything is worth one's attention and that everything is worth attention. And I love that about him.

TS:  Has your view of the process of selectivity, the amount of detail that you can use in a story or in a whole book, altered from book to book?

AM:  Well, I get ideas like that when I look over my earlier writing.

TS:  By earlier writing you mean...

AM:  The earlier published writing. When I have to do a reading, for instance, I will suddenly see how I would write this now. But, as I say, I don't *think* about writing, so I never *think* about selectivity of detail or anything like that when I'm doing something now. I just see when I have to read a passage from, say, *Lives of Girls and Women* that I would write this differently now.

TS:  You've referred to *Lives of Girls and Women* as "an episodic novel." Do you think that the sections of it work as stories as well as being parts of this episodic novel?

AM:  Well, for me to write them, they had to work fairly well as stories. I don't seem to be able to write otherwise. When I started writing *Lives* — I've probably told you this — I started writing it as a straight novel, and everything was working the way things work in the traditionally patterned novel except that it wasn't working for me, and I got about a third of the way into it.... And there again, I didn't *think* about what I was doing. I just went back and started tearing it apart and putting it into these little sections, because that's the way I wanted to tell the myself.

So it had to be done like that in order to be told to me in a that interested me most. I guess that's why I can't write a novel. lose interest. I don't know what it is about why I can't write a novel. God knows I still keep trying. But there always comes a point where everything seems to be getting really flat. You don't feel the tension. I can go on writing it so many words a day, and I pretty well know where it has to go, but I don't feel this pulling on the rope to get to the other side that I have to feel. And so I always do the same thing. I go back. I chop it up. I make it into these things that I can....People have suggested this is because I want to be able to manage everything and that I fear loss of control. And whenever anybody says anything that sounds at all negative, I always say yes, yes, this is my training, I have to agree [laughter] that I may indeed fear loss of control. But I don't think it's anything as simple as that.

TS: Is your sense of the form of a short story different from your sense of the form of a chapter?

AM: Yes, I suppose it is. But, as I say, I've never been able to really *master* writing chapters.

TS: In reading other people, are there other writers whom you might think of who...

AM: Well, usually when I read I don't *think* about how the person's doing it, too much. I probably haven't been able to figure out what the difference between a chapter and a short story is.

TS: Is a short story, however ironic it may be, more conclusive?

AM: Yes, I suppose it is. I suppose it is. And yet one reads.... You know there are all kinds of novels. There are all kinds of approaches to this, and I have certainly read novels in which the chapters could be very detached and conclusive.

Have you read *Sleepless Nights* by Elizabeth Hardwick? This is one of the books that has influenced or has been very *important* to me lately, that I read over and over. And one of the things she does is do chapters that....Well, some of them can be short stories. Some of them aren't. It's very loose, very loosely put together, and yet can be called a novel. So I just don't think there's any very, to me, satisfactory way of determining or defining.

TS: There are two other American writers about whom I'd

appreciate hearing your comments: Mary McCarthy and John Updike. I'm thinking of two books in particular: *The Company She Keeps* and *The Centaur*.

AM: Both those books I read a long time ago and *The Company She Keeps* even longer ago. I like *The Company She Keeps*. I like them both. I think when I read *The Company She Keeps* I was excited by the form, by the way in which she had handled that material.

TS: At what point would you have read that?

AM: Oh, I see what you're getting at. It was certainly [laughter] before *Lives of Girls and Women*. Yeah, and it may have influenced me that that kind of book was possible. Or am I thinking of *Memories of a Catholic Girlhood*, which also has some nice use of material in this chopped-up way?

*The Centaur* excited me greatly, mainly through something about the angle of vision. You see, I can't talk very well about writing. So in trying to say what excites me, I'm being imprecise. It was just something about the way the experience was looked at; though, there again, I didn't like the mythological parts. I didn't like that framework. I wanted to do without this. And that, I think, is my personal bias.

TS: Did you at some point form an impression of the tradition of the short story? Did you read Chekhov and Turgenev, for example?

AM: Sure, I read them, but without forming any [laughter] idea of a tradition. As I said, it finally began to get through to me that people wrote one kind of story in one decade and one in another. But I still wasn't seeing this, I don't think, from a respectable academic viewpoint. No, I would approach the Chekhov stories just as I would approach the Updike stories or the Welty stories, just to read stories for what they did to me. In reading all this I've been mostly a reader, very little a writer. Anything that gets through to me as a writer sort of gets through on a level that I'm not *thinking* too much about.

TS: It interests me that a younger writer at this time would probably not turn to Chekhov or Turgenev in the way that a writer of your generation and Hugh Hood's generation would turn to those writers.

AM: Well, you mean he wouldn't read them? Because it wasn't a matter of *turning* to, as for guidance or anything. It's just a matter of they were exciting reading that I came up against. Wouldn't that happen today? Would they not seem so exciting?

TS: I think younger writers would like them, but I don't know if they would find them as readily.

AM: Well, of course, I didn't find them through any university courses either. They'd be *more* apt now to find them through a university course, I think. But it might well be that they have writers to turn to, the writers of the '70s and '60s, who wouldn't be as important to me. Who do you think would be important for the younger writer today?

TS: I suspect that you were very important to Beth Harvor.

AM: Well, that's not too likely because we're not that far apart in age. I mean she'd be writing her stuff before she could get influenced by me, I think. We may have been influenced by some of the same people, though. That's possible.

TS: What sorts of influence do one's contemporaries have on you? People like John Metcalf, and Hugh Hood, and so on.

AM: Well, I'm not very often aware of influences, but I'm sure they're happening all the time. I think what it is is that you just pick up, oh, that's a good way of doing it. But with me I don't *think* about it, so I'm probably using things that other people have used first without even realizing I'm doing it. I think many of us do that. Or we pick up a tone that seems appropriate to a certain kind of material, and we try out that tone. Or perhaps we're given courage to go on using a kind of approach or material when otherwise we might worry that too much had been done of this.

A writer who uses what is obviously *personal* material — and I always say as *opposed* to straight autobiographical material — sometimes needs reassurance because there's bound to be a lot of criticism of doing this kind of writing. And if you see that other writers are going on and doing it well, and *you* are being excited as a reader by their work, then it cheers you up to do it yourself.

TS: In the '50s and '60s, were you aware of earlier Canadian writers, such as Stephen Leacock perhaps?

AM: Oh, I was aware of Stephen Leacock, but he wasn't important to me. But I remember reading Hugh MacLennan's *Two Solitudes* in high school and being very excited that this was a Canadian novel. I didn't discover Morley Callaghan at that time. It's odd that I didn't. There may have been a sort of eclipse of his work in the late ;40s. I'm not sure.

TS: He was doing a lot of radio work, then TV work, in the late '40s and the '50s.

AM: Aha. I suppose.

Oh! I know. Ethel Wilson. When I discovered Ethel Wilson, that was when I had just moved to Vancouver, and she was actually living in Vancouver, and I read "Lilly's Story" and "Tuesday and Wednesday."

TS: This was in the early 1950s.

AM: Early 1950s. It'd be about '52. And "Tuesday and Wednesday" is a story that I don't think is around much any more. It's like a short novel. I *was enormously* excited by her work because the style was such an enormous pleasure in itself. And I hadn't read, perhaps, a Canadian writer.... It was important to me that a Canadian writer was using so elegant a style. You know I don't mean style in the superficial sense, but that a point of view so complex and ironic was possible in Canadian literature.

TS: I'd also like to ask you about your childhood reading. You've written an essay entitled "Remember Roger Mortimer" about Dickens' *A Child's History of England*. I believe that one of your other early favourites was Montgomery's *Emily of New Moon*.

AM: Well, there are three Emily books — *Emily of New Moon*, *Emily Climbs*, and *Emily's Quest*—and they were all *very* important to me. I think *Emily of New Moon* is by *far* her best book. I'd like to write about it some day. It's about a child who wants to become a writer, and it even has a lot of examples of her attempts at writing, her poems and so on. It's close, in a lot of places, to being the book she should have written — in spite of having to follow certain conventions of what an entertaining novel should be and also certain conventions of all the things that you can't mention. In many ways there's great psychological truth in it, and it's also a very powerful book. And it's powerful in that she uses the grotesques, the near-grotesques, in not nearly so playful and popular-novelistic a way as she does in her other books.

I feel in that book she was getting very close to the book she should have written and never did write. There's a real sense of brooding and menace and even horror in that book which she just does not permit herself in a book like *Anne of Green Gables*. They're a bit like *Tom Sawyer* and *Huckleberry Finn*. You know how in *Tom Sawyer* everything is sort of popular-entertainment level, and in *Huckleberry Finn* we get down to some real stuff. Well, *Emily of New Moon* is a bit like that.

TS: Were there features of Montgomery's world, her fictional world, that connected in your mind with rural Ontario?

AM: Oh, very much so. The family structures, I think. I don't know if it would be a connection with rural Ontario. I suppose it would be. A connection with the sort of people she was dealing with, the old aunts and the grandmothers, the female power figures, which, as I say, she touches on really in *Emily of New Moon*, whereas she makes them palatable in her other books. A sense of injustice and strangeness in family life and of mystery in people that was familiar to me.

TS: Would you regard the form of books like *Chronicles of Avonlea* and *Further Chronicles of Avonlea* as similar to the kind of episodic form that you used in *Lives of Girls and Women*?

AM: Oh, I wouldn't have thought about that. Those books don't interest me much because I think they are very plainly pot-boilers. There may be just some similarity of structure. I'm not sure.

Montgomery's writing life I consider a tragedy because it's what happens to the real writer under certain circumstances where she feels her position as a minister's wife only allows her to get away with certain things where she couldn't overcome things in her own background and in herself, probably, and where she did write most successfully for the market.

TS: I'm especially interested in the form of short-story collections as a whole.

AM: That *is* an interesting question, and I've had editors with good ideas about this. I'm not very clear on how to do it myself. It's not something I have a real feel for, and I always want someone to help me. But I think the organization probably is very important, and here *I* need somebody who sees relationships between the stories which I might not be able to see.

TS: I'm interested in the differences between the order in which a group of stories was composed and the order in which they appear in the book. Could you look at the list of contents from *Dance of the Happy Shades* and tell me the order in which they were written?

AM: OK. Oh, well, as near as I can remember, the earliest story in this book is "The Time of Death," then "Day of the Butterfly." The next is "Thanks for the Ride." The next are probably "An Ounce of Cure" and "The Shining Houses" and, a bit later, "Sunday Afternoon." And then we skip to "A Trip to the Coast" and "The Peace of Utrecht," which were written sort of simultaneously but are very different stories.

TS: "Skip" in what sense?

AM: Well, you see, there were periods in here where I wrote hardly anything, due to things in my life, and writing blocks, and so on. These earlier stories — "The Shining Houses," "Thanks for the Ride," "Day of the Butterfly," and "A Trip to the Coast" — were exercise stories. "An Ounce of Cure" was not quite in that category, because it was a fun story.

The later stories are "A Trip to the Coast," "The Peace of Utrecht," and "Dance of the Happy Shades," which I wrote in the summer of '59. "The Peace of Utrecht" and "Dance of the Happy Shades" felt like the first real stories I had ever written. Then I wrote stories I consider "all real" [laughter]. The next one was probably "The Office." And then "Boys and Girls" and "Red Dress — 1946," which were written about the same time. And then the last stories for the book all were written the same winter.

TS: The last stories to be written were...?

AM: "Postcard," "Walker Brothers Cowboy," and "Images."

I think there is a progression in those stories, but they're not arranged that way. I think we did things like trying to not get all the stories that have a first-person narrator lumped together and things like that.

TS: So you strove...

AM: For variety. I think that my editor and I arranged those so that you wouldn't be getting a big lump of stories with this "I" person who obviously wasn't always the same person, so that the reader wouldn't be led to expect that this was a kind of segmented novel or something. So we had to do things like that.

TS: Over how many years, then, were the stories in *Dance of the Happy Shades* composed? Fifteen?

AM: "Day of the Butterfly" was written in 1953, and the last ones would have been written in 1967. So fourteen years.

TS: Are there any stories in that book which you think of as belonging, more properly, in the group with your earlier, uncollected stories?

AM: There's a story in here I don't like, called "A Trip to the Coast." I'd get rid of that. I might get rid of "The Shining Houses." I'm not *ashamed* of any of those stories. I just lump them in with earlier stories. "Thanks for the Ride" would be in that bunch too.

TS: I wasn't being pejorative.

AM: No, I know.

TS:  I just was interested in your sense of how your stories fall into groups and what you...

AM:  But I do make this distinction between when I started to write and.... "The Peace of Utrecht" was the story where I first tackled personal material. It was the first story I absolutely had to write and wasn't writing to see if I could write that kind of a story. I think every young writer starts out this way, where at first the stories are exercises. They're necessary exercises, and I don't mean they aren't felt and imagined as well as you can do them. But when a story takes over the way that one did with me, then you see, then *I* saw that writing was about something else altogether than I had suspected it was, that it was going to be less in my control and more inescapable than I had thought. Up until that time, it was probably "I will be a writer" [laughter]; and after that, "Some things have to be written by me."

TS:  You have a sense, then, of how, at certain points in your career, you began to write stories that were *different* kinds of stories.

AM:  Yes. Yes. Yes. There were definite changing points.

TS:  What points come to mind? What stories come to mind as breakthrough stories for you?

AM:  "Royal Beatings" was a *big* breakthrough story, a kind of story that I didn't intend to write at all. That led on to most of the stories in *Who Do You Think You Are?*.

TS:  Were there any of the stories in *Who Do You Think You Are?* that were composed before "Royal Beatings"?

AM:  Yes. Probably the real breakthrough came before with the first story that I wrote in that book, the second one in the book, "Privilege," which is about the school. But that began, oh, how should I say, on a not very deep fictional level, just with the desire, an almost documentary desire, and I thought I'd never.... It's the most personal story. I mean, it's a story about a school I actually went to and things that happened there. I just wanted to get that down. This is an impulse you sometimes have as a writer. There's a deeper level that you're not going to when you do that kind of writing, which doesn't mean it isn't valid. And then, when I went to "Royal Beatings," it opened up other areas. And the next thing that I wrote for that book was "The Beggar Maid," which was another sort of important turning-point story.

The stories in *Something I've Been Meaning to Tell You* are nearly all holding-pattern stories, except for the last story in the book, which is "The Ottawa Valley," and that was a big turning-point story.

TS: What do you mean by "holding-pattern"?

AM: Well, I mean I was going on doing the same things. I wasn't conscious of this, you know. You never are. When I say "exercise stories," it sounds like I'm really putting these stories down and I'm not. I think part of your writing career is spent doing exercise stories. But I think that's what most of them were. I was just waiting to get through to another level of what I wanted to do. Maybe I was making a *conscious* effort to get away from the personal material of *Lives of Girls and Women. Not* to do any more lives of girls and women; though every once in a while I'd fall off the wagon, and I would do a lives of girls and women type story. "Winter Wind," in that book, is that type of story, I think.

TS: What sort of story do you consider "How I Met My Husband" to be? Is it rather "a fun story" as you've termed "An Ounce of Cure" in *Dance of the Happy Shades?*

AM: It's a rather light story boiled down from a heavy, uncompleted novel.

TS: Were all of these stories written after *Lives of Girls and Women?*

AM: Yes. And they were an attempt, probably a mistaken attempt, to see "Oh, I can do this," and "I can do that," and "I can write this kind of story." Not quite as blatantly as that. But sort of "Let's see if I can use this material and make a story out of it," "Let's see what I can do with this idea." And I still do that. I'm writing a story that's kind of like that now. But you do see, looking back, that some stories were much more important than others. And this may not even mean that they're the more successful stories. They're just the ones that I *had* to write, while the other stories are stories I wrote because I'm a writer and this is what I go on doing.

TS: You mentioned that in shaping *Dance of the Happy Shades* you were striving for variety. Juxtaposition, almost.

AM: Yeah. I don't know if that's a good idea. There may be better ways to organize a book of short stories. The idea when we got this together was so the reader would sort of come up for air and then go into a new story.

TS: Could you have a look at the list of contents and just mention some of the points that jump out at you as being sharp juxtapositions or connections or...?

22

AM: Well, yes. "Walker Brothers Cowboy" is one of those — personal material cast in the form of a recollection of childhood. "The Shining Houses" is a back off, impersonal, I think it's a third-person kind of story. "Images" goes back very much to the same material as "Walker Brothers Cowboy." "Thanks for the Ride" then goes to a young *male* narrator, which I hardly ever do, and there again it's sort of a backing off. "The Office" — personal material — that's about my most autobiographical story, and yet it isn't on a very deep level. Then "An Ounce of Cure." "The Time of Death" was one of those "exercise stories." That really, I think, is a kind of imitation Southern story, if you want my real opinion. It's when I was writing like the people I admired, which I think is not a bad thing to do at a certain stage. After all, I wrote that when I was only about twenty-two. "Day of the Butterfly." I don't know about that. That's *such* an early story. Then "Boys and Girls," another of what I think of as "the real material" stories. "Postcard" is a story I like quite a lot, but it takes a big jump. It's one of those first-person-narrator stories where I've assumed a *persona* a long way from myself. I don't very often do that, so in a way it was kind of an interesting exercise, an interesting thing to do. "Red Dress — 1946." Again, adolescent recollection stuff. "Sunday Afternoon" is rather that way too. "A Trip to the Coast." That's the other imitation story. That's a story I really don't like.

TS: Imitation of...?

AM: Oh, of a whole genre. It wasn't a conscious imitation. But the tone of it is not *felt*. The tone of it is assumed. It's a trick. When I read it, it seems to me a trick story.

TS: Like a certain kind of magazine fiction?

AM: No, no. No, no, nothing like that. It's just like those paintings that are said to be "in the school of," "after the manner of." That's the kind of story it is. It's "after the manner of." And yet you can't even quite say whose manner, though the Southern bunch would be what you'd suspect. And I don't mean that I did it *that* consciously. But that's actually what happened.

And then "The Peace of Utrecht," which was probably, to me, the most important story in the book. "Dance of the Happy Shades" is also a fairly important story to me but backs off quite a bit. So it's just that I haven't lumped all of what I think of as "the real stuff," "the real material," together in one lump and put the other stories together. But I don't even know what to call the other stories.

TS:   You mentioned the use of the third person as a kind of backing off, or in connection with backing off.

AM:   Well, it is in the stories where it's used here, I think.

TS:   I was going to suggest that perhaps in your later work you seem to me to have discovered that through the use of the third person you can sometimes get closer.

AM:   Of course you can. Of course you can, sometimes. It just depends. And you get a *feel* for what you should do. But a lot of my stuff I write in both first and third person. Or I start off one way, and then I do it the other way. And sometimes I have to do it in both to get the final. I'm doing that right now. Rewriting in third person something I've written in first person because there were things I couldn't know until I wrote it in first person.

TS:   Writing in third person probably allows you to move around more in time. Is that important to you?

AM:   It allows you to move around a bit more, and it allows you to say things about other characters which if you say in first person you have to then somehow hedge or account for in ways that you don't if you're using third person. I don't know. You seem to somehow have to be a little more careful about the impression your first-person narrator is making.

There's a story of mine called "Memorial" in *Something I've Been Meaning to Tell You* which *is* a story that was very important to me. I shouldn't say those stories were all just.... They were all important, some more than others. But that story was important, and there's a dangerous weakness in it. There's a way in which it didn't work. And it's something about the narrator. I don't think that story *is* done in first person. But maybe it is. No, I think it's done in third person. But there's a kind of smugness about the point of view of the narrator which I did not sufficiently deal with. I thought I did. I was aware of this as a problem. But it isn't well enough dealt with. And this is one of the problems you get either when you use a first-person narrator or a third-person narrator who is very close to your own *persona*.

TS:   I'd like to return to that a little later on, in relation to your revisions to *Who Do You Think You Are?*; but, for the moment, I'd like to ask you, very briefly, about the order in which the stories in, or sections of, *Lives of Girls and Women* were composed.

AM:   OK. I remember that quite clearly. "Princess Ida" was the first. It was going to be a short story. Then I saw it was going to

24

work into a novel, and then I went on and on writing w
thought was a novel. Then I saw that wasn't working. So I
back and picked out of that novel "Princess Ida" in its or
form — I had changed it to make it into the novel — and I picked
out "Age of Faith," "Changes and Ceremonies," and "Lives of
Girls and Women." Then, having written all those separate
sections, I wrote "Baptizing." Then I went back and wrote the
first two sections, the one about Uncle Benny, "The Flats Road"
— which is called "The Flat Roads" in the paperback [laughter]
— and "Heirs of the Living Body." And then I wrote the
"Epilogue: The Photographer," which gave me *all* kinds of
trouble. I was about half as long again writing that as writing
the whole book. And I then plucked it out and decided to publish the book without it. Then — I'm terrible for last-minute
emergency calls to the publisher's — then I rewrote it and put it
in.

TS·   What did you do in rewriting it? What did you strive for?

AM:   God, I forget. My whole problem about it was that if this
was sort of a chronological, growing-up, traditional type of
novel, it had no place in the novel, it didn't fit in. It didn't fit in
either chronologically or...well, I could sort of tamper with it so
it was not too bad that way, but it sort of didn't fit in psychologi-
cally. Up until now this was not the story of the artist as a young
girl. It was just the story of a young girl. And this introduced a
whole new element, which I felt hadn't been sufficiently prepared
for. And yet, I found eventually that the book didn't mean
anything to me without it.

TS:   Did you make any revisions in the earlier stories so that the
artistic side of things was enhanced?

AM:   No. I didn't have time at that point. The book was in
galleys when I was doing all this stuff [laughter]. And I don't
think I would have anyway. I was too far beyond them. I just had
to feel that somehow this would....Sometimes I think that an
awkwardness has to be put up with for certain advantages it may
gain. I felt that the last section was an awkwardness, but it had to
be there.

TS:   In my reading of *Lives of Girls and Women*, I feel that the
emphasis is on a portrait of the girl *as a young artist*, rather than
a portrait of the artist *as a young girl*.

AM:   You mean there's a difference? Yes, I suppose there is. I
suppose that's what I mean.

TS:   Would you agree with that view?

AM:   Yes. That may then mean that the last section didn't need to be there after all. However, I want it there. I want it there, so it's going to be there.

TS:   On the other hand, it's because of the weight of that last section that I would reach that sort of reading of the book.

AM:   You mean that you *then* see something in the other sections that you might not have seen otherwise? Is that possible?

TS:   Well, I didn't see the other version. I just see the whole thing, as it now is, in the final version.

AM:   Well, you know it's just always so tricky to write about writers. I wrote, in that section, about the idea of the novel that she had in her head.

TS:   Did you choose the order of the stories in *Something I've Been Meaning to Tell You?*

AM:   Oh, I think so. I think we did maybe the same thing there, consciously trying to separate the "I," the first person, stories.

TS:   Was this an arrangement that you reached with...?

AM:   With my editor.

TS:   Was this the same editor as you'd had for *Dance of the Happy Shades?*

AM:   Yes.

TS:   Who was that?

AM:   Audrey Coffin. She worked for McGraw-Hill Ryerson.

TS:   How do you spell her last name?

AM:   Coffin. C-o-f-f-i-n.

TS:   Could you tell me the order in which the stories in *Something I've Been Meaning to Tell You* were composed, where it matters, and any salient connections or disruptions that you notice from one story to the next?

AM:   Well, "Material," which is a story I like — I'm always putting down this book, and then I find things in it that I do like — "Material" was the first story that I wrote for this book, or that was in this book. And then "Memorial" was the next. And they were both very interesting stories to me. They were both things, material, that I very much wanted to work with. Then I think probably the next one was "Something I've Been Meaning to Tell You," which isn't a very successful story, I don't think. That's a novel I wanted to write and was planning to write for years. The thing is, it's *very* much like the story I'm writing at the moment, where I'm trying to tell an awful lot of things. To me it's a discovery story, trying to find out how to *do* it, how to *tell* this kind of story.

TS: Have you given a name to this new story that you're writing?

AM: The working title is "The Ferguson Girls Must Never Marry."

TS: OK. How many pages in manuscript did you actually write of the title story of *Something I've Been Meaning to Tell You*?

AM: Oh, maybe fifty.

TS: And how far did you get in the telling of the story?

AM: Oh, I'd go over and over the same parts. I can't remember that. I really can't. But it wasn't working at all.

Then I wrote, rather quickly, some stories I'd been working with earlier. "The Spanish Lady," "Marrakesh," "The Found Boat," and "Forgiveness in Families" were all ideas I'd had for years and years.

TS: From the '6os?

AM: Yeah. And beyond that, some of them.

Then I wrote a story in here that I don't think works at all. It's a very embarrassing story, I think, called "Executioners," where, again, I was trying to find out how to *do* a certain kind of thing, and it didn't quite do it. And the story "Walking on Water," which, also, I'm not too happy with. I shouldn't probably have called these "holding-patterns" because actually they were experiments. I was trying very hard to learn things about writing, here, not in this intellectual way but by *doing* things. And "Walking on Water" was like that.

Then, right at the end, I wrote "Winter Wind" and "The Ottawa Valley." I think "The Ottawa Valley" is the most successful story in the book, though I put "Material" next to that. I like "The Ottawa Valley." And "Winter Wind" isn't too bad either. They were kind of, in a way, a going back to earlier material, though. They're autobiographical stories, where most of the stories in this book are not at all so.

I was trying out a lot of technical things in here, I suppose, without actually admitting that that was what I was doing. Now, when I look at the titles, I realize that.

TS: What about the connections or disruptions between stories in the order that they're presented here?

AM: Oh, I think we were trying here just to do a very simple thing of alternating the first-person stories rather than thinking

27

too much about the material, though I think I did want, they always want, and I want, what I feel is a strong story as the last story in the book. And my editor and some other people have liked "Something I've Been Meaning to Tell You" very much. So probably that was perceived as a strong story. My opinions of my stories, you know, are very personal and peculiar and not to be taken all that seriously.

TS:   I think *Something I've Been Meaning to Tell You* establishes a relatively new and more mysterious tone for your work.

AM:   Well, I hope it does. I hope it does something. Because I was certainly trying hard with this book. So scratch that holding-patterns business. Holding-patterns are when you're just staying in place and not trying. I *was* trying something very new, but I have since.... The truth is, one becomes very dissatisfied with everything, you know, with almost everything.

TS:   And sometimes you build into your stories that feeling of dissatisfaction with art.

AM:   Oh yeah. It's in "The Ottawa Valley," I believe. The last paragraph in this book is all about dissatisfaction with art. And I wrote a story called "Home," which has never been collected, which is sort of a final statement. It's an almost "I'm not going to write any more of this junk" kind of statement [laughter]. Well, no. It's an "I can't do it" or, even beyond that, "Nobody can do it" kind of statement. And every once in a while I write a story like this because it's what I feel. It's like the... you know all these people that are always making final concert tours and saying good-bye [laughter]. Then they're back with the next [laughter]. But I do quite *genuinely* feel that. I feel it right now. I sometimes feel just *tormented* by the inadequacy and impossibility and feel that maybe this is quite a mistaken way in which to spend one's life.

TS:   Not for me when I've got those books in front of me.

AM:   No, and.... Every once in a while I read that I'm a modest writer and a modest person. Not at all. This is not false modesty. It's the honest judgement that one has from time to time.

  In "The Ottawa Valley," I'm looking at all this material, I'm looking at real lives, and then I not only have to look at the inadequacy of the way I represent them but my right to represent them at all. And I think any writer who deals with personal material comes up against this.

TS:   Do you think that the titles of the title stories, like "Dance of the Happy Shades" or "Something I've Been Meaning to Tell You," have different connotations when they're used as the titles of entire books than when they're used as the titles of specific stories?

AM: Oh, yes, they probably do. I suppose there's always a great difficulty in the title for a volume of short stories. I think sometimes maybe they should have a different title altogether from the title of any of the stories. Still, some of my titles have been right for the books, I think. In fact, I think they all are.

TS: Didn't you originally plan to give *Lives of Girls and Women* the title *Real Life?*

AM: [laughter] Yes. And then a novel of that title came out in the spring list in the United States, so I couldn't do it. And yet I so much prefer, now, the final choice.

TS: And weren't you also thinking of giving *Who Do You Think You Are?* the title *True Lies?*

AM: No. That was never my choice. That was a publisher's suggestion. At least I don't *think* it was my choice. Sometimes I can't remember exactly what happened. I know that was considered, but I don't think it was very seriously considered by me.

One of the titles I have had chosen for a book, an idea I've had for a long time, is...the title was going to be *Learning Russian.* And I don't think any publisher would let me get away with that, because you can imagine where it would end up. And then the angry people who wouldn't learn Russian from reading it [laughter].

TS: Why was *Who Do You Think You Are?* given the title *The Beggar Maid* by your American publisher? Did you approve of that?

AM: They felt the colloquial put-down was not familiar to Americans. I had to accept that, though I think it probably is in certain parts of the U.S. anyway.

TS: I'd like to talk with you about the revision of *Who Do You Think You Are?.*

AM: Oh, it's the most confused revision in history. I don't know how I can do. It's very confused for me to think about how it happened. Well, anyway....

TS: The first version of the book contained a group of stories about Rose and a group of stories about Janet. Three of the Janet stories ("Connection," "The Stone in the Field," and "The Moons of Jupiter") were dropped from the second version; and the Janet stories that were retained were rewritten as third-person stories about Rose instead of first-person stories about Janet. One of the Janet stories that was retained ("Who Do You Think You Are?") was rewritten substantially. "Simon's Luck" was added for the first time.

AM: Well, there's really a rather simple reason for this. I wanted to do a group of stories all about Rose, and we didn't have enough. I hadn't yet written enough for a book. I had contracts with two publishers, my American and Canadian. The American publisher was willing to wait until I *did* write enough stories. My Canadian publisher felt that we had to get a book on the market for the fall season. This was probably a very sound business judgement. It meant that we were waiting a year for the American book, but the Canadian book had to come out right away. There weren't enough Rose stories. I had already got a bunch of these other Janet stories.

The thing is, those stories were all originally written with heroines of different names and appeared with different names in magazines. This isn't as important as it sounds, the name of the heroine. I often write about the same heroine and give her a different name and a different occupation and a slightly different background because of something I want to do in the story. But her psychological make-up is not different. And that's actually what I had done with all these stories.

So there were some of the Janet stories in which I recognized that I was using.... In fact, I *had* originally used a Rose heroine. The point is that we couldn't do a book with two-thirds of the stories about one heroine and one-third about another. So I very foolishly decided to do half and half, meaning that I had to change Rose into Janet for half of the book. Do you see what I mean?

TS: You changed Rose into Janet?

AM: Yeah. What we originally had was a two-thirds/one-third division, which wasn't going to work. Do you see?

TS: So which stories did you change from Rose to Janet stories?

AM: Oh, I forget [laughter].

TS: "Mischief"?

AM: I think I did change "Mischief." I think I changed "Providence." I'm not sure. It doesn't matter. The psychological truth was all there.

TS: And then you changed them back to Rose stories?

AM: Yeah. That's what I did. And this is all the exigencies of the publishing situation. Then what happened was that we had the book set up with half Janet and half Rose, and I was not happy with it at all. But we had a book for the fall list that way, and we'd gone too far to sort of go back. The book was in galleys. This is not a question of me being persuaded against my will. It's just a question of me being too stupid to see, or being not clear about what I would do next.

And then, suddenly, in September, with the book already in galleys, I saw that I could do two new Rose stories. "Who Do You Think You Are?" and "Simon's Luck" just came like that. And then I had enough for a book of Rose stories. So then we could jettison the stories that obviously weren't about Rose at all. And the stories that I had changed from Rose into Janet could be changed back to Rose — "Mischief" being one of them, "Providence" being another, and probably "The Beggar Maid." I'm not sure. It's terrible that I can't remember any better.

TS: No. I think "The Beggar Maid" was a Rose story.

AM: It was in the Rose bunch, eh? OK. There was some change.

I had to do an extensive rewrite on "Simon's Luck" right at the end to get it into the book. It was first a long three-part story with the same title. The three segments were called "Emily," "Sheila," and "Angela" — three women in Simon's life. "Emily" was the only segment published, and that became a Rose story for the book.

And then "Who Do You Think You Are?", which I believe I'd written as an entirely separate story, with different....I don't think it was a Janet story. I had a story with that title, formerly.

Anyway, all of a sudden I saw how all these would go together as Rose stories. The book was already in galleys. So I got them to pull it out at my expense, which was over $2,000. I then rewrote it. I wrote "Who Do You Think You Are?" in a weekend and rewrote everything else in a week. So that with the printers working overtime, which I paid for, they could get the book out into the fall season. A book cannot go on the Canadian market later than about mid-November, or its chances for Christmas sales are just dead. So we had to get it out by that time. All of which things, having been a bookseller, I understand.

You see it was mostly a....It wasn't an artistic decision as much....Well, it was. In the end it was *my* decision for what the book had to be. But the decisions before that were made from a

31

publishing point of view, with me going along with them because I couldn't, at that time, see how I could alter things. I couldn't see if I would ever get enough stories to make a Rose book. In this I was helped by the patience of my American publisher who seemed, with good reason, less commercially nervous than a Canadian publisher, and who was willing to wait to see what I could do.

TS: In the book's final form, sometimes the technique that you use is to have the narrator say that Rose thought such-and-such. At other times the narrator seems to have slipped directly into Rose's mind and, without saying "Rose thought," re-creates Rose's thoughts in a language that sounds just like Rose's at that appropriate time in her life. When this happens, the reader gets the impression that Rose herself is, in fact, the narrator, an impression that is reinforced by the fact that we know from the opening story that Rose has reached approximately age forty and is herself thinking about her past. But at other times the narrator adopts a superior, ironic tone towards Rose, even, I think, a superior tone towards Rose at age thirty-nine, not just Rose at age ten or twenty-two.

Is there some uncertainty in the presentation of narrative point of view in *Who Do You Think You Are?*? Is Janet still there, and can Janet *be* Rose?

AM: No, I don't think so. No, I don't think so. I don't think that has anything to do with it. There may *well* be an uncertainty, a problem that I had, but I don't think that hasty rewrite is the reason. I think there were just times when I felt that the story had to work that way, and I really can't tell you why.

TS: I'd like to move on to some, call them biographical, more general, paraliterary questions.

Have your sense of identity and your attitude towards the twenty years that you spent in Vancouver and Victoria changed now that you have been back in Ontario for several years?

AM: Goodness. I'm about to say "What was the question?" [laughter] Has my sense of who I am...

TS: Have your sense of identity and your sense of that time in Vancouver and Victoria changed after having resided here in Ontario now for several years?

AM: Yes, I see what you mean. Well, it's probably coming out in that I now have a very strong sense of wanting to write fiction about that time and seeing it in that distant, set-off, special way that I used to see Ontario when I lived in Vancouver and Victoria.

TS:  That time *and* that place?

AM:  This is the way I now see Vancouver and Victoria and the '50s and the '60s, which were my years there. They're the material that particularly interests me now.

TS:  At one reading, when you read "Spelling" at Western, in response to a question about regionalism in your writing, from, I think, a Wingham resident...

AM:  There's one in every crowd [laughter].

TS:  ...you said that you *only* thought of the Wingham material or regional material as "furniture" in your stories.

AM:  Yeah. Well, by that I mean I think of houses and streets and rooms and faces as what I put into the stories. But I never think I'm writing a story about Wingham or I'm writing a story about a Southwestern Ontario small town. Ever. I just use that stuff because it is familiar to me. It's what I know about.

TS:  And yet that level is one of the strongest levels to which your readers could respond.

AM:  Yes. The response is often a rather strange one, and I think sometimes they feel cheated by not having the church on the right street [laughter]. Then you do, constantly, get the thing about "But I grew up there, and life wasn't this bad." You know, a sort of more upbeat interpretation is called for.

I think this is a total confusion about what fiction is. They want a picture of the town, and they want a picture that they find agreeable, and I'm not concerned with any kind of comprehensive picture.

TS:  Has living in rural Ontario, again, reaffirmed any of your values?

AM:  When I first went back to Clinton, I remembered a lot of things that I had forgotten; and that's why I wrote some of the earlier material in *Who Do You Think You Are?*. It seemed to me that I wasn't finished with this. But I wasn't using the furniture. I *was* conscious of attitudes that I wanted to do more with, and the shape of people's lives, the shape of their stories, the whole business of how life is made into a story by the people who live it, and then the whole town sort of makes its own story.

TS:  Is your attitude, now, towards rural Ontario something like that double vision that we get of small-town Ontario in Stephen Leacock's *Sunshine Sketches of a Little Town*?

33

AM: What do you mean by "that double vision"?

TS: Partly sympathetic, partly ironic.

AM: I suppose it is. I don't think that it appears sympathetic to the people who live there. I would think of it as sympathetic. But I never worry at all about whether I'm being sympathetic.

TS: I've always wanted to ask you if that question in "Walker Brothers Cowboy," "Is this the way to Sunshine?", was an allusion to *Sunshine Sketches of a Little Town*.

AM: No. There's a village that has disappeared called Sunshine in Huron County. There are a lot of villages that are gone, you know. This is very interesting to go around and look at where they were. There's one called Prosperity on the most desolate-looking road. And then there was Sunshine and others like that.

TS: Had Sunshine disappeared at the time that the story was set?

AM: Well, it actually had but I didn't mean it. I just always liked the name, and it was a name that was important in my family because our kitchen chairs were made in the Sunshine chair factory [laughter]. So I wasn't using it for any particular symbolic reason.

TS: Has your attitude towards religion or sacred ritual developed or changed in recent years?

AM: You know, it's funny. I was just thinking about that this morning, because the story I'm working on now turns entirely on a point of religious ritual. And this is the first time I've *ever* written a story in which religion, the *observance* of religion and people's feelings about it, was the central thing. So obviously I've become more interested. But you see I never know what I think until I write.

TS: Del, in *Lives of Girls and Women*,...

AM: Yeah. There's a section in that on childish religious experience.

TS: ... tries various kinds of religion but moves on from them — in her mature years, as she looks back in the epilogue — and seems at that point to have accepted a religion of art.

AM: Yes. Well, that's the usual thing for young people, isn't it.

TS: For young people? To accept a religion of art?

AM: I would think so. Yeah.

TS: What about middle-aged people?

AM: Well, middle-aged people lose their faith in art.

TS: And find it again in religion?

AM: God knows [laughter].

TS:   Maybe He does [laughter].

I'd like to quote a short passage from John Metcalf's sto
"The Years in Exile" and get your reaction to this. The narrator
says,

> I have always disliked Wordsworth. Once, I must
> admit, I thought I disliked him for his bathos, his lugu-
> brious tone. But now I know that it is because he could
> not do justice to the truth; no philosophical cast of mind
> can do justice to particularity.
>
> I am uncomfortable with abstraction, his *or* mine.

AM:   Well, nobody could say it better. You must have known I
agree with that.

TS:   And yet, to offer one of those contradicting images that
you're fond of, I understand from Hugh Hood that you took
great pleasure in listening to passages from Wordsworth's *The
Prelude* when Hugh read them to you, that you were extremely
moved by what he read.

AM:   Well, I don't agree with John's opinion of Wordsworth, you
see, but I agree with everything else he says about the "philosophical cast of mind" and "particularity." I wouldn't have said
that about Wordsworth. I mean he certainly can get into it. But I
don't think he always does that.

TS:   Have you read Wordsworth over the years? Do you turn to
him occasionally?

AM:   No. I've read about as much as the average reading person
has read.

TS:   Sometimes I think of Hugh Hood as playing Coleridge to
your Wordsworth.

AM:   [laughter] To *my* Wordsworth? What do you mean?

TS:   [laughter] Well, I don't, obviously, mean the Wordsworth
that John Metcalf means.

AM:   I don't go on and on. I don't plan to live that long, either
[laughter].

TS:   I mean it in the way that Coleridge describes his intentions
versus Wordsworth's intentions, in that Coleridge comes from a
philosophical base...

AM:   Yes.

TS:   ... or tries to naturalize the supernatural, whereas ...

AM:   Well, I would have said Wordsworth did too....He defines
his intentions.

TS:   But it seems to me that Wordsworth tends, in his best work, to move out from particularity to show the mysteries inherent in the natural world.

AM: You mean you don't show those through particularity? I think he does.

TS: I mean that they're part of the particularity but that rather than...

AM: You see I think defining your intentions and going on about them is just a waste of time because you may be quite mistaken, not just mistaken in whether those are sort of good literary intentions but whether they actually are what you're doing. It seems to me you just can't know.

If I backed off and talked about this story I'm writing now and tried to figure out why I was trying to write this story, it would probably end up that I wouldn't write it. When it's all done, I can probably see where it went wrong. But that's about all. I guess I mean that, for me, too much thinking about what I'm doing is altogether a waste of time. And not even a very great temptation, though I sit around, you'd maybe think I was thinking, but I'm just having kind of a big, gloomy, empty-minded period [laughter] trying to get my story straight. I'm not *thinking* about writing.

TS: I have two further questions. Would you acknowledge possible influences of Joyce's *Dubliners* on *Dance of the Happy Shades*, particularly the possible importance of his story "The Dead" to the title story of your collection?

AM: I don't like *Dubliners* as much as I admire it. I've read "The Dead" a couple of times but not over and over as I've read the stories listed earlier. I'm always unconscious of influences, though. I read for pleasure, really for intoxication.

TS: There is a satiric reference in *Lives of Girls and Women* to the sort of writer who would compare sex to a train entering a tunnel instead of describing sex as it really is. Did you have a specific author and book in mind? I seem to recall a passage like that, I believe by Lawrence Durrell.

AM: I had no writer or passage in mind. I made that up. I make a lot of things up, though nobody seems to think so.

TS: Is there anything else you'd like to add at this point?

AM: No, I don't think so.

TS: Well, thank you very much.

London, Ontario<br>
27 April 1981

# "Clear Jelly": Alice Munro's Narrative Dialectics

## ROBERT THACKER

BEGINNING with her first collection, *Dance of the Happy Shades*, Alice Munro has received consistent praise for her style. Yet, strangely enough, most such comments have come from reviewers — of the several articles which treat Munro's work, only three have focused upon her style, and none has analyzed her narrative technique.[1] But a close examination of her early uncollected stories and those contained in *Dance of the Happy Shades* suggests that Munro's style developed from her first stories on; its development, moreover, is best seen through an examination of narrative technique. By the time her first collection appeared, Munro had perfected a distinctive, retrospective narrative approach that she has used throughout her subsequent work. In her stories, it is the means by which past and present commingle, the vehicle by which the narrator's humanity is communicated, and, finally, the means by which each narrator, and several other individual characters besides, are allowed their articulate moments. Simply put, it is the catalytic factor in Munro's substantial art.

Munro's first published stories appeared in the University of Western Ontario's undergraduate literary magazine, *Folio*, while she was a student there. Two of these, "The Dimensions of a Shadow" and "The Widower," reveal no real portents of her later success with the short story. The third-person omniscient narration is heavy-handed and Munro's narrative tone didactic, although she does show some facility with descriptions of physical detail.[2] The remaining story, however, entitled "Story for Sunday," reveals a glimpse of the narrative technique that became her hallmark, while at the same time it shares some of the others' flaws. As the story begins, the youthful protagonist, Evelyn, is hurrying to Sunday school, where she is a teacher's assistant. While Munro's omniscient third-person narrator concerns herself with the story's setting, as in the previous story, she concurrently reveals Evelyn's sense of anticipation over seeing Mr. Willens, the Sunday school superintendent, once again. Later, while Evelyn waits for the service to begin in church, the narrator tells us that "Today when she [Evelyn] looked at the pictures it was not quite the same; even in the depth and stillness of the moment she remembered Mr. Willens."[3] And, drawing upon Evelyn's memory, the narrator flashes back to the source of the girl's anticipation: the previous Sunday, having returned to an isolated room to retrieve her gloves, Evelyn happened upon Willens. He complimented her on her helpfulness and then took her in his arms and kissed her. As a result, the impressionable Evelyn has transformed him into a special being: "He was not handsome; his face in profile was somewhat flat, almost convex, not handsome at all, but beautiful." In so saying, Munro's narrator has made a key distinction: memory has transformed Willens into a romanticized being. Because of his attention the previous week, Willens has inadvertently altered Evelyn's view of herself. For example, looking at the other girls in church, who were concerned with mere boys, Evelyn considers herself superior because "She moved in a clear, cold flame of love which they [the other girls] could not even see." Of course Evelyn plans to position herself for another kiss, but, upon returning to the isolated room once again, she finds Willens re-enacting their kiss with the church's piano player, Myrtle Fotheringay. Overall, "Story for Sunday" is not profound literary art; it is significant only because it shows Munro, at a very early stage in her career, consciously manipulating past and present, holding the two realms together for the reader to see. Hence, through this commingling of past and present, Evelyn is allowed an articulate moment.

During her first few stories, Munro appears to have experimented with a variety of narrative stances, fluctuating from the first-person point of view to that of the third and back again; this continued through the *Dance of the Happy Shades* stories and continues still. But in the early stories, the shifts in narrative perspective are often marked. In "Story for Sunday," Munro uses third-person narration but is primarily concerned with Evelyn's thoughts and feelings. Her next published story, "The Idyllic Summer," also uses third-person narration, but Munro treats its protagonist in a far more objective manner.[4] It deals with the relationship between a wholly cerebral classics professor and his somewhat retarded daughter who is, therefore, primarily emotive. Munro uses the professor's letters to his colleagues in order to display the character's pious and pompous manner, while she describes the daughter, Clara, through her narrator's third-person analyses of the girl's actions and of the setting. The focus is on Clara, the inarticulate character, since her father is able to speak for himself. Yet "The Idyllic Summer" displays Munro dealing with the two character types seen throughout her stories: the articulate character speaking for himself and the inarticulate character rendered through third-person objective description and carefully delineated setting; and, in her next two stories, Munro concentrated on each separately. Thus, Munro's approach to her subject varied during this period, just as it was later to do in the stories composed after "Thanks for the Ride," alternating between a focus on individual character's thoughts and feelings as they present them and an emphasis on less articulate characters rendered through their actions and setting.

In her next story, "At the Other Place," Munro adopts for the first time the first-person point of view, a narrative stance which later became dominant in her first two books. It is, as well, the first in which a conventional family is depicted and also the first in which an immediate sense of place is vividly described. Because Munro's ability to present setting evocatively figures in her characterization, it is worth noting that from her very first stories on she handled setting well. Thus, in "At the Other Place," her narrator creates a definable texture of place for the reader, replete with sights, smells, and colours:

> It was a very hot day, but there had not been enough hot weather yet to burn the country up. The roadside bushes were still green and the money-musk was blooming unfaded in the long grass. Haying-time was over, but in some of the fields the coils were still standing. No one was working anywhere; the country was all hot and still in the sun, in the plum-blue shade of the heavy oaks and maples. The cows were lying down in the pastures, the horses dozing on their feet, under the trees. We passed a field of buckwheat in flower; it smelled as sweet as clover.[5]

Munro reveals here a finely attuned sense of surface detail which allows the reader to recreate mentally the scene she is describing. Through these figurative images, the reader is able to grasp the sensual context of the story which, in turn, lends the dramatized scenes a further sense of immediacy.

Moreover, "At the Other Place" is the first story in which the narrator's voice reveals two personae: though the narrator is ostensibly a child, her perceptions and the resulting descriptions are not strictly those of a child. Hence, her distinctions are often quite discerning; they are more mature in their judgement than the narrator's age would indicate, and she couches them in language sophisticated beyond her putative years. These two aspects of the narrator's sensibility, the child and the remembered child, are produced through the same sort of approach to past and present seen in "Story for Sunday," although here, instead of simply allowing the discrepancy between past and present to be inferred, Munro is deliberately cultivating it.

The story describes an afternoon outing to "the other place" owned by the narrator's family, the place where her father grew up. Within the story, the immediacy of the child is recreated through memory and through the narrative approach taken, and when combined with the weighing understanding of the older narrator (the adult who was the young girl), the resulting descriptions and evaluations are a merging of past and present. Thus, when considering her father, who is a farmer, dressed incongruously in his Sunday best, the narrator allows that

> ...my father, in a stiff blue shirt and suit with wide stripes, looked shrunken and stooped, red and grizzled in the face, much less his own man than he was in overalls and mechanic's cap. About this time I began to be puzzled and sad when I saw him in his good clothes — for when we saw him in the fields or holding the reins of a team or even sawing wood he was sure and powerful, a little more than life-size. (p. 131)

Not only does the narrator reveal her sophisticated perceptual and linguistic sense here, but she also shows that the immediacy of the story is feigned: "About this time...." It is an active reminiscence.

While visiting the other place to have a picnic and to care for the family's sheep, the narrator liked to explore the house where her father grew up. Reflecting, she recalls that she "sat on the window-ledge, looking through the open doorway at the big hard-maple that had been there when my father was little, and the slow movement of its branches, the way the sunlight caught on its leaves, gave me a forlorn and beautiful feeling of time and changes, and changelessness..." (pp. 131–32). Once, when her father came to the house to inspect an old wood stove, the narrator states "He did not look around or grow thoughtful as I thought he should..." (p. 132). Because of her own pensiveness, revealed here, the narrator is not entirely the twelve- to fourteen-year-old she seems to be throughout. Rather, as the story's narrator, she is nominally a child, narrating her immediate perceptions and thoughts; but, upon closer examination, we see that she is actually an adult, or at least older adolescent, remembering her experiences on a particular day "At the Other Place." So, just as she uses memory in "Story for Sunday," Munro here holds up past and present together. And by giving the story an appearance of immediacy — she is not trying to hide the fact that an older narrator is remembering — Munro is lending to her narrator a unique ability. The remembering narrator in "At the Other Place" recreates the immediate reality of the story while, at the same time, she is able to infuse the narrative with the incident's subjective importance, realized only as she matured. Thus, her comments about her father, quoted above, unite both past and present and so, by their interaction, expand Munro's meaning.

Surveying the stories chronologically, it is apparent that Munro came to use the retrospective narration first seen in "At the Other Place" with increasing frequency; indeed, in later stories she experimented with the technique, shaping and adjusting it to fit her subject, and as her narrators became more articulate, her art became more complex. But this represents only her overall direction — other stories written at this time reveal a different emphasis. In an unpublished interview, Munro comments that in her early stories she was more interested in setting than in character, and her next story, "The Edge of Town," reflects this concern.[7] Its protagonist, Harry Brooke, is an incessant talker who ironically cannot communicate with those around him, neither the townsfolk, nor his own family. Having adopted the third-person point of view, Munro is concerned with setting from the story's very beginning:

> Up here the soil is shallow and stony; the creeks dry up in summer, and a harsh wind from the west blows all year

long. There are not many trees, but wild-rose and black-berry bushes in little pockets of the hills, and long sharp sword-grass in the hollows. On an August day if you stand on the road leading out from the town, you can see miles and miles of brown blowing grass, and dust scooped up from the roads, and low, bumpy hills along the rim of the sky, which might be the end of the world. At night the crickets sing in the grass, and every second day, at supper time, a freight train goes through the town. (p.368)

In this setting, Munro places Harry Brooke, whom she treats objectively, never directly venturing into his thoughts. She delineates Harry's isolation by employing setting as a symbolic index of character and, in a manner analogous to the style of Eudora Welty, transforms details of setting into symbolic counterpoints for character.[8] And, having been born and raised in the same sort of social environment in which she places Harry, Munro describes his place in the town knowingly, unequivocally, as she presents the town's reaction to his babblings:

His expectancy, his seeking, made them wary, uneasily mocking. In a poor town like this, in a poor country, facing the year-long winds and the hard winters, people expect and seek very little; a rooted pessimism is their final wisdom. Among the raw bony faces of the Scotch-Irish, with their unspeaking eyes, the face of Harry was a flickering light, an unsteady blade; his exaggerated, flowering talk ran riot amongst barren statements and silences. (p.371)

The opening passage, previously quoted, underscores this one of detached analysis. Living in such an environment brings about the "rooted pessimism" Munro sees in the townspeople, and their stoicism, indeed, serves to set apart and objectify Harry Brooke, whose questions violate their "barren statements and silences."

The fact that "The Edge of Town" is sandwiched in between two stories which use the internalized first-person retrospective technique, "At the Other Place" and "Good-by, Myra," shows that Munro was working concurrently on two separate ways of rendering character. She chose to present characters like Harry

Brooke in this story and Clara in "The Idyllic Summer" objectively, through their actions and through setting; such treatment is, indeed, in keeping with the characters' noncommunicative situations. Another story in which she uses this technique is "The Time of Death."[9] But elsewhere, however, Munro chose to present first-person narrators who articulate their own experiences and, thereby, derive their own understanding. These narrators are found in "At the Other Place" and, as will be seen presently, in "Good-by, Myra." By working on each approach separately, therefore, Munro was developing greater skill with two major components of fiction, setting and character, so that, in her mature stories, like "Thanks for the Ride," she is able to fuse observer and participant within one narrative voice. Thus, Munro followed two separate, but by no means divergent, approaches to narration in her early stories.

Because "Good-by, Myra" is the first story which reveals a remembering narrator actively shaping the stuff of her memories in a somewhat covert manner, presenting an impression of immediacy and a detached understanding to the reader, it should be considered in some detail. The story deals with the development of a relationship between Helen, the narrator, and Myra Sayla, the outcast of Helen's grade-six class. Myra is an outcast because of her family background and her younger brother's dependence upon her while they are at school. As Helen tells us: "Jimmy Sayla was not used to going to the bathroom by himself and he would have to come to the grade-six door and ask for Myra and she would take him downstairs."[10] Jimmy's dependence extends to the playground as well, because his class-mates pick on him, and so the Saylas spend play periods standing together along the dividing line between the boys' and girls' playgrounds. Moreover, they are separate in that they do not fit into the Scots-Protestant ethos of the town; their parents are Eastern European immigrants, and the family is Roman Catholic. And, when a well-meaning teacher attempts to intercede with the grade-six girls on Myra's behalf, the girls, who had previously ignored Myra, turn on her as an object for derision.

Helen takes part in mocking Myra and does so without any apparent qualms. But one day, while walking to school, she notices that Myra is ahead and is slowing down to wait for her, so she befriends Myra, stating that "A role was shaping for me that I could not resist playing." The other girl's "humble, hopeful turnings" (p. 55) affect Helen, and she leaps to the superior role they afford her. Throughout their meeting, Helen responds to Myra as an individual; prior to this she had thought of Myra only as an odd presence: "It was queer to think that Myra, too, read the comics, or that she did anything, was anything at all, apart from her role at the school." A bond is forged between the two when Helen persuades Myra to keep the prize she found in Helen's Cracker-Jack. Forcing it upon Myra, Helen suddenly realizes the implications of her act: "We were both surprised. We looked at each other; I flushed but Myra did not. I realized the pledge as our fingers touched; I was panicky, but *all right.* All right, I thought, I can come early and walk with her other mornings. I can — I can go and talk to her at recess. Why not. *Why not?*" (p.56). Despite this realization, Helen has some misgivings about the friendship; she is wary of her peers' reaction. But her fears are inconsequential since Myra, having become ill with leukemia, stops attending school shortly thereafter.

Miss Darling, the grade-six teacher, organizes a "birthday party" for Myra — despite the fact it is March and Myra's birthday is in July — to be held at the hospital. Typically, Myra's disease grants her new status among her class-mates: "The birthday party of Myra Sayla became fashionable" (p.57). After the party is over and the girls are leaving, Myra calls Helen back to her bed. She then offers Helen a brush and comb set that the latter had noticed, and they make plans to play together when Myra returns from her treatment in London. Helen, however, is apprehensive, since she has premonitions that Myra will never return:

> Then I stood beside the bed wanting to say something else, or to ask something. Outside the hospital window, in the late sunlight, there was a sound like birds calling, but it wasn't, it was somebody playing in the street, maybe chasing with snowballs of the last unmelted snow. Myra heard, too; we were looking at each other. At that clear carrying sound her face changed, and I was scared, I did not know why.
> "When you come back — " I said....

Here Helen is faced with the life outside and the fact of Myra's impending death, which she intuits. Helen "understood the

44

demand she [Myra] made. And it was too much." As Helen leaves, she "called back quickly, treacherously, almost gaily, 'Good-by!' " (p.58). The demand Myra made on Helen is that of personal commitment, something which, as Helen herself suggests, is too much for an eleven-year-old to bear. Yet, by narrating "Good-by, Myra," Helen is remembering and purging herself of guilt. In the words of another of Munro's narrators, Myra has been "lifted out of life and held in light, suspended in the marvelous clear jelly that [Munro] has spent all [her] life learning how to make. It is an act of magic, there is no getting around it; it is an act, you might say, of a special, unsparing, unsentimental love. A fine and lucky benevolence." Like the character being spoken of here, Myra "has passed into Art. It doesn't happen to everybody" ("Material," *SIB*, p.43).

Such is the intention of Munro's own art. She creates a dialectic within the first-person narrator: Helen, the girl who knew Myra as an eleven-year old, and Helen, the older person actually narrating the story, combine to give the story two levels of reality. Because of Helen's memory and her detailed description, then, the texture of the story that the reader comes to understand in "Good-by, Myra" is a commingling of the remembered event, vividly described so as to lend immediacy to it, and Helen's detached understanding of it, an understanding that is detached because of the time which has passed since Helen knew Myra. The dynamic interaction between these two aspects of the narrator, the dialectic between them, is at the core of Munro's rhetoric; it is the way by which she creates her own "clear jelly."

Although Munro used the retrospective technique tentatively in "At the Other Place," its first use in a thoroughgoing way is in "Good-by, Myra." Remembering Myra as she was in the school yard, Helen retrospectively recalls the Saylas in mythical terms: "Over their dark eyes the lids were never fully raised; they had a weary look. But it was more than that. They were like children in a medieval painting, they were like small figures carved of wood, for worship or magic, with faces smooth and aged and meekly, cryptically uncommunicative" (p.17). As perceptive and descriptive as this passage is, it is not the product of the mentality of an eleven-year-old girl. The language and diction are too refined, the narrator's understanding of the scene's ramifications is too acute. In passages such as this, Munro combines her first-person narration with omniscient description. Yet the omniscience does not jar the reader, because it is a suitable intrusion, subtle and illuminating. The central simile contained here expands the reader's consciousness of the Saylas quickly and unobtrusively. This technique embodies the net effect of human memory: the reader is presented with Myra not as she actually *was*, but as she *is* remembered by Helen. Although the two images of Myra may very well be one and the same, they do not have to be, since memory tends to blur the picture, disregarding and enhancing details to achieve a desired impression. Helen is scared and does not know why because she has instinctively recognized the reality of another person's impending death, and the knowledge is beyond her intellectual scope. Yet, retrospectively, the sensibility of the older Helen is able to grasp the reality of Myra's eventual death; this recognition is implied throughout the story's last paragraph, as Helen "treacherously" calls "Good-by!" to Myra (p. 58).

"Good-by, Myra," furthermore, is central to this consideration of Munro's developing narrative technique because of major revisions she made before publishing it again, retitled "Day of the Butterfly," in *Dance of the Happy Shades*. When the two versions are compared, therefore, they reveal the direction in which their author was moving. In the stories written and published after "Good-by, Myra" — many of which were included in *Dance of the Happy Shades* — Munro moved more and more toward this retrospective first-person narrator as the teller of the tale. And, although this narrator was first seen in "At the Other Place," Munro's first use of it in a consistent and somewhat covert manner — she neither draws attention to nor provides specific information about the older narrator — was in "Good-by, Myra." So, in revising this story in order to sharpen the memory of the older narrator, Munro is revealing her main concern. Her narrators, her remembering narrators, inform, judge, understand, and, ultimately, illuminate — and so theirs is an essential presence in her fiction, a catalytic one. Thus, Munro's desire to sharpen the narrator's understanding of Myra Sayla is in keeping with the development of her distinctive narrative voice. "Day of the Butterfly" bears a greater similarity to those stories *Dance of the Happy Shades* in which Munro's retrospective narration is most refined — "Boys and Girls," "Red Dress — 1946," "Walker Brothers Cowboy," and "Images" — than to the early stories. Thus, the earlier version of this story is a

46

harbinger of things to come, while the revision suggests an author whose grasp upon her narrative voice has become far more firm in the interim between drafts.

The two versions diverge at the point when Helen describes the "clear carrying sound of somebody playing in the street" (*DHS*, p. 110). In the earlier version, Helen echoes Myra's plans for her eventual return, but in "Day of the Butterfly" she does not. In "Good-by, Myra," the sound makes Myra's face change, which in turn frightens Helen; but in the revision the sound "made Myra, her triumph and her bounty, and most of all her future in which she had found this place for me, turn shadowy, turn dark" (p. 110). In the first version, Helen's feelings are ambiguous; she is frightened by Myra's facial change but does "not know why" (p. 58). However, in the revision there is no ambivalence: Helen knows that Myra will go to London and die. Helen's fright in "Good-by, Myra" represents her intuitive awareness of the eventuality, but in the revision, the sharpened memory of the adult narrator states the realization more emphatically. Moreover, the sharpened delineation of Helen's memory has transformed the presents lying on Myra's bed. In the earlier version, they are without subjective significance, but in "Day of the Butterfly," Helen finds them threatening: "All the presents on the bed, the folded paper and ribbons, those guilt-tinged offerings, had passed into this shadow, they were no longer innocent objects to be touched, exchanged, accepted without danger." Helen's memory here is more exact, her realization is more profound; by characterizing the presents as "guilt-tinged offerings," she links them significantly to the girls' previous cruel treatment of Myra — treatment to which she was a party. Helen's recognition here does not differ in kind from the earlier version, yet its personal exactness leads both the narrator and the reader to a deeper understanding of the relationship. Moreover, Helen's attempt to withdraw quickly from the room, while explicitly stated in the first version, is more subtle in the second, and, likewise, though Helen tries to give the present back to Myra in the first version, in the second she mentally denies the "guilt-tinged offering": "I didn't want to take the case now but I could not think how to get out of it, what lie to tell. I'll give it away, I thought, I won't ever play with it. I would let my little brother pull it apart." In this instance, too, the scope of Helen's realization is broadened; because the rejection is thought rather than stated, Helen's older

47

self is shouldering more responsibility for it. Perhaps Helen recalls her own role when she and her peers were taunting Myra.

Finally, the most important change Munro made is seen in the last paragraph of "Day of the Butterfly." In "Good-by, Myra," Helen's final goodbye is allowed to stand alone, while Helen thinks only of getting outside to the spring air. In "Day of the Butterfly," however, Helen's reaction to a nurse's admonishment to leave is far more explicit:

> So I was released, set free by the barriers which now closed about Myra, her unknown, exalted, ethersmelling hospital world, and by the treachery of my own heart. 'Well thank you,' I said. 'Thank you for the thing. Goodbye.'
>
> Did Myra ever say goodbye? Not likely. She sat in her high bed, her delicate brown neck rising out of a hospital gown too big for her, her brown carved face immune to treachery, her offering perhaps already forgotten, prepared to be set apart for legendary uses, as she was even in the back porch at school. (p. 110)

Myra may be "immune to treachery," but Helen certainly is not. Moreover, since Myra is the subject of the reminiscence which comprises the story, she has been "set apart" for Helen's own "legendary uses." In comparing the two versions, then, it is possible to chart Munro's expansive delineation of memory when applied to a crucial childhood event. Helen's recollections in "Day of the Butterfly" are more precise; the adult recollections of the mature narrator's voice are presented with a higher degree of comprehension in the second version. This second, older narrator (the older narrator in "Good-by, Myra" is the first), the Helen in "Day of the Butterfly," recognizes the "treachery" in her own heart, which she does not attempt to avoid, and she understands her "treachery" better than the first older Helen does. It is a recognition that, as the narrator, she cannot deny: Helen must deal intellectually with her childhood responsibility. Another noteworthy difference is in the differing tones surrounding the two retreating Helens. In "Good-by, Myra," Helen impetuously departs, quickly calling "Good-by!" (p. 58), while the second Helen is more cerebral and more serene, as if she is aware of her responsibility toward Myra. Thus, her farewell is not an excla-

48

mation; instead, it is a flat statement: "Goodbye" (p. 110). Overall, Munro's revisions produced a more thoughtful evaluation of her narrator's memories.

In an unpublished interview, Munro comments on the differences between the two versions: "I've just changed the rhythm to get the voice of the narrator. I began to do that a lot better.... They [the changes] matter a lot to me. I don't decide to make the changes; it's just [that] when I start rewriting I start hearing the narrator's voice."[11] Her comments reveal the author's awareness of the separate narrators in the stories and, more importantly, her recognition of her own narrative development. Implicitly, the comments also recognize a change in the narrator's situation dictated by the author's own perceptive growth during the interim between drafts. Thus, it is fair to say that as Munro changed, her perception of Helen's responsibility changed; and the sharper focus apparent in "Day of the Butterfly" reflects the change. The shift lies with the author and the narrator rather than with the story's essential intent, since Helen's moral responsibility toward Myra remains unaltered.

As indicated earlier, Munro developed as a narrative craftsman along two separate, but by no means divergent, lines. That is, while she tended increasingly toward the type of narrative seen in "Good-by, Myra,"[12] she still occasionally wrote stories in which characters are presented objectively, without recourse to memory, through a third-person narrator. Such stories as "The Time of Death" and "A Trip to the Coast" bear a tangible relationship to "The Edge of Town" since, in each, setting and atmosphere predominate and characters are treated symbolically.[13] They are also Munro's least successful stories in *Dance of the Happy Shades*. Their presence, however, is key within Munro's work because they forced her to observe in a detached manner. Commenting on a story written just after "Good-by, Myra," "An Ounce of Cure" (a story which is patently a first-person reminiscence), Munro says:

> One thing in it I think is interesting, now that I look back
> on it: when the girl's circumstances become hopelessly
> messy, when nothing is going to go right for her, she gets
> out of it by looking at the way things happen — by
> changing from a participant to an observer. This is what
> I used to do myself, it is what a writer does; I think it

may be one of the things that make [sic] a writer in the first place. When I started to write the dreadful things I did write when I was about fifteen, I made the glorious leap from being a victim of my own ineptness and self-conscious miseries to being a godlike arranger of patterns and destinies, even if they were all in my head; I have never leapt back.[14]

This statement reveals Munro's essentially rhetorical approach to fiction, because, like their author, her protagonists are both participants, and observers. Through the interaction of these two modes of perception, Munro is able to present coherently the whole significance of a story's dramatized events. Thus, it is not remarkable that in some stories she prefers to simply observe — as in the third-person stories — without reference to the participant's thoughts or emotions. These stories, as well, allow her to concentrate on setting and atmosphere as the primary determinants of character, especially in "The Time of Death."

In "Thanks for the Ride," Munro brings her two separate narrative approaches together within one story. Dick, the story's narrator, is one of her finest characters; he is both participant in and observer of the story's action, a "pick-up" liaison, and he is Munro's sole male first-person narrator.[15] Lois, his partner in their evening's activities, is almost wholly inarticulate, and so her character is defined by Dick's observations of the town's environment, her physical appearance, and her home and family.

Because of his function within the story, Dick is a commingling of both first-person commitment and third-person detachment. As the story opens, he is sitting in the single café in a small Ontario town near, presumably, Lake Huron, with his cloddish cousin, George. The pair have been thrown together by circumstances and are planning an evening together, though Dick is not overly enthusiastic. His descriptions of the café and of the town's physical appearance are those of a detached third-person narrator:

My cousin George and I were sitting in a restaurant called Pop's Cafe, in a little town close to the Lake. It was getting dark in there, and they had not turned the lights on, but you could still read the signs plastered against the mirror between fly-speckled and slightly yellowed

cutouts of strawberry sundaes and tomato sandwiches.
(p. 44)

> It was a town of unpaved, wide, sandy streets and bare
> yards. Only the hardy things like red and yellow nastur-
> tiums, or a lilac bush with brown curled leaves, grew out
> of that cracked earth. The houses were set wide apart,
> with their own pumps and sheds and privies out behind;
> most of them were built of wood and painted green or
> grey or yellow. The trees that grew there were big
> willows or poplars, their fine leaves greyed with the dust.
> There were no trees along the main street, but spaces of
> tall grass and dandelions and blowing thistles — open
> country between the store buildings. The town hall was
> surprisingly large, with a great bell in a tower, the red
> brick rather glaring in the midst of the town's walls of
> faded, pale-painted wood. (pp. 46–47)

There is nothing in these descriptions that suggests the first-
person narration, except possibly "surprisingly"; they serve to
define the setting and, as such, later act as a symbolic counter-
point for the inarticulate Lois, who is apparently as rough as her
environment and is roughly used by boys up from the city, boys
like Dick and George. Indeed, this is *her* town. Later, after they
have met Adelaide, Lois' friend, and have located Lois walking
down a street, the characters go to Lois' home so that she can
change. Dick follows her into the house in order to wait for her,
and his observations reveal how adroitly Munro welds his roles
of observer and participant together:

> She opened the front door and said in a clear, stilted
> voice: "I would like you to meet my family."
>   The little front room had linoleum on the floor and
> flowered paper curtains at the windows. There was a
> glossy chesterfield with a Niagara Falls and a To Mother
> cushion on it, and there was a little black stove with a
> screen around it for summer, and a big vase of paper
> apple blossoms. A tall, frail woman came into the room
> drying her hands on a dishtowel, which she flung into a
> chair. Her mouth was full of blue-white china teeth, the
> long cords trembled in her neck. I said how-do-you-do to

her, embarrassed by Lois's announcement, so suddenly and purposefully conventional. I wondered if she had any misconceptions about this date, engineered by George for such specific purposes. I did not think so. Her face had no innocence in it that I could see; it was knowledgeable, calm, and hostile. She might have done it, then, to mock me, to make me into this caricature of The Date, the boy who grins and shuffles in the front hall and waits to be presented to the nice girl's family. But that was a little far-fetched. Why should she want to embarrass me when she had agreed to go out with me without even looking into my face? Why should she care enough? (pp. 49–50)

Here, in this paragraph, is the essence of Munro's narrative art. Having written stories like "The Edge of Town," in which her third-person narrator described, analyzed, and pronounced, and having written stories like "At the Other Place" and especially "Good-by, Myra," in which her remembering narrators both participated in the action and articulated its significance, Munro brings the two separate approaches together in the finely wrought "Thanks for the Ride." Dick is, as far as the reader can see, observing, describing, participating, and remembering, seemingly all at once. He is both descriptive and thoughtful as a narrator, as the two separate parts of this paragraph show: at first he describes the room, and, this description accomplished, he falls to musing over Lois' expectations. Hence in her finest stories — of which this is the first — Munro's adroit narrators communicate by varying their perspective: describing, reacting, confirming, denying, and, above all, remembering — as each is needed. Thus, her stories are best understood through an analysis of her rhetoric. Munro's narrative technique, usually subtly adjusted for the needs of each story, defines the dialectical basis of her style.

An example of these adjustments is the manner by which Munro communicates Lois' entrapped plight in the small resort town, for she seems to don her Saturday-night finery for almost every city boy up during the summer in the (apparently futile) hope that he will be "The Date." Since Lois is presented objectively, from Dick's point of view, Munro draws upon Dick's own curiosity about her character: he is inexperienced in pick-up affairs and so relates to Lois as a person, not as an object. In addition, Dick's presentation of the town's physical appearance, quoted above, underscores Lois' character, since she is certainly the human counterpart of those "hardy...red and yellow nasturtiums." Despite the fact that Lois utters little more than a dozen lines during the entire story, the reader is perfectly aware of her multitude of reasons for an "abusive and forlorn" (p.58) cry at the story's end. Since he is describing what he observed from memory, Dick lends subjective weight to objective facts. Thus, when he first comes into Lois' house, he notices "the smell of stale small rooms, bedclothes, frying, washing, and medicated ointments. And dirt, though it did not look dirty" (p.50). Having, as he does, an urban middle-class background, Dick is unaccustomed to Lois' mode of life at the edge of poverty. But his memory lends subjective weight to his initial impressions. Noting Lois' grandmother, whom he likens to a "collapsed pudding," Dick enlarges on his impression:

> Some of the smell in the house seemed to come from her. It was a smell of hidden decay, such as there is when some obscure little animal has died under the verandah. The smell, the slovenly, confiding voice — something about this life I had not known, something about these people. I thought: my mother, George's mother, they are innocent. Even George, George is innocent. But these others are born sly and sad and knowing. (p.51)

This is not to suggest that Dick could have not had such thoughts while glancing at Lois' grandmother peering in from the edge of the living-room, but one doubts that they would be so well articulated. Thus, through her exact descriptions, Munro is here — as she is throughout her other stories — juggling reminiscence so that it gives the appearance of immediacy. That is, should the readers care to think about it, they will see that the entire story is written in the past tense, and so Dick's emotions are, indeed, recalled in tranquility. But Munro's physical descriptions and other exact details lend such clarity to the presentation that readers think the events are unfolding before them. This ability, based on her narrative technique, allows her to fashion art out of a pick-up affair, a first kiss, or a runaway horse — commonplace events all.

This retrospective technique, which allows the older person who was the younger boy or girl to comment on what happened, to become, as she says, a "godlike arranger of patterns and destinies," is not, by any means, unique to Munro. A more widely known and recognized example of it is James Joyce's "Araby," one of the stories of childhood in *Dubliners*.[16] In her unpublished interview with Munro, Jill Gardiner presented the author with Cleanth Brooks and Robert Penn Warren's analysis of the technique as it functions within Joyce's story.[17] Munro's response was as follows:

> The adult narrator has the ability to detect and talk about the confusion. I don't feel that the confusion is ever resolved. And there is some kind of a central mystery, as in "Walker Brothers Cowboy," that is there for the adult narrator as it was for the child. I feel that all life becomes even *more* mysterious and difficult. And the whole act of writing is more an attempt at recognition than of understanding, because I don't understand many things. I feel a kind of satisfaction in just approaching something that is mysterious and important. Then writing is the art of approach and recognition. I believe that we don't solve these things — in fact our explanations take us further away.[18]

Such a statement certainly calls into question the thematic analyses offered by critics which purport to define Munro's vision of the world because, as her devotion to the short story suggests, Munro sees the world as one of flux. Thus, her pronouncements are few and her insights tentative and fleeting. Conversely, the central importance of her rhetoric takes on a greater validity in light of this statement — narrative technique is, after all, the vehicle for Munro's "approach and recognition."

A passage from "Thanks for the Ride" underscores this point. Sitting in a car parked on a lonely country road, passing a bottle of bootleg liquor back and forth, Dick observes Lois and tries to understand her:

> Each time Lois handed the bottle back to me she said "Thank you" in a mannerly and subtly contemptuous way. I put my arm around her, not much wanting to. I

was wondering what was the matter. This girl lay against my arm, scornful, acquiescent, angry, inarticulate and out-of-reach. I wanted to talk to her then more than to touch her, and that was out of the question; talk was not so little a thing to her as touching. Meanwhile I was aware that I should be beyond this, beyond the first stage and well into the second (for I had a knowledge, though it was not very comprehensive, of the orderly progression of stages, the ritual of back- and front-seat seduction). Almost I wished I was with Adelaide. (p.53)

Here Dick is describing, observing, participating, and remembering. Without subjecting this passage to extended rhetorical analysis, it could support a study of diction and syntax which led, through an understanding of Dick's position as narrator, inductively to a well-grounded presentation of theme. The adjectives define Lois: "contemptuous," "scornful," "acquiescent," "angry," "inarticulate"; Lois is all of these. But in using them, Dick is both "approaching something that is mysterious and important" — Lois — and revealing his position as a narrator. These adjectives, and others like them throughout the story, attest to the fact that Dick, the narrator, is recalling the entire evening after he has heard Lois' "abusive and forlorn" cry: " 'Thanks for the ride!' " (p.58). It was only after he left Lois that he recognized her to be a "mystic of love." But, however personally important to Dick, his ruminations mean nothing at all to Lois, who knows nothing of them. So far as she is concerned, Dick was just like all the rest of the city boys, perhaps even worse, since he showed her a glimmer of a relationship based on something other than sex and then dashed that hope. His penultimate description of Lois, "this mystic of love," who "sat now on the far side of the carseat, looking cold and rumpled, and utterly closed up in herself" (p.57) is exactly apt. She looks "cold and rumpled" because that is the way she is, that is the way she has every right to be.

Munro's retrospective narrative technique allows the reader to understand both Lois' defiant isolation and Dick's palpable regret, the two emotions held in tandem. This effect is the product of technique. Whatever view of life she has and is reflected in her stories comes, as she said, from "just approaching something that is mysterious and important," and that, indeed, is achieved through her craft, her adroit use of a distinctive, retrospective narrative technique. Because it is not tied to time, it ranges about the narrator's awareness in life and memory and illuminates as it evaluates. In "Thanks for the Ride," it is seen for the first time in its full flower.

That Munro continued to use and refine this technique subsequent to the late 1950s is apparent in the balance of the stories contained in *Dance of the Happy Shades*. Five of these, especially — "The Peace of Utrecht," "Boys and Girls," "Red Dress — 1946," "Walker Brothers Cowboy," and "Images," in the order of their composition[19] — are her most mature and refined stories in that collection; they are so because they reveal Munro's retrospective narrative technique employed in a dextrous and subtle manner. This ability certainly owes to the writing experience provided by earlier stories and outlined here.

Having evolved this technique by the time she published *Dance of the Happy Shades*, Munro has used it consistently in her subsequent work. Throughout *Lives of Girls and Women*, Del Jordan, its narrator, treads a fine line between the two points of view found in stories like "Day of the Butterfly." Her older voice seldom intrudes overtly; instead, it is subtly present to instruct, clarify, and expand the younger narrator's pronouncements. For example, in the last segment of "Baptizing," when Del and Garnet French recognize their differences and tacitly reject one another, the submerged older voice comments, "We had seen in each other what we could not bear, and we had no idea that people do see that, and go on, and hate and fight and try to kill each other, various ways, then love some more" (p. 240). Such covert intrusions, which embody the older Del's knowledge, are found throughout *Lives of Girls and Women*. Consequently, the technique Munro employed in *Lives of Girls and Women* is a distillation of that one she developed through her early work, for it is essentially the same as the technique employed in the stories considered here.

Munro's next published work, *Something I've Been Meaning to Tell You*, is another matter. It startles a reader to find such a range of narrative points of view, for Munro's narrators are constantly shifting in age, demeanour, and station in life. Some of the stories bear a direct relation to Munro's earlier work, focusing upon some remembered childhood experiences, like "The Found Boat" and "The Ottawa Valley." Others, especially

"Tell Me Yes or No," suggest a new direction; in that story, the narrator imagines her lover is dead, which alters the reader's impression of the story's reality. Another consideration in regard to this collection is that Munro's range has widened in that she is often concerned with the question of marriages gone sour, as in "Material" and "The Spanish Lady."

But despite the wider range found in the collection, Munro's basic narrative technique here is still essentially the same as that developed by the end of *Dance of the Happy Shades*. Within each story, there is usually a polarity of perception, either the narrator's or the central character's, and it is partially resolved through some sort of reconciliation or epiphany. Although the narrators reveal a wider range of human types, the technique employed to communicate each of their situations has some precursor in an earlier story. For example, the dramatized reminiscent technique found in "Material," "Memorial," and "The Ottawa Valley" was first used in "The Peace of Utrecht," first published in 1960 and later included in *Dance of the Happy Shades*. By rendering her narrators' remembrances dramatically, though, Munro was treating overtly the dual-voiced retrospective technique she had employed covertly in "Day of the Butterfly" and "Thanks for the Ride." Thus, *Something I've Been Meaning to Tell You* reveals Munro using essentially the same narrative techniques she had perfected by the time she published her first collection.

And while *Who Do You Think You Are?* reveals a far greater dependence on the third-person narrator than Munro's previous work, it, too, continues the use of her characteristic retrospective technique. There, the narrator juxtaposes Rose's younger, innocent view of herself and of her life with a more definite and comprehensive understanding, which derives from her subsequent experience. Thus, as third-person narrator, Munro presents Rose's initial impression in concert with the character's eventual understanding — and so she fulfills the weighing role seen within the first-person narrators of "Day of the Butterfly" and "Thanks for the Ride." Because of the detachment occasioned by the third-person narrator, Rose's story is less immediate to the reader than is Myra's or Lois' and Dick's, to be sure, but the narrative technique used in *Who Do You Think You Are?* is derived from Munro's experience in the earlier stories.

Thus Munro's distinctive narrative technique, which she had perfected by the time her first collection appeared, is the basis of her felicitous style — it has enabled her to create a dialectic between present and past, between experience and understanding. This, in turn, has enabled her to transform commonplace, everyday experiences — like a girlhood acquaintanceship, a pick-up affair, or a first date — into finely wrought art. Munro's narrative dialectics, then, by balancing one point of view against another, allow her to create her own "clear jelly," which presents a comprehensive understanding to her readers. And this, in the words of Munro's narrator in "Material," "is an act of magic, there is no getting around it; it is an act, you might say, of a special, unsparing, unsentimental love. A fine and lucky benevolence" (*SIB*, p. 43).

NOTES

A slightly different version of this essay was presented to the 5th Biennial Conference of the Association for Canadian Studies in the United States, Washington, D.C., on 29 Sept. 1979.

[1] W. H. New, "Pronouns and Propositions: Alice Munro's Stories," *Open Letter*, 3rd Ser., No. 5 (Summer 1976), pp. 40–49; Helen Hoy, " 'Dull, Simple, Amazing and Unfathomable': Paradox and Double Vision in Alice Munro's Fiction," *Studies in Canadian Literature*, 5 (1980), 100–15; W. R. Martin, "The Strange and the Familiar in Alice Munro," *Studies in Canadian Literature*, 7 (1982), 214–26. These critics alone attempt to define the workings of Munro's narrative art. Others writing on Munro have emphasized themes, her similarities to other writers, and her "vision"; they appear to have been under the egregious influence of the prevailing thematic approach taken by critics of Canadian literature over the past decade. The inapplicability of this approach to a stylist like Munro illustrates its very limited usefulness.

[2] Alice Laidlaw, "The Dimensions of a Shadow," *Folio*, 4 (April 1950), [n. pag.]. Alice Laidlaw, "The Widower," *Folio*, 5 (April 1951), [n. pag.].

[3] Alice Laidlaw, "Story for Sunday," *Folio*, 5 (Dec. 1950), [n. pag.].

[4] Alice Laidlaw Munro, "The Idyllic Summer," *The Canadian Forum*, Aug. 1954, pp. 106–07, 109–10.

[5] Alice Laidlaw, "At the Other Place," *The Canadian Forum*, Sept. 1955, p. 131. All further references to this work appear in the text.

⁶ Munro uses the father's clothing here as a subjective symbol of the man. This is a technique which she uses often in the later stories included in *Dance of the Happy Shades*, for example, "Images," p. 36. In this, the most recently composed story to be included in the volume, the narrator's consideration of her father's boots as an extension of his personality corresponds to this earlier instance.

⁷ Jill Gardiner, "The Early Short Stories of Alice Munro," M.A. Thesis New Brunswick 1973, p. 173. Gardiner's interview with Munro is included as an appendix to the thesis. Alice Munro, "The Edge of Town," *Queen's Quarterly*, 62 (Autumn 1955), 368–80. All further references to this work appear in the text.

⁸ See Mark Schorer, "Technique as Discovery," *The Hudson Review*, 1 (Spring 1948), 67–87; rpt. in *Myth and Method: Modern Theories of Fiction*, ed. James E. Miller, Jr. (Lincoln, Nebr.: Univ. of Nebraska Press, 1960), pp. 86–108. At one point, talking about the "cultivated sensitivity" of the styles of Welty, Katherine Anne Porter, and Jean Stafford, Schorer states that the values in each writer's style lie "in the subtle means by which sensuous details become symbols, and in the way the symbols provide a network which is the story, and which at the same time provides the writer and us with a refined moral insight by means of which to test it" (p. 106). Munro's style is of the same sort because the "network which is the story" in Munro's case is an aggregate of setting, character, and theme, strung together by her retrospective narrative technique, which provides perspective.

⁹ Alice Munro, "The Time of Death," *The Canadian Forum*, June 1956, pp. 63–66; rpt. [with minor revisions] in *DHS*, pp. 89–99.

¹⁰ Alice Munro, "Good-by, Myra," *Chatelaine*, July 1956, p. 17; rpt. [revised — "Day of the Butterfly"] in *DHS*, pp. 100–10. All further references to this work are from *Chatelaine*, unless indicated otherwise, and appear in the text.

¹¹ Gardiner, p. 176. The second parenthetical insertion is Gardiner's.

¹² Of the thirteen stories written after "Good-by, Myra" and included in *Dance of the Happy Shades*, only three—"Sunday Afternoon," "The Shining Houses," and "A Trip to the Coast" — employ a detached third-person narrator; the other ten use the remembering first-person narrator, as does the whole of *Lives of Girls and Women*.

¹³ In both "The Time of Death" and "A Trip to the Coast" [*DHS*], pp. 89–99, 172–89), Munro uses setting symbolically, in the former story by the way in which she handles the first snowfall of winter and in the latter by the way she handles the first few droplets of rain.

¹⁴ Alice Munro, "Author's Commentary," in *Sixteen By Twelve*: *Short*

*Stories by Canadian Writers,* ed. John Metcalf (Toronto: Ryerson, 1970), p. 125.

[15] Alice Munro, "Thanks for the Ride," *The Tamarack Review*, No. 2 (Winter 1957), 25–37; rpt. in *DHS*, pp. 44–58. All further references to this work are from *Dance of the Happy Shades* and appear in the text. It is worth noting that Munro did not revise this story prior to its publication in *Dance of the Happy Shades*, as was the case with the other stories published originally in the 1950s and included there.

[16] James Joyce, "Araby," *Dubliners* (1914; rpt. Harmondsworth, Eng.: Penguin, 1964), pp. 27–33.

[17] Cleanth Brooks and Robert Penn Warren, "Interpretation," in *Understanding Fiction*, 2nd ed. (New York: Appleton-Century-Crofts, 1959), p. 192.

[18] Gardiner, p. 178.

[19] This order of composition, as with that used throughout, reflects that given by Munro in John Metcalf, "A Conversation with Alice Munro," *Journal of Canadian Fiction*, 1, No. 4 (Fall 1972), p. 58; this order is corroborated by Gardiner, p. xii. For those stories not mentioned by Munro, I have adopted date of first publication to establish order of composition.

# "Treacheries of the Heart":
# Memoir, Confession, and Meditation
# in the Stories of Alice Munro

## MARGARET GAIL OSACHOFF

IN AN INTERVIEW with John Metcalf, Alice Munro was asked
"How far is your work autobiographical?", to which she
replied:

> I guess I have a standard answer to this ... in incident
> — no... in emotion completely. In incident up to a
> point too but of course, in *Lives of Girls and Women*
> which is a... I suppose it could be called an autobio-
> graphical novel... most of the incidents are changed
> versions of real incidents. *Some* are completely invented
> but the emotional reality, the girl's feeling for her
> mother, for men, for life is all... it's all solidly auto-
> biographical. I would not disclaim this at all.

She went on to say that "Sunday Afternoon" and "Boys and
Girls" use autobiographical material and that "The Peace of
Utrecht" was "my first really painful autobiographical story."[1]
Of the twenty-eight stories in *Dance of the Happy Shades* and
*Something I've Been Meaning to Tell You*, eighteen are in the first
person, and the use of this type of narration here and in *Lives of
Girls and Women* strengthens the impression that they are auto-
biographical. One of Munro's most distinctive characteristics is
her mastery of her first-person narratives; and two critics,
Douglas Barbour and Brandon Conron, have commented on
the compelling presence of the speaking voice in her stories.[2]
However, they do not distinguish the different ways in which
Munro uses voice, nor do they recognize that the narrator's
relationship or attitude to her autobiographical material often
influences the voice of the story.

In a story called "Home," Munro has her narrator / writer dwell on one of the problems that Munro herself must have to face when she uses material from her past — the problem of voice. *"A problem of the voices, the way people talk, how can it be handled?"*[3] is a question that concerns both the narrator of "Home" and Munro when they write their stories. Munro wants to present her material truthfully and recognizes the difficulties that face her in the attempt. Trying to capture exactly the images and voices of her past is her moral duty as a writer, and yet it is a process that she distrusts and one that preys on her conscience. She says:

> ...even as I most feverishly, desperately practise it, I am a little afraid that the work with words may turn out to be a questionable trick, an evasion (and never more so than when it is most dazzling, apt and striking), an unavoidable lie.[4]

Exploring the lives of others by writing about them involves the writer in "unavoidable lie[s]," and yet, paradoxically, those lies have a "pure reality" or truth about them. In "The Shining Houses," Mary

> ...found herself exploring her neighbour's life as she had once explored the lives of grandmothers and aunts — by pretending to know less than she did, asking for some story she had heard before; this way, remembered episodes emerged each time with slight differences of content, meaning, colour, yet with a pure reality that usually attaches to things which are at least part legend. (*DHS*, p. 19)

There can be a danger in turning memories into legends, and Munro works out her own concerns regarding the use of autobiographical material in her fiction by having some of her narrators conscious of the problems that are involved in using autobiographical material.

Even though a majority of her short fiction is written in the first person, there are significant differences among the stories. The speaking or "confiding voice," as Munro calls it in "Thanks for the Ride" (*DHS*, p. 51), is often present in her first-person narrations. The urge to tell one's story is strong; and depending on what the story is about, on the reason for the telling, and on its resolution, the stories can be called memoirs, confessions, or meditations. Such a distinction is important if we are to recognize the complexity of Munro's use of voice and its relation to her concern with the proper use of autobiographical material in fiction.

Most of the memoirs are found in her first collection of stories, *Dance of the Happy Shades*, and her first novel, *Lives of Girls and Women*, is a memoir.[5] Most of the confessions and meditations are in *Something I've Been Meaning to Tell You*. Thus, it can be seen that as Munro matures as a writer her use of voice in her first-person narratives shows more variety and her narrators become more self-conscious.

Munro calls "Dance of the Happy Shades," which started as an anecdote that someone told her at a family dinner party, a story "done in the form of a memoir more or less as a matter of convenience." However, she goes on, "The *I* of the story is a masquerade, she is a little middle-class girl I never was, an attempt to see the story through the eyes of the relative who told it to me."[6] When Munro talks about "the form of a memoir," she is alerting us to the idea that it is the narrator's memories of the past that are being used, that it is fiction we are reading rather than autobiography. The "I" of a story is not Munro, although the narrator and writer may have memories and concerns in common. A memoir is usually a story about childhood told by an adult who looks back on some memorable or traumatic event in the past. The point of view of a child or an adolescent is changed by the passage of time, and that changed person, the narrator, is sometimes evident in the present.[7] Childhood and adolescence are seen from the perspective of experience and maturity. The narrator in a Munro memoir tells an "I remember when" story, but there is no evidence of a listener.

The most straightforward way to deal with a retrospective view of a past event is simply to set it down as a fictional autobiography or memoir. But if the emotion that charges the memories of a particular event is stronger, the story becomes a confession. The narrator of a confession is a speaker with a confiding voice, who tells of some "treachery of my [her] own heart" ("Day of the Butterfly," *DHS*, p. 110) or of some wrong she has done. In a memoir, the treachery and guilt are minor or go unrecognized as such. A confession, on the other hand, is told because of inner necessity, and the narrator appeals for understanding, shares a burden with the listener, and perhaps wants absolution of guilt or reconciliation with the past. In a confession, there is a sense of emotional urgency in the telling and a strong impression that the narrator is actually speaking to someone.[8]

A meditation has the same sense of a speaking voice, but here the thoughts or words are instigated by the narrator's own need for clarity and are usually aimed at herself or at an imaginary listener. Words are organized to be spoken but remain in the speaker's head; the narrator thinks thoughts that she will never communicate to anyone. The difference between a confession and a meditation is the difference between a monologue and a soliloquy. The motivating force behind the narrator's words in Munro's meditations is the desire for truth, for self-knowledge, and for order through art. Whereas the guilt that instigates a confession is the guilt that arises out of harm (real or imagined) that the narrator has done someone, in a meditation the concern or even guilt that a narrator feels is usually associated with the question of the proper use of people and experiences as raw material for art. The treachery of the heart involved in the wrong use of autobiographical material is a frequent concern of the narrators in Munro's meditations.[9] As for the memoir — the narrator does not have guilt as a motivating force; she simply wants to tell a story about her past, and she does not concern herself with the moral or artistic scruples that could arise if she were self-conscious about her use of autobiographical material.

Like *Lives of Girls and Women*, "Day of the Butterfly," "Boys and Girls," and "Red Dress — 1946" are memoirs of childhood. They are told from the perspective of an adult who is remembering some important event in the past. Each of these stories involves what could be called a treachery of the heart, but none is a confession or meditation. None of them has a confessor listening to a confiding voice, and none deals with the moral qualms of a narrator using autobiographical material in her fiction. In "Day of the Butterfly," Helen remembers withholding friendship from Myra, an outsider in all school activities. Myra seemed not to have noticed Helen's treachery and offered herself as material for a future story: "She sat in her high bed...her brown carved face immune to treachery, her offering perhaps

64

already forgotten, prepared to be set apart for legendary uses, as she was even in the back porch at school" (*DHS*, p. 110). This idea of a person being "set apart for legendary uses" and the guilt of the narrator who uses such material is the subject matter of later Munro meditations, but here there is no such guilt. "Boys and Girls," too, contains one minor example of a treachery of the heart or "unexorcised guilt" (*DHS*, p. 123), as it is called by this narrator. Her desire, as a young girl, to tell stories to decrease the ordinariness of her life is the reason for her guilt (this desire put her brother in danger once), but there is no sign in this story of the qualms of conscience that often beset a Munro narrator in her use of autobiographical material. In "Red Dress — 1946," the narrator's treachery consists of her decision not to tell her mother "everything" (*DHS*, p. 160) about her near "defeat" (p. 151) at her first high-school dance. However, she felt that such a deception would protect her mother, and she has never felt any real guilt for the treachery. This story is an episode in the formation of a young girl's traditional "feminine" sensibility, and, like the other two stories, it is a bit of the past remembered by an adult narrator in the present.

"Dance of the Happy Shades," on the other hand, fails as a memoir because it is told in the present tense. In this story, the narrator is a girl, about fourteen perhaps, who takes piano lessons from the same woman as did her mother before her. Her observations in the present tense are apt but not believable, coming as they do from the mind of a young teenager. When she speaks of Miss Marsalles in the "old days" (*DHS*, p. 213), she gives far more detail than she would have access to about the house in Rosedale, the quality of the music played, and food served at the annual recitals. Some of the details could have been supplied by her mother or her sister, but statements such as "But on the whole the affair in those days had solidity, it had tradition, in its own serenely out-of-date way it had style" (p. 214) are not appropriate to the age of the narrator. The description of Miss Marsalles, "In this full light she looks like a character in a masquerade, like the feverish, fancied-up courtesan of an unpleasant Puritan imagination" (p. 217), is not one that would come from the mind of a young girl, however precocious. Only if she were an adult looking back on Miss Marsalles and her recitals would such perceptions and such a choice of words to voice internally those perceptions be appropriate. Only in retrospect would she talk of "the ceremonies of their childhood" and "the touch of absurd and slightly artificial nostalgia" (p. 215) or say "people who believe in miracles do not make much fuss when they actually encounter one" (p. 223). If the story were told entirely in the past tense by a mature woman in the present — another story about another treachery of the heart — the summation at the end that tells us about "that one communiqué from the other country where she [Miss Marsalles] lives" (p. 224) would be more convincing and appropriate.

"Images" is a similar kind of story about childhood, but, because it is told in the past tense by an adult in the present, it is a true memoir and a more successful story. The narrator was about five when she encountered Joe Phippen and his whiskey-loving cat, and she saw his world in terms of a fairy-tale. For her it was a world of power and danger and magic spells, and Munro vividly captures that child's perception as remembered by her when she is grown up. The description of the grandfather in bed waiting to die and Mary McQuade tending him is couched in language that an adult would use, but it captures the perceptions of the child:

> ...my grandfather lay in near-darkness all day, with his white hair...and his white nightshirt and pillows, making an island in the room which people approached with diffidence, but resolutely. Mary McQuade in her uniform was the other island in the room....she merely waited and breathed, making a sound like the fan made, full of old indefinable complaint. (*DHS*, p. 30)

Her attitude toward Mary shows a child's logic: Mary said that she was asked to come to look after the narrator's mother, but "I doubted that she was asked to come. She came, and cooked what she liked and rearranged things to suit herself, complaining about draughts, and let her power loose in the house. If she had never come my mother would never have taken to her bed" (pp. 32–33). There are reminders that the child is not the actual narrator. About the previous summer the narrator comments: "It was called, even that summer, my grandma's house, though my grandfather was then still alive," and "I was so young then I was put to sleep in a crib" (p. 30). About the time that is the focus of her remembering she says:

66

We did not yet have electricity. It came in soon afterwards, maybe the next summer. But at present there was a lamp on the table.

Now that he [her father] was married and settled down to farming he just kept the one [trap] line, and that for only a few years. This may have been the last year he had it. (p. 35)

After a while there was a bush behind us, the afternoon darkened. It did not occur to me, not till long afterwards, that this was the same bush you could see from our yard.... (p. 37)

It is the separation between the child subject and the adult narrator that makes "Images" a better story than "Dance of the Happy Shades," and it is also what makes "Images" a memoir.

"Winter Wind" and "How I Met My Husband" have the double perspective used in "Images." In "Winter Wind," the adult narrator tells her story in order to understand her grandmother and focuses on one incident to help her gain that understanding. That incident occurred when the narrator was a high-school girl and her grandmother was still alive. Information from a time after the storm is given to us in parentheses (Aunt Madge, the grandmother's sister, lives on in a nursing home [*SIB*, p. 194]; Betty Gosley, the narrator's best friend, became pregnant and married a dairy farmer the following winter [p. 198]; in this community, even now, happiness is described in terms of material possessions [p. 199]). The last two paragraphs are in the present tense and both start with "I understand" (*SIB*, pp. 205–06). Now that she is an adult, the narrator understands her grandmother in a way she could not before. The narrator of "How I Met My Husband" is a woman recounting an event in her life that occurred when she was fifteen. Now she is a married woman with children and with the household appliances and conveniences that she admired in the Peebles' house in the past. From that vantage point, she can make statements and judgements about her past because she, like the narrator in "Winter Wind," understands more now than she did then. For instance, there is her judgement of the lie she told to give Watters, the air-man, more time to get away from his fiancée:

67

I lied for him, and also, I have to admit, for me. Women should stick together and not do things like that. I see that now, but didn't then. I never thought of myself as being in any way like her, or coming to the same troubles, ever. (*SIB*, p. 161)

And from the perspective of a mature woman, she is able to say at the beginning of the last section of the story: "I didn't figure out till years later the extent of what I had been saved from" (p. 64). It is clear to us, however, that she has been saved from humiliation and from a great deal more; and although there is something sad and romantic about young and unrequited love, the reader can see that in marrying the mailman, who never did have a letter from Watters to deliver to her, she made the better choice. The fact that the narrator has never told her husband why she used to wait for the mail makes the reader, in the role of confidant/confidante, know more than the husband, but such a treachery of the heart seems small and beyond reproach — more whimsical than treacherous really — and not what confessions are made of. Both the implied story that the husband tells his children and the story that the narrator relates are memoirs rather than confessions because of the "happy" ending and because there is no sense of a listener in the story.

One essential feature of the confession is the confiding voice. In "Thanks for the Ride," Lois' mother tells the story of her husband's horrible accident in a "slovenly, confiding voice" (*DHS*, p. 51). Such a voice is what distinguishes a confession from a memoir, but since this is Dick's story, the woman's voice is allowed little scope, and the story is a memoir similar to "Boys and Girls." Again in "The Time of Death," a story which is told in the third person, Leona has an urge to tell her story, her aim being to deny her part in the scalding death of her retarded son, and she does at one point attempt to begin: "Leona drank some tea and refused to eat, and talked, beginning like this, in a voice that was ragged and insistent but not yet hysterical: I wasn't hardly out of the house, I wasn't out of the house twenty minutes — " (*DHS*, p. 89). Allie McGee knows the truth, but thinks that "...it was not a time for any sort of accuracy" (p. 91). Shifting the focus from Leona to Allie at this point puts an end to Leona's confiding voice.

Two of Munro's stories, "Something I've Been Meaning to Tell

You" and "Executioners," have the potential to be confessions but are not. In the first story, the voice doesn't even begin to speak. This third-person narration has the content of confession but lacks the confiding voice. Like Mr. Malley in "The Office," Et seems to be an artist who works, through telling stories, with people's lives as her raw material. She wants to tell Arthur the "truth" about Char's love for Blaikie and the cause of her death and thus dispel Arthur's image of her: "Sometimes Et had it on the tip of her tongue to say to Arthur, 'There's something I've been meaning to tell you.' She didn't believe she was going to let him die without knowing. He shouldn't be allowed" (*SIB*, p. 23). He is the only person left to tell, but she keeps putting it off. If she did open her mouth, perhaps a confiding voice would come out, but Et does not allow that to happen. In the case of "Executioners," Helena has no one left to whom she can tell her secret. She is now over sixty, and she has never told anyone of her part in the fire that consumed Howard Troy and his father when she was a child. She ends her "I remember when" story by saying,

> Sometimes I sit in the dark, drinking whiskey and water, thinking uselessly and helplessly, almost comfortably, about things like this that I had forgotten, or could not bear to think about for a long time.
> When everybody is dead who could have remembered it, then I suppose the fire will be finished with, it will be just as if nobody had ever run through that door. (*SIB*, pp. 154–55).

As long as Helena is alive and has memory, the fire cannot be "finished with." It is possible that she feels to blame for the fire because she had wanted to punish Howard in the most horrible ways for his sexual taunts; she had wanted his punishment to be not "clean and magical" but gruesome and personally inflicted (p. 149). Such material is fit for confession, but Helena has no one to talk to, and her memories have been with her so long that she is "almost" comfortable with them, and perhaps the whiskey takes the edge off the pain.

"The Spanish Lady," a story that does use the confiding voice, opens with the narrator writing and then throwing away two letters that show two opposite reactions that she can have towards her husband Hugh's affair with their best friend,

Margaret. She thinks of her life in terms of literature and says, "Life is not like the dim ironic stories I like to read, it is like a daytime serial on television. The banality will make you weep as much as anything else" (*SIB*, p. 176). As she thinks back over her friendship with Margaret, the story unfolds in such a way as to suggest that she is talking to someone to ease her pain, and she explains more than is necessary if the account is only for herself. She describes Hugh and Margaret:

> They are both shy, Hugh and Margaret, they are socially awkward, easily embarrassed. But cold underneath, you may be sure, colder than us easy flirts with our charms and conquests. They do not reveal themselves. (p. 179)

The "us" and "our" suggest that the listener is a kindred spirit, an "easy flirt," like the narrator, with more than his or her share of charm and conquest. She does confess that she has had affairs but blames her infidelity on Hugh's coldness. However, only the retrospective parts of the story sound like confession, and the description of her actions in the present break the confessional tone:

> A howl comes out, out of me, amazing protest.
> I put my arm across my open mouth and to stop the pain I bite it.... (p. 181)

Like Eileen in "Memorial," who makes order of her experiences by turning them into funny stories for friends, this narrator has the habit of making her experiences into anecdotes to relate to Hugh: "I can't think what to do with this man [the Rosicrucian whom she meets on the train] except to make him into a story for Hugh, a curiosity, a joke for Hugh" (pp. 186–87). She would like to be able to say something about the death of the old man in the Vancouver train station. She feels that his cry and his death are a message of which she knows the meaning but can't deliver. Usually a ready talker, the narrator is at a loss for words. However, if turning people into funny stories is a kind of treachery of the heart, perhaps here the narrator is true to herself and to the old man by being silent.

"An Ounce of Cure" has both the tone and form of a confession. Using the confiding voice, Munro writes the story to sound as if a woman is actually telling someone about an embarrassing episode from her adolescence. It opens with "My parents didn't drink" (*DHS*, p. 75), and soon the narrator addresses her listener parenthetically: "I showed the most painful banality in the conduct of the whole affair [her teenage crush on Martin Collingwood], as you will see" (p. 76). Other parenthetical comments keep the listener involved. When the narrator remembers Kay, who administered black coffee to sober her up after her "debauch," she says, "I met, and recognized, that tone of voice years later, in the maternity ward" (p. 83). At one point, she addresses the listener: "If you think that news of the Berrymans adventure would put me in demand for whatever gambols and orgies were going on in and around that town, you could not be more mistaken" (p. 87). At another point, she asks a question: "Why is it a temptation to refer to this sort of thing lightly, with irony, with amazement even, at finding oneself involved with such preposterous emotions in the unaccountable past?" She then provides the answer that the listener or reader might have in mind: "...with adolescent love, of course, it's practically obligatory" (p. 77). The narrator makes it clear that she did not enjoy this escapade. However, it did get her over her crush — a "splendidly unexpected" result of the "affair." What got her back to reality was her aesthetic consciousness of the event: "...I felt that I had had a glimpse of the shameless, marvellous, shattering absurdity with which the plots of life, though not fiction, are improvised. I could not take my eyes off it" (pp. 87–88). Whether she was waiting to see if the plots of life would turn into the plots of fiction is not clear. When she meets Martin again years later, the adult narrator tells us in the last paragraph, he is an undertaker and she is married to another man. Except for their roles in the "debauch," neither has a part to play in the drama of the other person's life. While the narrator seems to be too concerned with the literary or artistic aspects of her "story" for it to have the spiritual urgency of a confession, it does have a confiding voice that holds our attention.

"Forgiveness in Families" is a confession, too. Val, the narrator, is a mature woman who tells an implied listener about her hippie brother and the "disaster" which is his life. The confiding tone is there, especially at the beginning. The narrator uses phrases such as "So as I say" and inserts the kind of questions the listener would ask her:

He [Cam] was born the week I started school, and how's that for timing?...I was going to school for the first time and all other kids had their mothers with them and where was mine?...

It wasn't his fault getting born and it wasn't his fault throwing up at my wedding. Think of it. (*SIB*, p. 93)

I will skip over what he did between getting born and throwing up at my wedding except to say....

Now. Jobs. The question comes up...what is he going to do, how is he going to make a living? (p. 94)

The narrator's treachery of the heart, which is her reason for telling us about her brother, is a complex one. When their mother is improving after a serious illness, Val finds that she feels somehow disappointed that "...Cam didn't kill her after all, with his carelessness and craziness" as she expected. She realizes that she is disappointed that their mother didn't die and that she doesn't have Cam to blame for yet another "disaster." "That was the real shock to me," Val says, "why I kept shaking. Not whether Mother lived or died. It was what was so plain about myself" (p. 104). She sees something about herself that she does not like and does not want to face up to: she is not a better person than Cam, although she has always thought that she was. Their mother credits Cam with saving her life, and Val must practise the art of forgiveness — for her, a kind of martyrdom. She confides in her listener: "I had a strange feeling, like I was walking on coals and trying a spell so I wouldn't get burnt" (p. 105).

"Forgiveness in Families" seems to be a confession that verges on meditation. If it weren't for the listener, who seems to be actually there attending to Val's words, it could be seen as one. The treachery of the heart is an actual one involving a mistake or misjudgement on the narrator's part toward her brother. She perceives at the end of the story that she has badly overvalued her own morality and mistaken his. "Postcard" has a similar ending. Like Val, Helen experiences a revelation about herself that presumably will make a drastic change in her life. This story about what happened "Yesterday afternoon" (*DHS*, p. 128) has the confiding voice of a confession, but there is no listener. At the end Helen seems to address someone, "Oh, Buddy Shields, you can just go on talking..." (p.146), but she is not speaking to Buddy, and she is not likely to tell anyone of her insight into what went wrong with the relationship between Clare and herself. Basically, the story is Helen's meditation on her lack of judgement spoken to herself for her own benefit. "Executioners" could also be considered as a meditation of this type, with Helena's treachery of the heart consisting of the violence in herself that is at the core of her most vivid memory, a treachery that no one guesses and that she cannot reveal to anyone except herself. However, Munro's most interesting meditations are those that leave behind the question of the guilt involved in the actual misjudging of others or of oneself and tackle the problem of the use of autobiographical material in art.

"The Office," although it is a memoir, can be considered as a forerunner of later stories such as "Material" — stories about a person using another person and his or her life as raw material for a story. The narrator here is a writer of fiction who, as a tenant, encounters Mr. Malley, the owner of the office. Assuming that she can use such material in her writing, he tells her of the scandalous sex life of the chiropractor who had the office before she did. Then he tells her about his own life.

> It occurred to me that he was revealing his life to me in
> the hope that I would write it down. Of course he had
> probably revealed it to plenty of people for no particular
> reason, but in my case there seemed to be a special, even
> desperate necessity....He looked to me to say yes.
> (DHS, p.68)

Although this story lacks the confiding voice that is necessary to make it a confession, this statement provides the motivation of most confession: the speaker wants the listener to say *yes* you couldn't help it, *yes* I understand, *yes* you did what you could. Mr. Malley wants to confess, but the narrator does not want to listen; and in trying to avoid being Mr. Malley's confidante or confessor, the narrator makes him dislike her. The notes that he puts on her door recounting her supposed nefarious activities are all fabrications of his fertile imagination, and she "wondered a good deal about that chiropractor. It was not comfortable to see how the legends of Mr. Malley's life were built up" (p.71). He makes it impossible for her to stay, and she leaves knowing that

73

the next set of stories or "legends" will be about her.

She pictures him "arranging in his mind the bizarre but some-how never quite satisfactory narrative of yet another betrayal of trust. While I arrange words, and think it is my right to be rid of him" (p. 74). Like George in "Thanks for the Ride," who rear-ranges facts a bit when they make him uneasy and manufactures a new "truth," Mr. Malley also rearranges facts and manufac-tures a new "truth" to suit himself. In this way, he is similar to the narrator of "The Office" or to any other writer, including Munro, who uses autobiographical material and shapes it into satisfactory narratives to suit his or her purposes. Mr. Malley considers the narrator's failure to co-operate in the making of legends a "betrayal of trust" or a kind of treachery. On the other hand, the narrator uses Mr. Malley and his eccentricities as mate-rial for a story and thinks it is her right to do so. This could be considered a treachery of the heart, but unlike the narrators in later Munro stories, the narrator of "The Office" is not conscious of her attitude toward her autobiographical material, and Mr. Malley does, although not in the way he had hoped, get into her story. This narrator does not recognize the questions of morality that are inherent in her own arrangement of words, and this lack of self-consciousness puts her in the same category as Helen, who uses Myra and her illness in a story, in "Day of the Butterfly," or as the narrator of "The Spanish Lady," who used to turn the people she met into funny stories to tell her husband.

Helen, the narrator of "The Peace of Utrecht," is also an arranger of words and is also guilty of a treachery of the heart. She and her sister Maddy had withdrawn all emotion in dealing with their sick mother, their services to her becoming "parodies of love" (*DHS*, p. 199). Helen had not even come home for her mother's funeral. Harbouring considerable guilt, Helen remem-bers the past and would like to talk about it, but Maddy stops her by saying, "No exorcising here..." (p. 191). However, although exorcism of the past or reconciliation to it through confession is not possible for them, exorcism of another kind is possible. Now that she is dead, the mother has become "one of the town's possessions and oddities, its brief legends" (p. 194), even though her daughters had been ashamed of her and had considered her a "particularly tasteless sideshow" (p. 195). The source of legend is "the unsatisfactory, apologetic and persistent reality" (p. 197) which the mother fulfills admirably. To make their memories bearable and manageable, the daughters now make their mother into a "character" in a story. They have an outlet that Helena in "Executioners" does not have. Helen and Maddy entertain Fred Powell with stories of their childhood:

> [We make] this strange man a present of our childhood, or of that version of our childhood which is safely preserved in anecdote, as in a kind of mental cellophane. And what fantasies we build around the frail figures of our child-selves, so that they emerge beyond recognition incorrigible and gay. We tell stories together well. (p. 193)

Fred compliments the sisters on their good memories, but what they exhibit is not memory but a kind of deception, a talent for disguise, imagination, or artistry (or "translation" — a term that Munro uses in *Who Do You Think You Are?* ["Who Do You Think You Are?", p. 206]) that transforms the reality into something manageable in the same way that Lois' mother in "Thanks for the Ride" or Mrs. Fullerton in "The Shining Houses" do in creating their "legends." The making of legends out of experience seems to be an activity that is necessary for the emotional survival of ordinary people as well as of writers. But because such an activity departs from "truth" and is a kind of treachery of the heart, it results in guilt in Munro's self-conscious narrators.

Such guilt is the subject of "Material." The narrator of this story is a middle-aged woman who used to be married to Hugo, a writer who has become well known. Because she gives details of her past life that she would not need to remind herself of, the story seems to be a confession that is confided to a listener. However, it is possible that the story is a meditation and that the listener is inside her own head, or equally possible is the idea that the listener is an imagined Hugo. On the cover of the book of his stories that she has bought are a photograph of him and a biography, and these initiate her memories. She gives a picture of Hugo as a selfish, talented man who left her to clean up the "messes" and took the time to read and write. She knows that Hugo's biography is fabricated out of half-truths about his life, and her bitterness is evident when she says, "Look at Hugo's picture, look at the undershirt, listen to what it says about him" (*SIB*, p. 29). She continues: "After he quit [the short-lived job painting telephone poles], Hugo found a job marking Grade Twelve examination papers. Why didn't he put that down?" (p. 30). The reason is implied: such a mundane job wouldn't enhance the image he wants to project. Halfway through the next paragraph, the narrator addresses Hugo directly for the only time:

> Put that down, Hugo. *Recorder player....* Look at you, Hugo, your image is not only fake but out-of-date.... you should have shaved your head, shaved your beard, put on a monk's cowl; you should have shut up, Hugo. (pp. 30–31)

After reading the story in which Hugo has turned Dotty, the unlucky daughter of their former landlady, into Art, the narrator wants to write him a letter acknowledging him as a talented writer in order to make up for her previous lack of faith in him. She says, "I respect what has been done. I respect the intention and the effort and the result" (p. 43), but what she feels must be quite different because all she can write is, *"This is not enough, Hugo. You think it is, but it isn't. You are mistaken, Hugo"* (p. 44). What appears first to be a treachery of her heart turns out, in her opinion, to be a treachery of Hugo's. As she got to know her, the narrator came to like Dotty as a person, whereas Hugo merely used her as a source of funny anecdotes and callously let her basement flood and the water ruin her furniture. Even now, long after that incident, the narrator thinks that Hugo misused Dotty. She has "ironical objections" to his story about Dotty: "Dotty was a lucky person.... she was lucky to live in that basement for a few months and eventually to have this done to her.... She has passed into Art. It doesn't happen to everybody." Perhaps when the narrator writes, *"This is not enough,"* she means that this story of Hugo's (or any story) is insufficient as expiation of his treachery toward Dotty. Art is not enough; Art is not a substitute for sympathy and understanding. Maybe she is even suggesting that it is somehow wrong to use as raw material someone's lived and suffered life and turn it by "an act of magic" into Art. Or perhaps she feels that, although Hugo shows "a special, unsparing, unsentimental love" in capturing Dotty in "the marvelous clear jelly" of his Art (p. 43), it is impossible for a man of Hugo's character to be honest enough to reveal the truth

76

of his material. Indeed, it may not be enough to be a sympathetic writer; any writer may fail. Also, believing that men know "how to ignore or use things" and that men have authority and are not "*at the mercy.* Or think they are not" (p. 44), the narrator may see Hugo's story as another example of men's exploitation of women and, thus, proclaims, "*This is not enough.... You are mistaken.*" Her bitter complaint, then, is aimed at Hugo both as a writer and as a man. For her, art is a moral activity, and this story is her corrective to Hugo's faulty vision and misuse of Dotty as material. Thus, her story, which takes the place of her letter to Hugo, is partly memoir and partly a meditation on the right use of the past as raw material for art.

If "Material" can be seen as a meditation on the relation of life to art, then "Tell Me Yes or No" can be seen as one on the relation of art to life. In "Material," the "listener" is disguised, and only once does the narrator address Hugo directly, even though it is possible that the whole meditation is aimed at an imagined Hugo. However, in "Tell Me Yes or No," there is no disguise; the voice is not a confiding voice, and the whole story is addressed to the narrator's former lover, who is not present. By composing in her mind or writing about her relationship with him, she exorcises him from her life. As with the narrator and her desire to "*get rid, of*" her mother in "The Ottawa Valley" (*SIB*, p. 246), the narrator here must get rid of her lover, must get him out of her life even to the point of imagining him dead. As in "Material," parts of this story read like memoir. For instance, this narrator explains what kind of person she was, young and innocent although she was already a wife and mother, when she first met the man who was much later to become her lover. She goes on to describe in detail the day two years ago when they met again and became lovers. Of course, he would know about all this and have no need of the detail. But she does. She needs it badly. She needs to kill him off the way a writer of fiction or television scripts often kills off a character — and she needs to make his death "solid."

She imagines how she found out about his death in a newspaper and supplies a clue to what she is doing to him: "The thing we old pros know about, in these fantasies, is the importance of detail solidity...." If she describes finding out about his death in detail ("A heart attack, that will do" [*SIB*, p. 109]), his death will be solid and real and true — at least as solid and real

77

and true as was their relationship, which seemed to consist mainly of an exchange of letters. She loved him, she claims, for "artistic" reasons. He gave coherence and unity to her life:

> I loved you for linking me with my past.... If I could kindle love then [when they first met in the 1950s] and take it now there was less waste than I had thought. Much less than I had thought. My life did not altogether fall away in separate pieces, lost. (p. 113)

Becoming involved with him gives her the feeling that, like a character in a novel, she leads a life where no event is a "waste." Nevertheless, she says that now she enjoys not waiting for his letters anymore, and her freedom seems to depend on his "death." Just reading about it in the newspaper is not enough, however. She must, in imagination, visit the city ("this city of my imagination" [p. 124]) where he lives and hear more details from his wife (she tells the narrator that death was caused by a heart attack at his desk the previous March while she was at work) in order to make the death "solid" for her. The narrator describes parts of the city in vivid and particular detail in the present tense as though she is actually there at the time of thinking or writing but gives us a clue to what she is doing when she says, "Dusk is the time I would choose, to loiter not far from the open windows [of your house]..." (p. 118). She also describes the man in the present tense as though he were alive: "Amusing and informative you are, so skilled you verge on elegance...," and "...I would say that you are uncompromising," and ". . . there is something chivalric about you." She slips into the present tense when describing her love for him — "the way I am in love" and "at any moment the ties may be cut" — but then corrects herself by saying "have been cut" (p. 116).

The present tense is not appropriate if he is actually dead or if she has finished killing him off in her imagination and, thus, ended her love. Evidently, she needs still more detail to make his death absolutely real: a newspaper report, a visit to his city, and an encounter with his wife are not enough. To receive from his wife a bag of love letters written by another woman to this man is what the narrator needs to make her completely free. So she invents Patricia and her letters, supplies Patricia with a daughter, and imagines Patricia's appearance much spoiled by crying over the lack of communication from her lover. The narrator, in effect, projects her own situation and feelings on to the invented Patricia and in this way frees herself from that situation and those feelings. The narrator addresses her lover:

> She suffers according to rules we all know, which are meaningless and absolute. When I think of her I see all this sort of love as you must have seen, or see it, as something going on at a distance; a strange, not even pitiable, expenditure; unintelligible ceremony in an unknown faith. Am I right, am I getting close to you, is that true?

He is not dead (he can still "see it"), but he is dead to her.[10] If his distance and dread of involvement are his "tricks and trap doors" (p. 124), she has some of her own: her inventive imagination and her ability to turn him into the subject of her fantasy or meditation. If he can escape from her through silence, she has her revenge by exposing him and their relationship through words.

The narrator in "The Stone in the Field" avoids such temptation. This story, which is a Munro novel in miniature, is basically a memoir, except for the last paragraph where the narrator reflects on her material. Her greatest temptation is to make a romantic connection between the mysterious hermit and one or more of her aunts:

> I would have made a horrible, plausible connection between that silence and the manner of his death [cancer of the tongue], between the silence of all of them, the failure to speak what was on their minds, and the manner of his death.

If she had been younger, she might not have been able to resist such a temptation, such a treachery. When she was young, "everything could click into place so satisfactorily, in my head." Not so now. Now, she implies, she sees such plausible but romantic connections as a kind of horrible betrayal of her material: "Now I can only say, my father's sisters behaved in such a way....my mother's cousins behaved in another way...."[11] That is all she can say, all that is allowable in conformity with the truth as she sees it.

"Home," an uncollected story, deals with this issue more

explicitly and serves as a kind of summary of Munro's concerns about the truthful and proper use of autobiographical material. "Home" is another story in the first person which combines memories of the past with events in the present. The narrator visits her old home, which is still lived in by her father and stepmother, and remembers what it used to be like. In this way, the story is a memoir, but a substantial part of the story (four passages in italics) is taken up with the concerns of the narrator as writer, and even though she addresses a "you" here, these serve as meditations on the morality of using autobiographical material in fiction. Munro, in the guise of a narrator, addresses a "you" who seems to be the reader or, more likely, another part of herself:

> It is not love I would compel for them [the people who live in the town from where she comes], but respect. I would like you to see through this parody, self-parody, to something that is not lovable, not delightful. I can't get it, I can't quite bring it out. (p.142)

She wants to write without sentimentality about the people she knows best and bring their real but often unlovable selves to our attention. She does this through voice and image and worries and frets about the accuracy and truthfulness of her description of her memories of these people in her fiction. Another worry is that her raw material (the town and its people) has faded for her because she has "used it up" and "drained" it of messages. She has "escaped things by this use" (p.143) and seems to feel guilty for having done so. Such is the predicament of the narrator in "The Ottawa Valley," too. That narrator also tries to work out or sort out her memories of her mother through a retrospective account in the form of "a series of snapshots": "...it is to reach her that this whole journey has been undertaken. With what purpose? To mark her off, to describe, to illumine, to celebrate, to *get rid* of, her; and it did not work..." (*SIB*, p.246).

The narrator of "Home," on the other hand, seems somewhat regretful that she has got rid of her past by using it as the source of her fiction. She had planned to end this story with the words, "And so I went away and wrote this story" (p.152), but instead she describes her oldest memory and then ends by addressing the listener for the last time:

*You can see this scene, can't you, you can see it quietly
made, that magic and prosaic safety briefly held for us,
the camera moving out and out, that spot shrinking,
darkness. Yes. That is effective.*

*I don't want any more effects, I tell you, lying. I don't
know what I want. I want to do this with honour, if I
possibly can.* (p. 153)

Fearing that she is guilty of a treachery of the heart in her use of
"tricks" and "skill" to transform the past into autobiographical
fiction, the narrator wants to write in a way that will get respect
for her subjects and assure honour — not glory but a sense of
integrity and honesty — for herself. Munro wants — and gets —
the same for herself in her remarkable first-person stories.

NOTES

[1] John Metcalf, "A Conversation with Alice Munro," *Journal of Canadian Fiction*, 1, No. 4 (Fall 1972), p. 58.
[2] Douglas Barbour says that these "exercises in memory" "move
through the chaos of experience & refuse to give it the false form which
assumes the world is safe." The suspense in the stories arises not from
a reader wondering what will happen next but from his or her desire to
find out "what she *will say* next" ("The Extraordinary Ordinary,"
*Open Letter*, 3rd ser., No. 3 [Late Fall 1975], p. 109). And Brandon
Conron says that Munro's "technique allows an intimate rapport
between reader and narrator" ("Munro's Wonderland," *Canadian
Literature*, No. 78 [Autumn 1978], p. 123).
[3] Alice Munro, "Home," in *74: New Canadian Stories*, ed. David
Helwig and Joan Harcourt (Ottawa: Oberon, 1974), p. 142. All further
references to this work appear in the text.
[4] Alice Munro, "The Colonel's Hash Resettled," in *The Narrative
Voice: Stories and Reflections by Canadian Authors*, ed. John Metcalf
(Toronto: McGraw-Hill Ryerson, 1972), p. 182.
[5] Since *Lives of Girls and Women* is more like a novel than a collection of
short stories, and since it adds nothing new to a discussion of memoir,
it is not dealt with in this essay. Neither is the third-person narrated
*Who Do You Think You Are?*. However, because they enhance my
discussion, I use one story that was subsequently collected in *The
Moons of Jupiter* and one story that has not yet been put in a collection.

[6]"The Colonel's Hash Resettled," p. 183.

[7]Roy Pascal distinguishes memoir from reminiscence — the former "concerns itself with public events" and the latter with "private relationships" — and both of these from autobiography proper, whose "attention is focused on the self, in the memoir or reminiscence on others" (*Design and Truth in Autobiography* [London: Routledge and Kegan Paul, 1960], p. 5). In Munro's fiction, such distinctions are not necessary. All the memories concern the narrators personally, and the content is private relationships and not public events. Of all the terms available, I have chosen memoir since it is the term used by Munro herself.

[8]Pascal says that confession is like autobiography but focuses on the internal life. It started as a religious form of autobiography, and in his *Confessions* St. Augustine created "the coherent history of his own soul" (p. 22). When used as a literary rather than a religious term, confession does not necessarily imply an admission of sin or wrong-doing. In describing parts of his life that are normally withheld from others, the writer seeks purgation or absolution as the goal, but "forgiveness" is gained through self-perception and understanding rather than through the ritual of religious confession. Although in this case confession can have self-justification as a motive, with Jean-Jacques Rousseau's *Confessions* autobiography became "a search for the true self, and a means to come to terms with it" (p. 39). Unlike autobiography, in fictional confession there is the convention of the listener as in the actual act of the religious confession.

[9]A meditation is a type of devotional literature, the most famous example being the *Meditations* of Marcus Aurelius (translated by A.S.L. Farquharson, introduction by D.A. Rees [London: Dent, 1961].) Meditations are reflections on moral and spiritual topics. They have no order, narrative, or consecutive arrangement and, thus, are not a type of autobiography. They are private soliloquies intended for no eyes but the writer's own, and it is this aspect, plus the moral (but not religious) nature of the meditation, that is useful in an examination of voice in Munro's stories.

[10]Conron understands the lover to be actually dead and the narrator to visit his city and actually receive a bag of letters from his wife (pp. 120–21).

[11]Alice Munro, "The Stone in the Field," *Saturday Night*, April 1979, p. 45. Rpt. in *The Moons of Jupiter* (Toronto: Macmillan, 1982), pp. 19–35.

# Alice Munro and A Maze of Time

## JOHN ORANGE

THE WAY ALICE MUNRO tells her stories has evolved over the years
from a relatively conventional and straightforward narration by
a first-person narrator to a much more complicated, subtle, and
experimental narrative technique, often involving a third-person
limited narrator, as in *Something I've Been Meaning to Tell You*,
*Who Do You Think You Are?*, and half of the stories in *The
Moons of Jupiter*. Besides gradually creating a distance between
author and narrator, Munro has also increasingly manipulated
her use of narrative time as a structural device in the telling of the
stories. Her shift over to the use of a third-person narrator is
related to her disruption of narrative time, and it is useful to
explore how changing her use of both of these techniques frees
Munro from the limitations of first-person narration, so that she
can explore a different set of themes without losing touch with
her basic strengths and concerns as a writer. In other words, by
increasingly departing from a first-person narrator, Munro also
departs from conventional linear development in the telling of
the story. By freeing herself to shift time schemes and, thus,
create a seemingly random narrative line, she expresses her
vision more clearly by emphasizing a set of themes that are only
anticipated in her earlier works.

Eleven of the fifteen stories in *Dance of Happy Shades* are
written in the first person, and all but one of the narrators are
female. The first story in that collection, "Walker Brothers
Cowboy," is told by a young girl who speaks in the present tense.
Events, then, are necessarily arranged in chronological order,
and the reader experiences the adventure in the story in just the
way the narrator does. Consequently, both reader and narrator
learn from the experience in the same way and at the same time.
The technique is effective in communicating the young girl's new

awareness of the complexity and sadness of adult life, and, thus, the story signals her movement from a state of innocent wonder to one of vague anxiety and sadness. The story is also about the passage of time and what is lost to time. Details such as maple tree roots cracking the sidewalk, the references to dinosaurs in the area, and the geological history of the Great Lakes underline the notion of transience and loss in the personal lives of Ben, Nora, and the two mothers. The final description of the day passing and the weather changing to rain beautifully captures the relationship between the movement of time and the child's dim perception of the sorrows of adult experience awaiting her.

The next story, "The Shining Houses," contains the same theme (among others) in that old Mrs. Fullerton and her property are about to be displaced by a seemingly inexorable "progress" of time, even though she seems to the narrator to be the very spirit of the place. Once again, the story is structured by a linear and chronological sequence of events as they impress themselves on Mary, the central consciousness in the story. In both stories, although the passage of time is one of the themes, the treatment of that theme is conventional and straightforward. The reader's awareness of time passing is delimited by the narrative point of view.

The other stories in the collection which deal with rites of passage, the child's apprehension of a darker adult world awaiting her (him in one case), are told in chronological, linear sequential fashion. "Images," "Thanks for the Ride," "An Ounce of Cure," "Day of the Butterfly," "Boys and Girls," "Red Dress — 1946," and "A Trip to the Coast" all move from past time to pluperfect time, or memory time, in a conventional manner, and the emphasis in these stories is on the quality of the experience being described rather than on the tricks time itself plays on people. The stories focusing on adult experiences, such as "The Shining Houses," "Postcard," and "The Peace of Utrecht," bring the theme of fugitive time more to the foreground, as might be expected since memory is what shapes adult lives as opposed to childhood awareness. However, there are few ruptures in the linear structuring of the stories.

"The Peace of Utrecht" is perhaps the most interesting in this regard. The narrator tells her story inside of two time frames — one consisting of the events of the last three weeks, the other of the events of childhood more than ten years ago. *"After all this time"* is italicized (p. 195), as if to emphasize the theme and the functioning of memory in the story. The narrator is trying to "complete the picture" (p. 200) by putting distant and recent memories together, and, once she feels she has done this, she can then offer her sister, Maddie, advice in what seems to be very recent past time. It is the action of memory which has been instrumental in fusing episodes across time which leads to the narrator's new understanding. In this story, Munro breaks up the linear or chronological arrangement of episodes, however slightly, and this story creates a rather different impression than the others in the volume.

*Lives of Girls and Women* is again narrated in the first person, and the stories are arranged so as to give the impression of a chronological development in the age and character of the narrator. However, because each section is also self-contained, a short story in a story sequence, Munro is free to move two steps forward in time in one story and a half a step back to start the next. Also, she can insert interpolated stories told by other characters to fill in pluperfect time. Despite this more fluid use of time, the reader, nevertheless, has the impression of a linear sequence in the development of the sensibilities, knowledge, and understanding of Del, the narrator.

At the heart of this use of a first-person narrator ranging back through memory time to tell a story is the implicit assumption, or at least the *impression* left in the reader, that human experience can be understood, that the world has an implicit order. The fact that Del becomes a *writer*, and that *she* is the sensible consciousness through which the story is told, reinforces the reader's assumption that the events of the story have some implicit, or even explicit, meaning in that the writer has set her experience into the form of a story. (The meaning is, in fact, sometimes stated too explicitly in a paragraph, often near the end of the story, when Munro and/or the narrator explains the theme of the story!)[1] When remembered events are selected and placed in a linear sequence, the reader is encouraged to assume a cause / effect relationship among those events and to develop an understanding of the story by a process of logic which relates events to character development. Del as writer has an impulse to shape and, thereby, to find (give?) meaning in her experience, even at an early age.[2] The question becomes: is this choice of narrative point of view and its consequent linear-chronological arrangement of events the most effective way to accomplish Munro's desired ends, or even to display her real strengths as a writer? The answer to that question can be found in her statements on her purpose in writing and in her more recent choice of narrative point of view.

The invention of a "double sense of present time," as Margaret Laurence calls it, in which the narrative voice has to speak as a child and an adult simultaneously,[3] is not new to fiction. Usually, the narrator, often the implied writer of the story after he or she has reached maturity, describes an event as *experienced* by a child or adolescent but written in the *style* of an adult who is more detached and judicial than the child could have been at the time of the event. The adult is usually in the process of working out a solution to the problem (and the confusion) which the child faced, and this is suggested by the very act of organizing the memory and then, more importantly, by writing it down. Brandon Conron has stated that Munro's early stories "depend partly for their effect on a bifocal point of view,"[4] where an adult, after a lapse of time, gains "new insights and perspectives between an incident and its recording."[5] Munro, when questioned about this device, has qualified the conventional function that it serves:

> The adult narrator has the ability to detect and talk about the confusion [of the child]. I don't feel that the confusion is ever resolved. And there is some kind of a central mystery, as in "Walker Brothers Cowboy", that is there for the adult narrator as well as it was for the child. I feel that all life becomes even more mysterious and difficult. And the whole act of writing is more an attempt at recognition than of understanding because I don't understand many things. I feel a kind of satisfaction in just approaching something that is mysterious and important. Then writing is the act of approach and recognition. I believe that we don't solve these things — in fact our explanations take us further away.[6]

Given the way the device of first-person narrator in double perspective works, especially when the events are arranged by memory into chronological sequence, do these stories have the effect that Munro outlines? It could be argued, for example, that

86

the narrator of "Walker Brothers Cowboy" has learned a great deal about her father's inner life, about time, and about how adulthood dawns on adolescence at the end of that story. *Most*, perhaps *all*, of the confusion of the child has been cleared up for both the narrator and the reader. The story has shape, a rhetorical structure, and, therefore, it amplifies its meaning and even suggests life can be finally known in some final way. If there is a residue of mystery in the story it is, I would say, very slight.

It is obvious, however, that Munro's strengths as a writer lie in the direction of recognizing unacknowledged realities, mysterious depths in the ordinary, the paradoxes at the core of human psychological responses,[7] our capacity for self-delusion, and the "super realism or magical and mysterious suggestion of a soul beyond the objects depicted."[8] Her writing style places emphasis on the surface textures, the sensory qualities of life which are multifarious, transitory, and arresting, simultaneously. Our memories tend to give our experiences of life a legendary quality, and at the heart of a legend is a secret. Munro also explores the secret selves inside the roles and public masks we wear only to discover even deeper and often unfathomable depths to the human personality. Life does *not* have implicit meaning, nor is it understandable when we focus solely on this side of her writing.

Perhaps, then, Munro has decided that a first-person narrator setting down memories in a more or less linear sequence is not the only way, or even the most desirable way, to communicate her vision. Whatever the reason, she changed her narrative point of view to that of third-person limited omniscient in five of the thirteen stories of *Something I've Been Meaning to Tell You*, and in all of the stories in *Who Do You Think You Are?*. It is clear, also, that many of the stories in these two collections have a more mysterious, cryptic quality to them. The reader experiences a disquieting sense that meaning is hidden, blurred, even obscured because of the way the story is told. Abrupt shifts in time and settings, as well as a more *associative* (as opposed to linear, logical) set of links among memories and thoughts in characters' minds, leaves one with the impression that experience *cannot* be understood, and that, ultimately, any pattern of meaning and significance in human action can only be partial, and temporary, and probably illusory. Without even the security of a linear, sequential narrative form to fall back on, the reader is left more on his/her own — i.e., with ironic distance that does not provide answers and yet with a much stronger sense of the bewilderment and frustration felt by the central characters.

*Something I've Been Meaning to Tell You* signals a transition in Munro's writing in that it contains three different kinds of stories. On the one hand, we find the conventional narratives containing familiar themes and settings such as "How I Met My Husband," "The Found Boat," "Executioners," "Winter Wind," "The Ottawa Valley," and "Forgiveness in Families." Those stories all follow a conventional linear form. A second group of stories might include "Material," "Tell Me Yes or No," and "The Spanish Lady." The women who tell these stories seem to be less confident in their ability to draw meaning from their experiences, and they narrate the episodes in a more disjointed, associative way, leaving the reader with the impression that they have not yet completely worked through this pain, nor have they come to any satisfactory understanding of its causes. Their final but uneasy state of mind is echoed, in fact, in all of the stories in the collection. Perhaps Eileen's thought in "Memorial" says it best:

> *I have not worked through anything*, Eileen thought. And further: *I do not believe things are there to be worked through.*
>
> People die; they suffer, they die....Illness and accidents. They ought be respected, not explained. Words are all shameful. They ought to crumble in shame. (p. 221)

There are other similar passages in the stories:

> Never mind. I invented her. I invented you, as far as my purposes go. I invented loving you and I invented your death. I have my tricks and my trap doors, too. I don't understand their workings at the present moment, but I have to be careful, I won't speak against them. ("Tell Me Yes or No," p. 124)
>
> And how is anybody to know, I think as I put this down, how am I to know what I claim to know?...
> But that only takes care of the facts. I have said other

things.... Yet I have not invented it, I really believe it. Without any proof I believe it, and so I must believe that we get messages another way, that we have connections that cannot be investigated, but have to be relied on. ("Winter Wind," p. 201)

What we say and feel no longer rings true, it is slightly beside the point. As if we were all wound up a long time ago and were spinning out of control, whirring, making noises, but at a touch could stop, and see each other for the first time, harmless and still. This is a message; I really believe it is; but I don't see how I can deliver it. ("The Spanish Lady," p. 191)

...it is to reach her [my mother] that this whole journey has been undertaken. With what purpose? To mark her off, to describe, to illumine, to celebrate, to *get rid*, of her; and it did not work, for she looms too close, just as she always did. She is heavy as always, she weighs everything down, and yet she is indistinct, her edges melt and flow. Which means she has stuck to me as close as ever and refused to fall away, and I could go on, and on, applying what skills I have, using what tricks I know, and it would always be the same. ("The Ottawa Valley," p. 246)

The fact that most of these passages come at the end of the stories indicates that Munro is underlining the difficulty, even the futility, of tying up human experience, even in stories, into neat packages of meaning. Munro consciously avoids a didactic and rhetorical direction in these stories, presumably because she is trying to avoid creating the illusion that experience can be delimited or that her narrators have reached any final conscious (i.e., articulated) explanation of how life works. That is not to say that the *stories* have no meaning. They are designed so that their very form will reinforce the theme of the complexity, and, ultimately, the unfathomable depth, of any human experience. Our understanding even of ourselves can only be tentative and tenuous, according to these stories.

The third kind of story in this collection presents narrators who are unable to control even their memories, let alone understand events in their present lives. "Something I've Been Meaning to Tell You," "Walking on Water," "Marrakesh," and "Memorial" are stories told in the third person by a narrator who limits the reader's knowledge to that of a central character who is forced to live inside of herself (himself in one case) because the world outside has become completely mysterious to her. These narrators, mostly old people, travel through present events in their lives uncomprehending, bewildered, fascinated, afraid, and suddenly jolted into the past and given a memory which helps them, or startles them, or sometimes throws them into even more confusion. Consequently, the reader comes away from the story, especially after first reading, feeling much the way the character felt. The world has begun to tumble. Things happen at random. Memories both illuminate and conceal meanings. Time and space are askew.

In this kind of story, Munro best captures the sense of hidden mysteries. One way she does this is by abrupt shifts of narrative time, often without transitions or precise dating. The title-story, for example, begins with an episode which occurs in present narrative time, followed by one in the recent past ("The day before" [p. 1]), then one in "that past June" (p. 4), and then it moves into the distant past when "Et remembered the first time she understood that Char was beautiful," "just a couple of weeks" before her brother drowned (p. 5). There follows a reference to the drowning incident and an abrupt shift to a time about four years later, which may or may not be concurrent with the time of Char's affair with Blaikie Noble in the summer of 1918, depending upon how one reads the paragraphs between the reference to the drowning and the date given two paragraphs later. The subsequent references to time become rather indistinct, as though they make sense only to one who has lived through the events being remembered: "Before Christmas" (p. 11), "One afternoon" (p. 12) (presumably much later since Char is married to Arthur), "Arthur was almost bald now and Et's own hair was thin and dark" (p. 14), "After the blueing episode" (p. 15) (1918), "the week before the Labor Day weekend" (p. 20), "in later years" (p. 8). The story ends in a time period sometime later than when it began, but the reader has no firm sense just how long after unless he/she goes back through a maze of references to time to figure it out. The function of the *seemingly* random shifts in time is to reinforce the sense of hidden (or secret) information which Et is hiding from the reader, possibly even from herself. The idea that Et may have murdered her sister is only faintly glimpsed at first. The way the story is narrated, we are offered a suspicion which becomes a conviction only upon second reading.

The story "Walking on Water" also contains abrupt leaps in time from present to far past, to recent past, to present, to more recent past, to dream time etc., but in this story, the shifts are usually triggered by fears or associations in Mr. Lougheed's mind. The protagonist looks for some firm ground in a world which keeps shifting underneath him often by locating himself in time ("The time set was Sunday morning. Today was Friday. Ten o'clock had been the exact time picked..." etc., [p. 68]). However, his mind keeps jumping to other times, and the story-line follows his almost random train of thoughts. Waiting for Eugene to finish meditating, for example, Mr. Lougheed remembers having walked by him in the past, and, at that time, he looked away in embarrassment. The omniscient narrator follows the old man's train of thought:

> He did not look to see the expression on Eugene's face. Rapt, was it supposed to be? He was as alarmed, as appalled, in the furthest corner of himself, as if he had seen somebody making love.
> That had happened, too. (p. 69)

(The simile is presumably the narrator's, but Munro makes it seem as though the association also occurs to her protagonist.) We are then told about how one day Mr. Lougheed inadvertently saw Rex and Calla copulating, and immediately we are told of the first time he became a voyeur when he was a boy and he paid to watch "one of the Brewer boys and his younger sister" (p. 70). The story moves along in this manner, forward and backward in time, through a recurring dream, until the episode when Eugene tries, and fails, to walk on water. At the end of the story, Mr. Lougheed is so baffled and confused that "he doubted his powers" to get to "the top of the stairs," and he considers retreating to the safe refuge of "an apartment building" (p. 92).

Another story involving an elderly person's sense of psychological dislocation is "Marrakesh," and, once again, the story is told in a way that makes the reader feel the protagonist's profound alienation from the rapidly changing world around her. Social roles, sexual activity, conventional moral values, and even conventional wisdom have all changed radically, and Dorothy finds herself becoming a voyeur peeping in at life, which is passing by in front of her. Like Eileen in "Memorial," Dorothy is left on her own to muster whatever resources of faith and understanding that she can. The ironic distance of both author and reader is sustained not only by Munro's reluctance to intervene in her own voice, but also by the dislocations in narrative time and abrupt shifts among seemingly unrelated episodes. However, the reader feels a good deal of sympathy for the central characters, and Munro's strong compassion for them also becomes conspicuous, precisely as a result of these same techniques. They serve to put us in these characters' psyches more completely, so that we experience the world as they do. At the same time, the rhetorical direction of the story is submerged or hidden, so our first response is the one Munro's writing intends to evoke — "approach and recognition."[9]

In some ways, these more experimental stories in *Something I've Been Meaning to Tell You* anticipate the kind of stories that are interwoven in the next collection, *Who Do You Think You Are?*. The setting is that of the early stories, and, just as in *Lives of Girls and Women*, we follow the development of a girl through adolescence and into adulthood; even many of the themes are similar to those in the first two books. However, the stories are told in a very different way, and they produce very different effects. The narrative point of view is third-person limited omniscient in that it focuses primarily on Rose's experiences and her psychological and emotional responses to her environment. Munro even gives herself more latitude in this book to intervene in her own voice in order to heighten ironic distance between Rose and the reader. Apparently, Munro had originally intended to increase that distance by having some of the stories centre on a writer named Janet who writes stories about a character named Rose, whose life closely parallels her own. The Janet stories were to be narrated in the first person and the Rose stories in the third person.[10] Clearly, that design would have pushed Munro's presence as author even further into the background. Although the design of the book was changed at the last minute, it is fair to say that Munro's intention to step back from her characters is clear. Ironic distance allows a writer to suspend judgement, as it were, and, therefore, there is no need to give precise rhetorical direction to the stories. Or, looked at from another vantage point, one way to avoid giving a story a rhetorical-didactic focus is to inject ironic distance, thus leaving the reader on his/her own to interpret the story's meaning.

Added to this use of third-person narrative point of view, we find Munro's now consistent disruption of narrative time (except for "Wild Swans"), abrupt shifts in setting, and unpredictable endings to stories, which leave the reader dazzled, curious, and groping for understanding. In discussing her earlier story, "The Office," Munro said that she would not write that story the same way now:

> I'd like it *more open, less pointed, even less contrived*; I would like it to seem all artless and accidental, which means that I have adopted another fashion. By fashion I don't mean some currently popular tricks — though there's always a bit of that — but *a way of making the story that seems to get closer to what I want to say.* [emphasis added][11]

The underlying artistic vision, or what Munro "wants to say," in the more recent stories, then, is that patterns of interpretation of human experience, whether they are offered by memory, analysis, other people, or even by works of fiction, are all inadequate and often illusory.

The truth is that Truth is hidden — submerged for a variety of reasons. Consequently, in *Something I've Been Meaning to Tell You*, Munro emphasizes the theme that people tend to hide their "real selves" from others, and, more especially, that we all tend to live at a little distance from ourselves. We act out roles and scenes in which we do, and do not, believe. One of the most powerful passages in *Who Do You Think You Are?* involves a violent beating Rose receives from her father. Both seem to be acting out parts they only partially accept, and each knows the other is play-acting:

> He pushes her off the table. His face, like his voice, is quite out of character. He is like a bad actor, who turns a part grotesque. As if he must savor and insist on just what is shameful and terrible about this. That is not to

say he is pretending, that he is acting, and does not mean it. He is acting, and he means it. Rose knows that, she knows everything about him.

She has since wondered about murders, and murderers. Does the thing have to be carried through, in the end, partly for the effect, to prove to the audience of one — who won't be able to report, only register, the lesson — that such a thing can happen, that there is nothing that can't happen, that the most dreadful antic is justified, feelings can be found to match it? ("Royal Beatings," p. 16)

Rose plays "her part in this with the same grossness, the same exaggeration, that her father displays" (p. 17) and, significantly, later becomes a successful actress. Her role, however, is not her "identity." It is only who she *thinks* she is. It isn't until the last story that Rose seems ready to make a distinction between the two. Finally, as Munro said in an interview, what Rose "gets [is] a knowledge of herself."[12] That knowledge of an *authentic* self is hard won, however, and by no means easily articulated. In fact, the design of the stories insures that the reader will find it difficult to formulate exactly what Rose "knows" without including all the details of all of the stories.

The design of the stories also helps to emphasize the theme of the illusory nature of ordinary life. The sudden interview with Hat Nettleton at the end of the "Royal Beatings," because it is juxtaposed with the story of Becky Tyde and her father's death, makes one recognize how superficial our knowledge of history really is. The ending of "Half a Grapefruit" lists the upstanding citizens of Hanratty who are also labelled by occupation (accountant, undertaker, contractor) when Rose's memory depicts them as very different kinds of people than their public image suggests. In fact, most of the stories juxtapose the secret and public lives of characters in order to expose the illusory nature of "ordinary" life: the "minister" in "Wild Swans," Simon in "Simon's Luck," Flo, Rose's father, and a number of background characters are all hiding important dimensions of themselves.

Related to the theme of the illusory quality of our perceptions of people is Munro's examination of the distortions which some kinds of fiction create. Flo tells stories, for example, and one wonders how reliable they can be. Rose tells stories back, and one wonders how much she has added for effect.[13] Flo's hostility to all books, Rose's father's reluctant admiration of them ("Half a Grapefruit," p. 44), the comment on Katherine Mansfield's "The Garden Party" (p. 48), and the painting *King Cophetua and the Beggar Maid* ("The Beggar Maid," p. 77), are only a few of many references to art which not only help to define Rose's romantic imagination, but also allow Munro to examine the influence of art on the ways we perceive our own history and ourselves. How "real" are the local legends? Do they contain more "truth" than historical facts? Do they point to an unseen reality? Are they merely distortions? The design of Munro's stories themselves seems to imply that all things are real and that everything in life can be arranged for many different purposes and effects. Some stories distort more than others. Others, like Flo's warnings of a white slave trade, almost come true. J. R. (Tim) Struthers accurately sums up the impression that the stories create:

> Throughout Munro's fiction, characters and actions become exaggerated — momentarily assume romantic, melodramatic, gothic, or even absurd proportions — then diminish to their normal, ordinary forms. To present human beings only in their exaggerated forms, such as the "idiotic saintly whore" ridiculed in the [next] story, is to neglect their essential humanness and ultimately to distort reality. Conversely, to present reality as something plain and even tedious is to misrepresent it as well, by ignoring the splendour and the savagery that are shown when ordinary existence suddenly and surprisingly opens inward, capsizes, or is lifted up to reveal unimaginable mysteries, sources of celebration.[14]

In fact, Munro's use of abrupt breaks in narrative time and sudden shifts of place brings these issues to the foreground. It is as though we are being invited to ponder how stories are made, since, in many ways, we have to help to make each story ourselves. At the very least, we are encouraged to consider all the other possible ways that the parts of this particular story could be arranged. Thus, we find a more successful marriage of form and vision in these stories as opposed to the earlier, more conventional ones.

The juxtapositioning of episodes from different times also

adds an ironic commentary, and character and reader alike have to shift perspectives of reality as we move through life. What Rose felt at one time for Patrick, or Clifford, or Flo, or her father, is contrasted with the way she feels about the same character or event much later. But since we are given what amounts to stereoscopic vision of a character or event in two different times, the result is an ironic counterpointing which perfectly reinforces the themes of acting roles in real life based on illusion, illusions becoming real over time, stories containing truth etc. We are continually reminded how Flo behaved, for example, or what she said in the light of what happened to her much later, and vice versa.

It is clear, too, that death, or the shadow of approaching death, is present in all of the stories. Disruptions in narrative time signal the final end of time, throughout the collection. Rose's father is terminally ill. Simon and Ralph Gillespie die unexpectedly. Flo is put in a nursing home. A number of background characters are listed who die quietly, violently, mysteriously, predictably, even humorously. Flo's accounts of local *history* seem to centre on death:

> ...for then Patrick got to hear about a man who cut his own throat, *his own throat*, from ear to ear, a man who shot himself the first time and didn't do enough damage, so he loaded up and fired again and managed it, another man who hanged himself using a chain, the kind of chain you hook on a tractor with, so it was a wonder his head was not torn off. ("The Beggar Maid," p. 87)

Even Flo, in her own way, seems to understand that death is the mystery that makes all living and all life mysterious. It is no wonder we need our illusions. By jumping backward and forward in time, Munro reminds the readers of inexorable change and unfathomable fate. Yet there is that blind old woman who can spell "celebrate" and somehow still cling to some centre in herself, no matter how pathetic or how comical her performance is. She too, is a "wonder" ("Spelling," p. 183).

What this collection of stories conveys most powerfully is what Rose "gets" when she "gets herself." Rose shares Munro's understanding that we each struggle to find our way through a maze of events, places, other lives. The disruptions in narrative time in these stories, the constant rush of myriad details, the shifts of attention to assorted peripheral characters and stories, the quick slide show of places and events, all serve to reinforce the idea that our lives take terribly and wonderfully unpredictable turns in that maze. Seemingly secure paths can lead into wholly unfamiliar territory — that "other country" where people live inside of themselves ("Dance of the Happy Shades," *DHS*, p. 224). New landscapes of possible meanings continually come into view. At the centre of the maze is death, and what propels us through it is the rascal time.

NOTES

[1] In public talks Munro has mentioned this weakness and says, for example, that, given a second chance, she would delete the last sentence of "Postcard."

[2] In his study of *Lives of Girls and Women*, J. R. (Tim) Struthers has analyzed this pattern in the novel, so it need not be dwelled on here (J. R. Struthers, "Reality and Ordering: The Growth of a Young Artist in *Lives of Girls and Women*," *Essays on Canadian Writing*, No. 3 [Fall 1975], pp. 32–46).

[3] Margaret Laurence, "Time and Narrative Voice," in *Margaret Laurence: The Writer & Her Critics*, ed. William New, Critical Views on Canadian Writers (Toronto: McGraw-Hill Ryerson, 1977), pp. 158–59. In "Review of *A Bird in The House*" reproduced in the same volume (pp. 152–55), Kent Thompson examines the function of this device in Laurence's stories and it is quite different in intent than it is in Munro's stories.

[4] Brandon Conron, "Munro's Wonderland," *Canadian Literature*, No. 78 (Autumn 1978), p. 111.

[5] Conron, p. 115.

[6] Jill Marjorie Gardiner, interview with Alice Munro in "The Early Short Stories of Alice Munro," M. A. Thesis New Brunswick 1973, p. 178.

[7] For one of the extensive discussions on this and related topics see Helen Hoy, " 'Dull, Simple, Amazing and Unfathomable': Paradox and Double Vision in Alice Munro's Fiction," *Studies in Canadian Literature*, 5 (Spring 1980), 100–15.

[8] Conron, p. 110.

[9] Gardiner, p. 178.

¹⁰ See the J. R. (Tim) Struthers interview with Munro in this volume and also J. R. (Tim) Struthers, "Introduction: Almost a Patented Canadian Technique" in "Intersecting Orbits: A Study of Selected Story Cycles by Hugh Hood, Jack Hodgins, Clark Blaise and Alice Munro," Diss. Western Ontario 1982, pp. 24–25.

¹¹ Alice Munro, "On Writing 'The Office,' " in *Transitions II: Short Fiction; a Source Book of Canadian Literature*, ed. Edward Peck (Vancouver: CommCept, 1978), p. 261.

¹² Alan Twigg, "What Is," in his *For Openers: Conversations with 24 Canadian Writers* (Madeira Park, B. C.: Harbour, 1981), p. 19.

¹³ See "Half a Grapefruit" pp. 42–45. For a more complete discussion of this issue see Lawrence Mathews, "Who Do You Think You Are?: Alice Munro's Art of Disarrangement" in this collection of essays.

¹⁴ Struthers, "Introduction," pp. 14–15.

# "Changing Is the Word I Want"

LORNA IRVINE

IN *Lives of Girls and Women*, Del Jordan's mother haltingly puts into words her belief that body transplants allow an immortality that religions have never been able to assure:

> If we weren't thinking all the time in terms of persons, if we were thinking of Nature, all Nature going on and on, parts of it dying — well not dying, changing, *changing* is the word I want, changing into something else, all those elements that make the person changing and going back into Nature again and reappearing over and over in birds and animals and flowers — Uncle Craig doesn't have to be Uncle Craig! (p. 47)

Idiosyncratic as this passage sounds, it nonetheless focuses the reader's attention on the centrality of change in Alice Munro's fiction. Throughout, transformations of various kinds affect not only the characters she creates for us, and the situations in which they find themselves, but also the structure of the stories she writes. Her fictions are filled with flux, with process, with the deceived eye and the altered landscape, with the almost indecipherable moment of metamorphosis rather than with its results. Furthermore, the peculiarly jerky, I might even say breathless, pace of a Munro narrative reflects the kaleidoscope of moods that are the stories' contents. Particularly in *Who Do You Think You Are?*, the typically disrupted chronology, also a reflection and a cause of the variegations of the text, is emphasized by structural breaks in the actual spacing on the page. Indeed, so obsessive is the concern with change that it seems necessary to investigate it from a number of angles.

As Tzvetan Todorov and other structuralist critics of narrative have thoroughly illustrated, narratives are always constructed from varying kinds of transformations.[1] The major structural transformations, summarized by Todorov as those of status, of supposition, of knowledge, and of manner, more or less do cover the possible plots of fiction. We can observe them repeatedly in the fiction discussed here. But the problem that I am addressing has a slightly different perspective. It is Munro's insistent illustration of flux that fascinates me — the fluid relationships between order and disorder, between stillness and movement, and, perhaps most important, between revelation and secrecy. The privileging of change seems to me to account for the peculiar ambivalence of a Munro story, an ambivalence that makes the reader indecisive about the meaning of the fictional experience. Partly, Munro is simply doing what most writers do at some point in their fictions; that is, she dramatizes the difficulty of her craft. Like so many stories, hers, too, are about the act of writing. And this act is an ambivalent one. On the one hand, writing is the articulating of inarticulate experience, giving it order, revealing its hidden meanings, and holding it still so that it can be accurately observed. On the other hand, writing also creates disorder, suggests hidden meanings and can, as Munro's invariably does, refuse epiphany, stasis, closure. In the epilogue of *Lives of Girls and Women*, Del describes the resulting tension:

> I would try to make lists. . . .
> The hope of accuracy we bring to such tasks is crazy, heartbreaking.
> And no list could hold what I wanted, for what I wanted was every last thing, every layer of speech and thought, stroke of light on bark or walls, every smell, pothole, pain, crack, delusion, held still and held together — radiant, everlasting. (p. 253)

Yet although Del claims to desire epiphany, she assiduously avoids it, choosing instead to present, as I argue her author does, the transitory, the questions that "persist in spite of the novels" (p. 251). Just as the faces of the photographs taken by Del's fictional photographer shift and alter, so, too, do the boundaries of Munro's stories.

But apart from dramatizing the difficulty that writers have in making words mean what they want them to, Munro's obsession with change obviously indicates other concerns. These concerns relate to her perception of experience as a woman and to the lives of the women about whom she writes. In her article, "Child-Women and Primitives in the Fiction of Alice Munro," Beverley Rasporich writes: "...the shifting perspectives of her feminine voice may undermine a logical or consistent philosophy, but in a historical sense, they are an evocative and instinctive articulation of society in transition, and of women in search of themselves."[2] I, too, believe that Munro describes women who are in the process of transformation. As Del's mother claims: "There is a change coming I think in the lives of girls and women" (p. 176). In story after story, Munro creates girls and women who imagine change or actually experience it. Such concentration on social transformation insists on a fluid narrative, one that refuses closure in order to allow the female characters room to alter the insistent endings of, for example, the nineteenth century novel where women's fates are closed: death or marriage.[3] It insists, also, on a broken chronological development, such as occurs in *Lives of Girls and Women* and *Who Do You Think You Are?*, so that the female *Bildungsroman*, at least for Munro, does not follow a rigid plan. Again, change dominates. The abrupt alternations of past and present encourage a perspective that keeps even memory flowing.

If the social concerns of Munro's fiction encourage this fluid narration, I believe, to use Patricia Spack's phrase, that the female imagination[4] also tends to perceive change as paramount, to refuse to define the boundaries of the self. When Del compares herself to the rigid, purposeful Jerry Storey, she admits her shifting sense of self: "I whose natural boundaries were so much more ambiguous, who soaked up protective coloration wherever it might be found, began to see that it might be restful, to be like Jerry" (p. 200). This sense of ambiguous boundary permeates Munro's fiction, not only because she so often describes women, but also because she is a woman writer. As extensions of the rigidly masculine theories of development prevalent in the nineteenth century and much of the twentieth, today's theorists pay more attention to these perceptions of the female body. Dorothy Dinnerstein, in *The Mermaid and the Minotaur*, locates them in the early relationship with the mother, arguing that because the mother is imagined as a "global, inchoate, all-embracing presence before she is a person, a discrete finite human individual with a subjectivity of her own,"[5] in certain fundamental ways, female bodies seem forever impossible to contain. This fact is most clearly apparent in the mother-daughter relationship. As Nancy Chodorow also argues, "Because of their mothering by women, girls come to experience themselves as less separate than boys, as having more permeable ego boundaries. Girls come to define themselves more in relation to others."[6] In a Munro story, then, the relationships between mothers and daughters, among women peers, and, most notably, between a female perspective and the act of writing are all interwoven.

Such interweavings are, for instance, vividly portrayed in the final story of the collection *Something I've Been Meaning to Tell You*. In "The Ottawa Valley," artistic transformation is a metaphor for the changing mother-daughter relationship. The story is worth looking at in some detail. In it the narrator, a woman (only two of Munro's collected stories, "Thanks for the Ride" and "Walking on Water," are narrated by men or have a man as their central character), loosely links together a series of impressions of a childhood trip she has taken with her mother. Transience imbues everything — the train ride from Toronto to Ottawa, the Second World War, the narrator's childhood. At the centre are women's lives. Their centrality is simultaneously a contradiction and a proof of Del's mother's statement in *Lives of Girls and Women*: "All women have had up till now has been their connection with men. All we have had. No more lives of our own, really, than domestic animals" (p. 176). Apart from the narrator's mother, the two major women of the story, Aunt Dodie and Aunt Lena, are defined against men: Dodie as an abandoned bride, Lena as a repressed, frightened, irascible wife. At the same time, by writing about them, the narrator has transformed their dependence, has brought them to the forefront of the story she has to tell, has given them social meaning. In Munro's stories, women always matter. Yet the artistic transformation undertaken is something other than the "brownish snapshots" with their fancy borders described towards the end (*SIB*, p. 246). The boundaries of these women are not clear. Indeed, the narrator uses them to help to get her mother into focus. In some basic way, artistic transformation here is bound up with the figure of the mother as, for men, it is with the father.

The mother — that, of course, is what "The Ottawa Valley" is about. And about, too, the narrative connections among women, the ways in which stories connect them, the repetitions that make ambiguous the boundaries of female bodies (the narrator at the time of writing is the same age as was her mother on the trip), the transformations that make succinct summary, even closure, impossible. The last long paragraph, the last of the collection, reveals a female aesthetic. It describes the difficulty experienced by a female writer in changing the mother into art. Indirectly, it throws considerable light on the structure of a Munro story, giving reasons for its backtracking, for the fact that it so often loses itself, for its remarkable fluidity and ambiguity. Describing her mother as she remembers her at some point towards the end of the trip to the Ottawa Valley (significantly her mother's old home, the custodian of the past), "turning strange, indifferent...she darkened in front of me" (p. 244), the narrator moves into her summary statements on a note of ambivalence and secrecy. She denies her reminiscences the status of stories. "If I had been making a proper story out of this" implies a failure of proper narrative closure, a failure that somehow makes what she has to say less fictional, less story-like. Her desire to find out more, presumably about her mother, emphasizes the impossibility of holding memory still, of separating the self, of closing the story.

> The problem, the only problem, is my mother. And she is the one of course that I am trying to get; it is to reach her that this whole journey has been undertaken. With what purpose? To mark her off, to describe, to illumine, to celebrate, *to get rid*, of her; and it did not work, for she looms too close, just as she always did. She is heavy as always, her edges melt and flow. Which means she has stuck to me as close as ever and refused to fall away, and I could go on, and on, applying what skills I have, using what tricks I know, and it would always be the same. (p. 246)

Described by Dinnerstein and by Chodorow, this sense of permeable ego boundaries dominates female life. It is expressed by the narrator of "The Peace of Utrecht" when she remembers that at the very word, "mother," she felt her "whole identity, that pretentious adolescent construction, come tumbling down" (*DHS*, p. 194). More angrily, it is also expressed by Rose's friend, Jocelyn, about her pediatrician mother: " 'She is the sort of person who just covers everything with a kind of rotten smarminess. She sort of oozes over everything.... She has these rotten coy little names for all the parts of your body' " ("Mischief," *WDY*, p. 103).

These have been direct episodes and statements that reveal the centrality of the mother in Munro's writing. However, in other less direct and even more interesting ways, the stories are filled with a tension that I believe to have at its base female bodies, unclear boundaries, mother-daughter relationships, changing female lives. The tension I speak of has to do with secrecy, with the sense that certain lives are being lived more or less underground, that, if one looks carefully at anything, it will change as if by magic. Such tension, important as it is in Munro's work, is certainly not limited to texts by women. Frank Kermode has made of it a theory of narrative. In "Secrets and Narrative Sequence," he describes, through a close reading of Joseph Conrad's *Under Western Eyes*, the ways in which texts subvert the apparent clarities of their own structures. He writes: "... we may like to think, for our purposes, of narrative as the product of two intertwined processes, the presentation of a fable and its progressive interpretation (which of course alters it). The first process tends towards clarity and propriety ('refined common sense'), the second toward secrecy, toward distortions which cover secrets."[7] Fictional plots do indeed pull against themselves, suggesting just such complexities as Kermode describes. Yet the secrets they hide differ, as does the emphasis given to alternate stories. Because Munro's concentration on change seems to reveal not only aesthetic arguments about the stability of language and the difficulty of containing experience by words, but also a peculiarly female concern with bodily boundaries and with changing social structures, I suggest that the dominance of secrecy and alternate texts in her stories implies an underground that is characteristic of texts by women.

The story, "Memorial," illustrates, less obliquely than most Munro stories, the sort of tension I am attempting to get at. In it, two sisters, June and Eileen, represent the opposition between order and disorder, between clarity and confusion, between articulation and secrecy, between rigidity and change. Like the critic, one of the sisters, June, wants clarity, wants to be able to chew on experience in order to assimilate it and control it. The other sister, Eileen, believes such use of experience destroys its very texture. Eileen describes herself: "Compared to June, she did live irresponsibly. Eileen had to see this, she had to admit it. Her lazy garbage all thrown together, her cupboards under their surface tidiness bursting with chaos" (*SIB*, pp. 209–10). Not surprisingly, Eileen is a writer. Not surprisingly, too, the conflict is revealed, at about the middle of the story, to be about relationships with the mother.

> By majoring in psychology June had tried to get round the problem of their mother, just as Eileen had tried to do by the study of English literature. June had been more successful. Eileen was gratified by the high incidence of crazy mothers in books, but failed to put this discovery to any use. June, on the other hand, was able to present their mother to her friends with no apologies....
> (pp. 212–13)

Through Eileen, Munro denigrates June's approach to life. Now it is clear to the reader that June has most certainly not worked through the problem of the mother, that, like Eileen's, her own ego boundaries are far from solid, and that her rigidity is simply an alternate defensive gesture. But what is important about the story is that the conflict should be so dramatically contained within "Women's bodies" (p. 225), and that it should so absolutely merge these bodies with the figure of the mother and with the act of writing. Directly about the words used at Douglas's memorial service, indirectly about words and the mother, Eileen's comments about language emphasize secrecy, trickery, change, the very qualities that create the ambivalence of a Munro story:

> People die; they suffer, they die. Their mother had died of ordinary pneumonia, after all that craziness. Illness and accidents. They ought to be respected, not explained. Words are all shameful. They ought to crumble in shame.... No fraud in the words but what fraud now in saying them. Silence the only possible thing. (p. 221)

But it isn't silence that Munro wants. In story after story, she ironically undercuts every movement towards revelation, indeed, denies the epiphanic moment of clarity, stillness, fulfilled silence. The evocation of James Joyce's "The Dead," at the end of "The Time of Death," while it implies a kind of structural epiphany (the only one I know of in Munro's work), bears so little connection to the story that it follows as to seem by its very presence ironic. Without exception, the other stories of *Dance of the Happy Shades* and of *Something I've Been Meaning to Tell You* (as well as the individual segments of the singly narrated volumes, *Lives of Girls and Women* and *Who Do You Think You Are?*), although at various places suggesting an about-to-be-revealed meaning, invariably change direction, pull back from explanation in order to keep the narrative boundaries open and the story flowing. If one looks at the endings of the various stories, they present an array of indeterminate suggestions, all of which seem to support Kermode's argument that much narrative material is "less manifestly under the control of authority, less easily subordinated to 'clearness and effect,' more palpably the enemy of order, of interpretative consensus, of message."[8] Mystery, pretense, wish, doubt, invention, lies, deceit, tricks, secrets, fraudulence, absurdity, treachery, are some of the words that appear in the endings of Munro's stories. One, "Walker Brothers Cowboy," concludes in a way so typical that it is worth quoting at greater length. The story is of a young girl's afternoon with her father, as seen from the perspective of the girl's adult self. The recollections coalesce around a visit to an old woman and her aging daughter, women who somehow obliquely at the time, and indeed even in retrospect, combine with the narrator's mother. The story ends with a comment about the father:

> ...I feel my father's life flowing back from our car in the last of the afternoon, darkening and turning strange, like a landscape that has an enchantment on it, making it kindly, ordinary and familiar while you are looking at it, but changing it, once your back is turned, into something you will never know.... (*DHS*, p. 18)

The secret that imbues the story, that changes the known land-scape, is something that the mother must not be told.

The important words here — flowing, darkening, turning strange, enchantment, changing — all suggest secrecy and trans-formation. In context (similar words appear in almost every story), they reveal with varying emphases certain facts about women's lives: the sense many women have of being suppressed, of living underground; the discrepancy between what one appears to be and what one feels oneself to be; the vagueness experienced by many women about their ego boundaries; the tendency to merge with others. Throughout, numerous images also represent these sensations. The new houses of "The Shining Houses" hide the "old wilderness city" that is, nonetheless, still there, evoked by a few homes that remain, "dark, enclosed, expressing something like savagery in their disorder" (*DHS*, p.24). Because the story is about the sympathetic connections between two quite different women, the one old and the other young, the images used imply the dark underground that joins women's lives. In "Images," icebergs and shadows merge in the narrator's imagination; by the end of the story, she sees herself changed, "Like the children in fairy stories who have seen their parents make pacts with terrifying strangers...like them, dazed and powerful with secrets" (*DHS*, p.43). The pupa in *Lives of Girls and Women*, with its difficult, perhaps even pointless metamorphosis, dramatizes the changing lives of the girls and women of the story. Indeed, the very structure of *Lives of Girls and Women* illustrates the dichotomy perceived by Kermode. Presented as a *Künstlerroman*, the stories are only superficially chronological, for they are continually forced askew, pulled out of shape, darkened by a secrecy that has less to do with Del's general artistic development than with her development as a *woman* artist. As Kermode suggests about complex narratives, *Lives of Girls and Women* does move in two directions, the one showing the changes in Del from her early years, through her adolescence, to a kind of artistic awakening, the other backtracking, revealing discordant memories, illustrating underground lives: the lives of women, secret, mostly unarticulated. The women of the collection thus pull against the straightforward development of the plot and will not allow clarification to occur: Madeleine and her inexpressible rage; Aunt Elspeth and Auntie Grace in their enclosed, secret world; Aunt Nile, who "looked amazed and unhappy as someone who had never even heard of foreign countries, and who is suddenly whisked away and deposited in one, with everybody around speaking an undreamt-of language" (p.83); Mrs. Sherriff, eccentric, a little crazy; Miss Farris, whose cheerfulness completely hides a profound, suicidal despair; Fern Dogherty, with her "diffuse complaints, lazy movements, indifferent agreeableness" (p. 144), "letting loose those grand, inflated emotions she paid no attention to, in life" (p. 145); Naomi and her circle of friends, who guard, as their secret, the town gossip, and who, when they speak, "might mean something else" (p. 182). In the epilogue, Del expresses her sense of these lives: "People's lives, in Jubilee as elswhere, were dull, simple, amazing and unfathomable — deep caves paved with kitchen linoleum" (p. 253). For the writer, these lives are hardly to be understood. They are unclear, both individually and as a class, their boundaries shift, they change.

Secrecy also dominates the stories of *Something I've Been Meaning to Tell You*, illustrating in much the same way it has in the two earlier volumes the difficulty of establishing boundaries and the alternate plots that pull against the surface plot. The title-story revolves around various secrets: Char's love for Blaikie; Et's jealousy of Char; Et's love for Arthur; Et's lie to Char; Et's silence with Arthur. These secrets, each of which emphasizes the ambivalent relationship between the two sisters, give the story its peculiar vagueness. Images of haunting abound: "She could not tell if Char went paler, hearing this, because Char was pale in the first place as anybody could get. She was like a ghost now, with her hair gone white" (p. 1). Women's lives are not at all what they appear to be. "Material" pursues the problem from a different angle. The tone is established by references to the amorphous women (of whom the narrator had once been one) who are so obliquely connected with literature that they spend their lives looking after male writers "for the sake of the words that will come from them" (p. 25). Other women, like Dotty, seem only to be material for the kind of aesthetic transformations effected by men like Hugo. Yet all these women dó have lives of their own. Although she sees her own life, like the lives of the other women she mentions, as having no authority, as being secret, underground, the narrator insists on its validity. It is different from a man's. Speaking of the two men she best knows, she recognizes the quality of this difference: "Both of them have decided what to do about everything they run across in this world, what attitude to take, how to ignore or use things. In their limited and precarious ways they both have authority. They are not *at the mercy*" (pp. 43–44).[9] Women cannot so easily summarize, cannot hold still; they see with eyes more sensitive to the complexities and necessary contradictions of human existence. The same secret is shared by the narrators of "Tell Me Yes or No" and "Winter Wind": "And how is anybody to know, I think as I put this down.... Yet I have not invented it, I really believe it. Without any proof I believe it, and so I must believe that we get messages another way, that we have connections that cannot be investigated, but have to be relied on" ("Winter Wind," p. 201). Thus are brought together secrecy, narration, and women, alternative stories that argue against traditional authority. Change dominates the sequence; floating boundaries, ambivalence, open-endedness characterize the texts.

With an even greater emphasis on social transformation, *Who Do You Think You Are?* also keeps women's bodies central. Again, innuendo gives the stories a dream-like distance and maintains at the forefront secrecy and confusion. All the stories seem, as Rose describes an early memory, "like a dream that goes back and back into other dreams, over hills and through doorways, maddeningly dim and populous and familiar and elusive" ("Royal Beatings," p. 11). Women's bodies shift in and out of focus. In the background is the dead mother, her presence preserved in Flo, Rose's stepmother, a woman of "extraordinary hardness and softness" ("Royal Beatings," p. 9). Other Hanratty women are recalled through a sexual haze that transforms their bodies and makes their outlines unclear: simple-minded Franny McGill, whose body was the scene of incest; Ruby Carruthers, who had intercourse with most of the boys of the town. Socially, these women are doomed. Cora, at first an object of desire, later simply a fat and lazy housewife, absorbs more of the adult Rose's attention. She tries to hold Cora still in her memory, but she fails. Unlike the men described in "Material," she does not know what attitude to take nor how to ignore or use things:

> Rose would strain over these things afterwards, when she was alone, strain to remember them, know them, get them for good. What was the use of that? When she thought of Cora she had the sense of a glowing dark spot, a melting center, a smell and taste of burnt chocolate, *that she could never get at.* ("Privilege," pp. 33–34, emphasis added)

She is no more successful at getting at the more sophisticated women she meets later in life, Dr. Henshawe and Jocelyn, both of whom confuse her own sexual boundaries and change her social orientation. The terrible heaviness of the mother, with her flowing and melting edges and her suffocating closeness, so central to Munro's stories, is also inverted in *Who Do You Think You Are?*. Now a mother herself, Rose dreams a nightmarish vision of her daughter, Anna: "She was covered with clay that seemed to have leaves or branches in it, so that the effect was of dead garlands. Decoration; ruination. And the clay or mud was not dry, it was still dripping off her, so that she looked crude and sad, a botched heavy-headed idol" ("Providence," p. 133). As usual, secrecy pervades the text. Recalling herself as a young schoolgirl, "building up the first store of things she could never tell" ("Privilege," p. 24), Rose continues to use telling and not telling, in the way I have argued Munro does, as contradictory structures in the same narrative sequence. And again, the difference that Rose perceives between herself and Patrick, a difference that "seemed to involve not just a different pronunciation but a whole different approach to talking" ("The Beggar Maid," p. 87), emphasizes not just the class discrepancy between the two, but also the specificity of female experience: the wavering outlines of the body and the changing social possibilities reflected as they are in the structures of the narrative.

In recent literary theory, the authority of texts, their fathering, has been the subject of much debate.[10] What I am arguing in terms of Munro's fiction is a different theory of narrative sequence. As is particularly clear in the content of such stories as "The Ottawa Valley" and the whole of *Lives of Girls and Women*, Munro dramatically illustrates, through each writer-narrator, the ways in which texts may be imagined as being mothered and the different emphases that result from imagining writing in such a way. By extension, I suggest that it may be worthwhile to look at all of Munro's work as structural as well as contextual revelations of women's bodies, ego boundaries, and social status. When we do so, we discover the importance of change in this fiction, whether it be represented by specific physical or social transformations, by the fluidity of the narrative boundaries, or by the aesthetic movement between secrecy and revelation. Indeed, perhaps changing is the only word that can be used to describe adequately women's perceptions of their bodies and, in these days of constant attention to various women's movements, their position in contemporary cultures. Their writing about themselves must surely reflect these concerns.

I am grateful to the National Endowment for the Humanities for a grant which made the writing of this paper possible.

[1] See particularly the chapter "Narrative Transformations" in Tzvetan Todorov's book, *The Poetics of Prose*, trans. Richard Howard (Ithaca: Cornell Univ. Press, 1977), pp. 218–33.

[2] Beverley J. Rasporich, "Child-Women and Primitives in the Fiction of Alice Munro," *Atlantis*, 1, No. 2 (Spring 1976), 13–14.

[3] A particularly interesting analysis of such closures to texts is Nancy Miller's *The Heroine's Text: Readings in the French and English Novel, 1722–1782* (New York: Columbia Univ. Press, 1980).

[4] See Patricia Spacks, *The Female Imagination* (New York: Knopf, 1975).

[5] Dorothy Dinnerstein, *The Mermaid and the Minotaur: Sexual Arrangements and Human Malaise* (New York: Harper & Row, 1977), p. 93.

[6] Nancy Chodorow, *The Reproduction of Mothering: Psychoanalysis and the Sociology of Gender* (Berkeley: Univ. of California Press, 1978), p. 93.

[7] Frank Kermode, "Secrets and Narrative Sequence," *Critical Inquiry*, 7 (Autumn 1980), 86.

[8] Kermode, 87.

[9] One of the most interesting studies of the connection between authority and the writing of women occurs in the opening section, "Toward a Feminist Poetics," of Sandra Gilbert and Susan Gubar's *The Madwoman in the Attic: The Woman Writer and the Nineteenth-Century Literary Imagination* (New Haven: Yale Univ. Press, 1979), pp. 3–104.

[10] Apart from being included in the text just cited, this debate runs through the works of Harold Bloom, particularly *The Anxiety of Influence: A Theory of Poetry* (New York: Oxford Univ. Press, 1973), and *A Map of Misreading* (New York: Oxford Univ. Press, 1975), John Irwin, *Doubling and Incest/Repetition and Revenge: A Speculative Reading of Faulkner* (Baltimore: Johns Hopkins Univ. Press, 1975), Edward W. Said, *Beginnings: Intention and Method* (New York: Basic, 1975) and in much of the work of the deconstructionists. See also Dianne F. Sadoff, "Storytelling and the Figure of the Father in *Little Dorrit*," *PMLA*, 95 (March 1980), 234–45.

# "At least part legend":
# The Fiction of Alice Munro

CATHERINE SHELDRICK ROSS

"It's as if I must take great care over everything....
I have to know the design."[1]

THERE IS A REVEALING PASSAGE that appeared in the first, unpublished version of *Who Do You Think You Are?*:

> It seems as if there are feelings that have to be translated
> into a next-door language, which might blow them up
> and burst them altogether; or else they have to be let
> alone. The truth about them is always suspected, never
> verified, the light catches but doesn't define them, any
> more than it does the memory of lantern slides, and
> Milton Homer, diabolically happy on the swing. Yet
> there is the feeling — I have the feeling — that at some
> level these things open; fragments, moments, sugges-
> tions, open, full of power.[2]

Alice Munro's stories, we could say, are translations into the
next-door language of fiction of all those documentary details,
those dazzling textures and surfaces, of remembered experience.
In interviews, she has often been quoted as saying that she is very
concerned with the surfaces of life, that she would like to do in
words what the magic realist painters like Edward Hopper and
Alex Colville have done in painting.[3] That is to say, she wants to
present ordinary experience with such intensity that it stands
revealed as something extraordinary. This is why the stories are
always pushing toward that moment when "these things open;
fragments, moments, suggestions, open, full of power."

When "these thing open," the reader catches a glimpse of other levels of experience — powerful legendary shapes that lie behind the ordinary life presented in Munro's stories of growing up in Southwestern Ontario, of moving to the West Coast and back again, and of making accommodations to the adult world of marriage, parenthood, and finding a career. Words like "legendary," "ritual," and "ceremony" are used often, and with special force and resonance. Such words are clues to how Munro solves the problem of presenting exact documentary details, while giving her stories a satisfying shape. For the texture of her stories, she relies on her almost total photographic recall of experience. But, for the arrangement of her details, she turns to myths and legends, rituals and ceremonies.

At the centre of a story by Munro is quite likely to be a ceremonial event such as a school play, an annual party, a dance, a first date, a home-coming, or a memorial service. The encounter with death and the initiating into sexual roles are the two most important ritualized events used, and they are repeated with variation in the first four books. In "Boys and Girls," from *Dance of the Happy Shades*, they are combined, the ritual slaughter of an animal being the central event in a painful rite of passage that initiates the narrator into the knowledge of what it is to be a girl. Always, Munro succeeds in making the reader feel that she is not imposing these patterns but is discovering them in the material itself. The reader arrives at the understanding reached by Et in "Something I've Been Meaning to Tell You," who looks at her sister, Char, bending over the starch basin and recognizes "that the qualities of legend were real, that they surfaced where and when you least expected" (*SIB*, p. 6).

The introductory paragraph of the story "The Shining Houses," from *Dance of the Happy Shades*, may suggest Munro's own method of getting the design just right:

> Mary sat on the back steps of Mrs. Fullerton's house, talking — or really listening — to Mrs. Fullerton.... And Mary found herself exploring her neighbour's life as she had once explored the lives of grandmothers and aunts — by pretending to know less than she did, asking for some story she had heard before; this way, remembered episodes emerged each time with slight differences of content, meaning, colour, yet with a pure reality that

usually attaches to things which are at least part legend.
(p. 19)

In much the same way, perhaps, Munro works over the details of
her story, piling them up, smoothing them away, until the pattern
is deepened with each reworking and is finally illuminated and
revealed.

Munro's method of achieving design in her stories is easiest to
recognize in the first collection, *Dance of the Happy Shades*.
These stories, considered together, reveal three levels of experience. There is the ordinary, shapeless world of everyday experience that presents itself in the fiction as "real life."[4] These
everyday objects of "real life," observed with great intensity,
open to reveal sometimes a lower, imprisoning world of madness
and death and sometimes an upper, redeemed world of art and
ritual order. Very often, as in "Images" and "Dance of the
Happy Shades," the narrator's encounter with these lower or
upper worlds provides the story with an organizing design taken
from folk-tale and ritual. The structure for "Images" is the
familiar motif of the underground journey, which, in this story,
ends with the heroine's meeting a figure of death in an underground house and her initiation into secret knowledge of life.[5]
The young narrator makes this legendary journey without going
farther than the bush which is visible from her own yard. The
dazzling final sentence, which recapitulates the action of the
story, suggests in its diction the two worlds — not really separate
— through which the narrator moves: the fairy-tale underworld
of dangerous encounters, terrifying strangers, and death and the
ordinary world of knives and forks and good manners:

> Like the children in fairy stories who have seen their
> parents make pacts with terrifying strangers, who have
> discovered that our fears are based on nothing but the
> truth, but who come back fresh from marvellous escapes
> and take up their knives and forks, with humility and
> good manners, prepared to live happily ever after — like
> them, dazed and powerful with secrets, I never said a
> word. (p. 43)

"Dance of the Happy Shades," on the other hand, ends with a
message from an upper world of art and ritual. The narrator's

recognition that such a world exists to qualify her understanding of her routine life comes when she hears the serene music of a retarded child at Miss Marsalles' annual piano recital. This music, which is "something fragile, courtly and gay, that carries with it the freedom of a great unemotional happiness" (p. 222), is recognized as "the one communiqué from the other country where she [Miss Marsalles] lives" (p. 224).

A writer of romance or fantasy wanting to represent this contrast between different worlds might have his/her characters cross some clearly defined boundary into a quite separate, mysterious territory. The British author of children's books, E. Nesbit, remarks in *The Enchanted Castle*:

> There is a curtain, thin as gossamer, clear as glass, strong as iron, that hangs for ever between the world of magic and the world that seems to us to be real. And when once people have found one of the little weak spots in that curtain... almost anything may happen.[6]

In "Dance of the Happy Shades," however, the narrator, without ever leaving "the world that seems to us to be real," finds herself in a situation at Miss Marsalles' party where "things are getting out of hand, anything may happen" (p. 212). Munro's central characters often find themselves in circumstances where it seems that "anything may happen," but not because they have left their ordinary world behind them to go through the weak spot in the curtain. The effect is achieved instead through some tilt in their perception which lets them, but not the other characters in the story, see the ordinary as extraordinary. The central character sees patterns and attends to messages that are invisible and inaudible to the other characters—the younger brother, for example, in "Walker Brothers Cowboy" and "Boys and Girls," or the girl-friend, Lonnie, in "Red Dress — 1946," who never notice anything unusual. What is important is a way of seeing. Therefore, the central character's sense of being in contact with a legendary world is often expressed in terms of altered conditions of lighting: the familiar landscape may be illuminated or, as happens more often, it may be darkened by shadows of another world.

"Day of the Butterfly," for example, ends with a shift in the narrator's perception which allows her to see the shadow. Helen has remained behind in the hospital room after the birthday party which the class has given for Myra, who is ill with leuke-mia. Myra offers Helen one of her presents and speaks of getting better and playing with Helen after school. Just then, a sound outside the hospital room of "someone playing in the street, maybe chasing with the last snowballs of the year" makes Myra, and most of all Myra's future, "turn shadowy, turn dark":

> All the presents on the bed, the folded paper and ribbons, those guilt-tinged offerings, had passed into this shadow, they were no longer innocent objects to be touched, exchanged, accepted without danger.

The shadow that absorbs the moment, the presents on the bed, and even the narrator herself is death. Myra, however, seems to have already passed beyond death, having been transformed in the final image into a figure in a saint's legend, "her brown carved face immune to treachery...prepared to be set apart for legendary uses, as she was even in the back porch at school" (p. 110). Earlier in the story, Myra and her brother have been compared to "children in a medieval painting...like small figures carved of wood, for worship or magic..." (p. 101). This appearance of Myra as an icon brings the narrator, Helen, to an understanding of her own role as betrayer — this in a story which is about the problem of charity and the strangeness of discovering that one would rather run with the mob.

"Walker Brothers Cowboy" also ends with a shadow from another world. The shadowed landscape with an enchantment over it is an image used to convey the young narrator's sense of the larger shapes that lie behind routine life in Tuppertown. The initial walk to the shore to " 'see if the Lake's still there' " (p. 1) establishes the familiar landscape of the lakeshore, which is later revealed in an unfamiliar aspect. When the little girl and her father, Ben Jordan, reach the lake, the father is the one to shift the perspective from the ordinary view to a vision of the wide sweep of geological time and the glaciers which once gouged out the Great Lakes from a wide, flat plain. The little girl is dismayed by these open vistas of time and space:

> The tiny share we have of time appalls me, though my father seems to regard it with tranquillity....I do not like to think of it. I wish the Lake to be always just a lake,

with the safe-swimming floats marking it, and the break-water and the lights of Tuppertown. (p. 3)

The little girl wants the safety of the known and familiar and unchanged, but by the end of the story everything has changed. She begins to understand something of the mystery of time when her father takes her and her brother on a journey into his own past. He takes them to see Nora, a vibrant earth-mother figure, whom he should have married but did not, it is suggested, because she is a Roman Catholic. The child, watching her father's joking and whisky-drinking and watching Nora's hopeful dancing, glimpses a hidden part of her father's life. Finally, Ben says that they must go:

"We've taken a lot of your time now."
"Time," says Nora bitterly. "Will you come by ever again?" (p. 17)

The ending of the story comes to a focus in what the girl learns about the vast cycles of geologic time, the short span of human time, and the bitterness of wasted opportunities for love.

Thinking about these contradictions during the drive home, she feels her father's life "darkening and turning strange, like a landscape that has an enchantment on it, making it kindly, ordinary and familiar while you are looking at it, but changing it, once your back is turned, into something you will never know, with all kinds of weathers, and distances you cannot imagine" (p. 18). The word "enchantment" in this sentence serves much the same function as the word "marvellous" in the sentence quoted from "Images" in suggesting the transformation of the ordinary into something extraordinary. The landscape under an enchantment being recalled here is haunted by the ghosts of dinosaurs and fossils and glaciers — suitable spectres for the bedrock of Southern Ontario, which, according to *The Physiography of Southern Ontario*, is "among the oldest beds to harbour the petrified remains of plants or animals."[7] This landscape, a counterpart for the father's life, suggests in one unified image the various levels of being, from deep hidden deposits to overlying strata to observable surfaces, and the various layers of time, from the past to the familiar present. Drawing attention here to what is called elsewhere, in the story "Characters," "the landscape

117

under the one you see.... The lakes and shores we map and name but never saw,"[8] Munro succeeds in transforming the local Southwestern Ontario landscape into a place of legendary importance, shadowed by a significant past.

These shadows in "Day of the Butterfly" and in "Walker Brothers Cowboy" are signs from the lower world. In other stories from *Dance of the Happy Shades*, it is a character who represents the lower world, appearing often as an emissary of death, as, for example, Bram, the scissors-man, in "The Time of Death," the hypnotist in "A Trip to the Coast," and mad old Joe in "Images." In "Images," the little girl, accompanying her father along the river to check the trap-lines for dead muskrats, is taken into her deepest fears about death. An enchantment seems to come over the landscape, and suddenly a man appears, carrying an axe. Munro has said in a commentary on the story in *The Narrative Voice*:

> [The story] started with the picture in my mind of the man met in the woods, coming obliquely down the river-bank, carrying the hatchet, and the child watching him, and the father unaware, bending over his traps. For a long time I was carrying this picture in my mind, as I am carrying various pictures now which may or may not turn into stories. Of course the character did not spring from nowhere. His ancestors were a few old men, half hermits, half madmen, often paranoid, occasionally dangerous, living around the country where I grew up....I had always heard stories about them; they were established early as semi-legendary figures in my mind.[9]

The little girl, encountering this semi-legendary being, is transfixed, because old Joe with his axe and his underground house is the personification of her worst imaginings. She experiences not "fear so much as recognition" (p.38). In the course of this ritual journey, she has brought her knowledge of death from an instinctual to a conscious level and has incorporated it into herself to make her understanding of life more complete.

Recognition of another kind occurs in "The Peace of Utrecht" when the narrator recognizes on a conscious level something that she has in some sense already known about the total shape of her mother's life. The narrator, coming back from the West Coast to Jubilee on the summer after her mother's death, moves from the ordinary world to a world of silences, imprisonment, and death. Madness and hysteria are suggested by phrases such as "dim world of continuing disaster, of home" (p. 191), "keyed-up antics" (p. 193), "dreaming, sunken feeling of these streets" (p. 196), "once-familiar atmosphere of frenzy and frustration" (p. 200), and "the complex strain...the feelings of hysteria" (p. 201). The purpose of this movement into a special, dislocated world is to re-create the image of the mother, for "in the ordinary world it was not possible to re-create her" (pp. 200–01).

This recreation is complete following a horrifying ritual during which Aunt Annie displays, piece by piece, the mended and cleaned articles of the dead mother's clothing until finally the bodiless presence of a ghost is uncovered. What is revealed is the full horror and pathos of the life of the "Gothic Mother" (p. 200) struggling against the prison of her own body as she must have struggled against the repressiveness of the small town. Aunt Annie at last breaks the taboo of silence to tell Helen how her mother escaped from the hospital through the snow and was brought back and nailed down, a " 'board across her bed.' " Like the little girl in "Images," who returns from her journey underground with the understanding that "our fears are based on nothing but the truth," Helen listens, knowing that "what I would be told I already knew, I had always known." And when Aunt Annie tells this story, behind her "soft familiar face there is another, more primitive old woman..." (p. 208).

This image of the "primitive" mask beneath the everyday face, like the image cited earlier of the glacier-moulded "landscape under the one you see," suggests powerful and disturbing primitive shapes that lie under the surface. But there is also in the story another image that seems to beckon from a world of order and ceremony. The mother, like Miss Marsalles, costumes herself in brocades. The judgement of Jubilee on these "brocades and flowered silks, growing yearly more exotic" (p. 205), is that this was "extravagant, unnecessary from any practical point of view" (p. 200). But brocade in these stories is the emblem of the artist figure who, in defiance of the practical materialism of the town, envisions some higher world of art and order and beauty. In "Winter Wind," to broaden our examination now from *Dance of the Happy Shades* to include the next three books, the mother's extravagant designs on her cupboards of flowers and fish and sail-boats are a variant of these exotic brocades, as are Nora's lavishly flowered dress in "Walker Brothers Cowboy" and the bright, eloquent pictures of birds in this passage from "Privilege" in *Who Do You Think You Are?*:

> One thing in the school was captivating, lovely. Pictures of birds. Rose didn't know if the teacher had climbed up and nailed them above the blackboard, too high for easy desecration....(p. 29)

> A red-headed woodpecker; an oriole; a blue jay; a Canada Goose. The colors clear and long-lasting. Backgrounds of pure snow, of blossoming branches, of heady summer sky. In an ordinary classroom they would not have seemed so extraordinary. Here they were bright and eloquent, so much at variance with everything else that what they seemed to represent was not the birds themselves, not those skies and snows, but some other world of hardy innocence, bounteous information, privileged light-heartedness. No stealing from lunchpails there; no slashing coats; no pulling down pants and probing with painful sticks; no fucking; no Franny. (pp. 29–30)

Here the details of outhouse arrangements, cloakroom humiliations, and routine victimization suggests a lower, imprisoning world, more than ordinarily grim and sinister, but the pictures of birds seem to offer some release, a promise of "some other world of hardy innocence." They are another communiqué, we might say, from the other country where Miss Marsalles lives.

Related to this vision of brightness and clarity and innocence are those moments in the stories when the central characters perceive a pattern to experience that renders it luminous, as in this example from "The Peace of Utrecht":

> And now an experience which seemed not at all memorable at the time...had been transformed into something curiously meaningful for me, and complete; it took in more than the girls dancing and the single street, it spread over the whole town, its rudimentary pattern of streets and its bare trees and muddy yards just free of

snow, over the dirt roads where the lights of cars appeared, jolting towards the town, under an immense pale wash of sky. (pp. 201–02)

Similarly, in *Lives of Girls and Women*, Del says that she "loved the order, the wholeness, the intricate arrangement of town life, that only an outsider could see.... all these things, rituals and diversions, frail and bright, woven together — Town!" (p. 70). The artist is the one who perceives this order and wants to give it permanent form. Two frequently quoted passages express what Munro's kind of artist tries to do. The first is from the epilogue to *Lives of Girls and Women* where Del describes how she wants to write things down, make lists of ordinary details, capture "every last thing, every layer of speech and thought, stroke of light on bark or walls, every smell, pothole, pain, crack, delusion, held still and held together — radiant, everlasting" (p. 253). The second, from "Material" in *Something I've Been Meaning to Tell You*, is the description of Dotty in Hugo's story "lifted out of life and held in light, suspended in the marvelous clear jelly that Hugo has spent all his life learning how to make" (p. 43). In contrast with the images of the shadowed landscape associated with the lower world, the images in the passages just cited above suggest brightness and light: "colors clear and long-lasting," "Backgrounds of pure snow," "bright and eloquent," "immense pale wash of sky," "radiant, everlasting," and "held in light."

The artist, then, is the person most in touch with both the luminous order of the upper world and the shadowed landscape of the lower world. Hence, the artist can best perceive the patterns of these other worlds sometimes revealing themselves in this ordinary one. The artist figures represented in the stories are, like Munro herself, concerned with finding the right design to give order to events, usually events of the past. Miss Marsalles, for example, whose family home in Rosedale was furnished with a portrait of Mary, Queen of Scots, "brown misty pictures of historical battles," and Harvard Classics, is a guardian of the past and her home a repository of art and history. She lives "outside the complications of time" ("Dance of the Happy Shades," *DHS*, p. 214), giving shape to the past by her annual rituals. Likewise, Uncle Craig, in *Lives of Girls and Women*, is attempting, however misguidedly and ineptly, to give a ritualized order to events of the past. In his family tree, he wants to reveal "the whole solid, intricate structure of lives supporting us from the past." His files and drawers contain "a great accumulation of the most ordinary facts, which it was his business to get in order" (p. 31), but which he can never get in order because he has no sense of design, no way of revealing the significance of these ordinary facts. It is left to Del to fulfil Uncle Craig's purpose by becoming the kind of writer that Munro herself has become.

Initially, Del is interested in getting down the patterns of the lower world — what she calls "black fable" (p. 248). To this end, she changes Jubilee in her fiction into "an older, darker, more decaying town," inhabited by people whose speech is "subtle and evasive and bizarrely stupid" and whose platitudes "crackled with madness" (p. 247). In this description of Del's fiction, Munro may quite possibly be recalling her own early writing. In her first published story, "The Dimensions of a Shadow," Miss Abelhart, a spinster of the Tennessee Williams kind, breaks the "fetter" of the "neat routine of the little town" by refusing to go to a temperance meeting.[10] Instead, she goes for a walk where she meets a boy from her senior Latin class, the thought of whom "was never far from the surface of her mind, always wavering like a shadow, over her consciousness." Unexpectedly, the boy tells her what she has longed to hear — that he loves her. During this encounter, she recognizes on a conscious level that the town considers her "Barren and sterile and useless," and the "things that had lain so darkly hidden were given sound and shape and hung in frozen words on the air." The ending of the story is the disclosure that Miss Abelhart has gone mad and that the boy she has been talking to is a shadowy apparition that only she can see. The concluding sentence leaves her "alone in a bottomless silence." In this story, the pattern is clearly established of the break from the ordinary world of routine to a mad world, populated by shadows and by insubstantial outlines of repressed desire. And yet, because this pattern is archetypal, one can say about it what Del says about her novel: that "such people and such a story" seem "discovered, not made up ... as if that town was lying close behind the one I walked through every day" (p. 248). The patterns apparent in Munro's and Del's earliest stories are familiar because they deal with fundamental human experiences — the recognition of identity, the encounter with the dark shadow, and the like — those elements that have become central in the shared storehouse of story-telling conventions. In later stories, Munro fills in these patterns with a rich texture of the particularities of ordinary life.

Del also discovers the importance to a writer of paying close attention to ordinary life. During a visit with Bobby Sherriff, whose family is the model for the decaying Gothic family in her novel, she is brought up short by the "ordinariness of everything" (p. 250). She realizes that it is not enough to write a work that is pure design: she must test the design against ordinary life and find the patterns inhering there. Hence Del's comment about being "greedy for Jubilee," wanting to make lists and to write things down. And hence, also, her recognition of the need for design in order to make the ordinary objects eloquent: "...no list could hold what I wanted, for what I wanted was every last thing...held still and held together — radiant, everlasting" (p. 253).

Del's sense here of the value of ordinary objects is shared by other central characters and seems to be most strongly felt after an experience which removes these characters for a time from the ordinary world, allowing them to see their ordinary life with the enriched awareness of other levels of experience. Helen, Del, Rose, and others are drawn into special worlds created sometimes by sexuality, madness, or death and sometimes by art, ritual, or a vision of order. In *Lives of Girls and Women*, Del has a series of encounters with special worlds such as Uncle Benny's world, which is "like a troubling distorted reflection, the same but never at all the same," where "anything might happen" (p. 25). In *Who Do You Think You Are?*, various experiences expose Rose to the unpredictable power of other worlds: when she sees Patrick in his carrel, she has a "vision of happiness," "as if there existed a radiantly kind and innocent Rose and Patrick, hardly ever visible, in the shadow of their usual selves" ("The Beggar Maid," p. 95); when, on the other hand, she puts Flo into the Home in "Spelling," she has an insight into an old woman's "emptiness or confusion that nobody on this side can do more than guess at" (p. 183). The perspective supplied by the threat of death can make the central character appreciate the precious value of ordinary life, as in this passage in "Forgiveness in Families" from *Something I've Been Meaning to Tell You*: "Then you're dying, Mother is dying...and what you've had is all there is, and going to the Library, just a thing like that, coming back up the hill on the bus with books and a bag of grapes seems now

123

worth wanting" (p. 99). The result of the temporary withdrawal into some special world is often some new understanding that allows the central character to see the ordinary as extraordinary, charged with other levels of being. Del is representative in this respect in her discovery that people's lives, in Jubilee as elsewhere, are "dull, simple, amazing and unfathomable — deep caves paved with kitchen linoleum" (p. 253).

The return journey from the special to the ordinary world is important, therefore, because after this return the central character repossesses the ordinary world in all its particularity and with a newly acquired sense of its power. In "Baptizing," for example, Del thinks of Garnet French as a "solid intrusion of the legendary into the real world" (p. 215), but when their relationship ends she reports:

> As I walked on into Jubilee I repossessed the world. Trees, houses, fences, streets, came back to me, in their own sober and familiar shapes. Unconnected to the life of love, uncoloured by love, the world resumes its own, its natural and callous importance. (p. 240)

The corresponding passage describing Rose's repossession of the world in "Simon's Luck" is more explicit about the precious value of the ordinary world that would bring Rose back as much from the upper as from the lower world:

> It was those dishes that told her of her changed state....she thought how love removes the world for you, and just as surely when it's going well as when it's going badly. This shouldn't have been, and wasn't, a surprise to her; the surprise was that she so much wanted, required, everything to be there for her, thick and plain as ice-cream dishes, so that it seemed to her it might not be the disappointment, the losses, the dissolution, she had been running from, any more than the opposite of those things; the celebration and shock of love, the dazzling alteration. Even if that was safe, she couldn't accept it. Either way you were robbed of something — a private balance spring, a little dry kernel of probity. So she thought. (*WDY*, p. 170)

The ice-cream dishes in this passage have acquired the intensely felt presence possessed by objects in a magic realist painting.

A suitable quotation with which to conclude this essay demonstrates the ordinary landscape becoming, in Munro's writing about it, invested with a legendary force until "these things open...full of power." The passage comes from the final paragraph of an article written for the *Weekend Magazine* in which she is describing that mile or so of the Maitland River, called the Menesetung River by the Indians, that runs behind her father's land, west of Wingham, Ontario:

> We believed there were deep holes in the river....I am still partly convinced that this river — not even the whole river, but this little stretch of it — will provide whatever myths you want, whatever adventures. I name the plants, I name the fish, and every name seems to me triumphant, every leaf and quick fish remarkably valuable. This ordinary place is sufficient, everything here touchable and mysterious.[11]

The sequence of elements is significant: the "deep holes" that suggest a mysterious, lower level of experience; the available "myths" and "adventures" that provide the designs; the role of the writer in naming all the concrete particulars; and, finally, the revelation of the ordinary place as "touchable and mysterious." So, on a larger scale, do Munro's stories take this "little stretch" of home territory, find the legendary shapes that lie behind its everyday experience, and reveal the ordinary world as "remarkably valuable."

NOTES

[1] Alan Twigg, "What Is," in his *For Openers: Conversations with 24 Canadian Writers* (Madeira Park, B.C.: Harbour, 1981), p. 16.

[2] Galley of the first version of *Who Do You Think You Are?*, p. 231, quoted in Linda Leitch, "Alice Munro's Fiction: Explorations in Open Forms," M.A. Thesis Guelph 1980, pp. 169–70.

[3] See, for example, the following comment by Munro from the interview given in Graeme Gibson, "Alice Munro," in his *Eleven Canadian Novelists: Interviewed by Graeme Gibson* (Toronto: Anansi, 1973):

"I'm very, very excited by what you might call the surface of life....It seems to me very important to be able to get at the exact tone or texture of how things are" (p. 241).

4 *"Real Life,"* a rejected title for *Lives of Girls and Women*, is the phrase that concludes "Baptizing" in *Lives of Girls and Women* (p. 242).

5 See, for example, Stith Thompson, *Motif-Index of Folk Literature: A Classification of Narrative Elements in Folktales, Ballads, Myths, Fables, Mediaeval Romances, Exampla, Fabliaux, Jest-books, and Local Legends*, Rev. ed., Vol. 3 (Bloomington, Ind.: Indiana Univ. Press, 1955). Motifs FO–F199 are concerned with "Otherworld journeys" and include such classifications as "Journey to otherworld," "Access to upper world," and "Transportation to or from upper world."

6 Quoted in Stephen Prickett, *Victorian Fantasy* (Sussex: Harvester, 1979), p. 34.

7 L. J. Chapman and D. F. Putnam, *The Physiography of Southern Ontario*, 2nd ed. (Toronto: Univ. of Toronto Press, 1966), p. 3.

8 Alice Munro, "Characters," *Ploughshares*, 4, No. 3 (1978), 73.

9 Alice Munro, "The Colonel's Hash Resettled," in *The Narrative Voice: Stories and Reflections by Canadian Authors*, ed. John Metcalf (Toronto: McGraw-Hill Ryerson, 1972), p. 182.

10 Alice Laidlaw, "The Dimensions of a Shadow," *Folio*, 4 (April 1950), [n. pag.].

11 Alice Munro, "Everything Here Is Touchable and Mysterious," *Weekend Magazine*, 11 May 1974, p. 33.

# The Unimaginable Vancouvers:
## Alice Munro's Words

MICHAEL TAYLOR

I'm not an intellectual writer. I'm very, very excited by what you
might call the surface of life....

— Alice Munro

....everything is surface. The surface is what's there
And nothing can exist except what's there.

— John Ashbery

I don't know of anything so mighty as words. There are those
to which I lift my hat when I see them sitting prince-like on
the page.

— Emily Dickinson

ALICE MUNRO frequently pauses in mid-paragraph to tip her hat
to the physical charms of one or another of her words. In what
seems to be an act of excited serendipity, she often repeats a word
or phrase, after our having experienced it in its official place in
the narrative, in order to examine it more searchingly, insisting
that we give it its due as a thing in itself, as though it were an
object that had properties of its own, just like its cousins in the
phenomenological world. This savouring of the shape, and
sound, and feel of words, prince and commoner alike, occurs
especially often in Munro's novel, *Lives of Girls and Women* —
no more than appropriately so, I would suggest, when we
remember that Del, the book's narrator, is in the often painful
process of discovering herself as a writer, one who turns out to be
remarkably like her creator, Munro. In a typical moment of
slightly bashful linguistic confession, Del tells us that she "liked
the word *mistress*, a full-skirted word, with some ceremony

about it" (p. 185). Del is clearly responding here to what makes Emily Dickinson lift her poetic hat. But for us, as more worldly readers of the text, it is not the word "mistress" itself which we admire, but the words that Munro uses to convey Del's secret ecstasy — "a full-skirted word, with some ceremony about it." Both adjective and noun, "full-skirted" and "ceremony," make us think of "mistress" in its almost anachronistic, pristine full-ness: the word has been revitalized by the stately metaphor through which we perceive it. It is hard to imagine a more full-skirted word than full-skirted. And yet it should be obvious that the felicity of the matter does not depend solely on Munro's unusual choice of the word "full-skirted" (fine choice though it is); there is something essentially congruent with that choice not only in mistress's faded etymology but in its surface properties. We have only to substitute the more mundane word "girl-friend" to be made fully aware of the freight "mistress" carries.

Although there's nothing full-skirted or ceremonious about "girl-friend," Del's passion for words is by no means exclusively aristocratic. Like Munro behind her, she's just as alive to the equally interesting surfaces of far less ceremonious words than "mistress." She responds, for example, just as enthusiastically to a word that is at the other end of the sexual spectrum:

> ...the words themselves still gave off flashes of power, particularly *fuck*, which I had never been able to really look at, on fences or sidewalks. I had never been able to contemplate before its thrust of brutality, hypnotic swagger. (p. 167)

"Thrust of brutality," "hypnotic swagger" do for "fuck" what "full-skirted" and "ceremony" do for "mistress" — they revivify the word for us, re-expose us to its original power to shock: as with "mistress," there is a congruence between the illuminating metaphor and the sound, length and shape, the surfaces, of the illumined word — "fuck" *does* have its thrust of brutality, "mistress" *is* a full-skirted word. In similar, though much less startling fashion, the writer / narrator of "The Office," a short story in Munro's first book, *Dance of the Happy Shades*, responds to the blandishments of the surface of her word, "It was really the sound of the word 'office' that I liked, its sound of dignity and peace" (p. 60), while Ruth, in the short story "Labor

Day Dinner," provides one of the few instances in Munro's most recent collection, *The Moons of Jupiter*, of an appropriate imaginative response to the surfaces of words: "...to Ruth the word 'gynecologist' seemed sharp and appalling, and she saw the gynecologist's daughter dressed in an outfit of cold, jagged metal" (p. 151). In those instances in Munro's work where this congruence is missing — where the word's surface resists the enveloping play of fancy — we realize that the writer has merely exercised, in a somewhat disdainful fashion, the prerogative of her profession and decided that a word should simply be what she wants it to be. Hence, in the title-story of *Something I've Been Meaning to Tell You*, the fitful course of the love affair between Char and Blaikie takes precedence over the word's phonemic reality:

> Char and Blaikie seemed to her the same kind of animal — tall, light, powerful, with a dangerous luxuriance. They sat apart but shone out together. *Lovers.* Not a soft word, as people thought, but cruel and tearing. (p. 14).

The reality of love may be cruel and tearing but the word "lovers" itself cannot ever be. It may be more than mere coincidence that the considerable success of "Something I've Been Meaning to Tell You" as a short story depends upon its insistent and sinister refusal to spell out in so many words the misery of Char's love for Blaikie and her desperate marriage to Arthur: the story is full of tantalizing somethings that are never told, including the specific something that Et fails to tell Arthur in the last paragraph. There is no room here in a story of such ominous silences for the kind of quirky celebration of the surface of words that distinguishes *Lives of Girls and Women*.

Sometimes — to change the angle of approach slightly — Munro's delight in the surface attractions of words takes the form of an unexpected, and unexpectedly apposite, extended literal interpretation of simple meanings. Here, for example, is a cadenza on the word "attack," whose original meaning has all but disappeared in such commonplace phrases as "heart attack," always rendered in conversation as a single word, "heartattack":

> Heart *attack*. It sounded like an explosion, like fire-works going off, shooting sticks of light in all directions,

shooting a little ball of light — that was Uncle Craig's
heart, or his soul — high into the air, where it tumbled
and went out. (*LGW*, p. 46)

Later, Del remembers how she once responded to the news that
someone's mother had died during an operation:

Her mother died. She went away for an operation but
she had large lumps in both breasts and she died, my
mother always said, on the table. On the *operating* table.
When I was younger I used to imagine her stretched out
dead on an ordinary table among the teacups and
ketchup and jam. (p. 77)

This time, Munro italicizes the less important word *"operating,"*
but it is clear that the word which strikes Del's fancy is the
unitalicized, super-ordinary word "table," whose connotations
for her until that point had always been drably domestic. This
determination to invest the ordinary with a magical fascination
occasionally leads Munro into easy indulgences, as in this
concoction with which Rose in *Who Do You Think You Are?*
gets herself back into Flo's good graces: "The suave dreamy
custard," she rhapsodizes, "the nipping berries, robust peaches,
luxury of sherry-soaked cake, munificence of whipped cream"
("Spelling," p. 181). Usually, however, Munro's attempts to
rescue words from their often dull or cliché-ridden lives produce
the kind of zestful originality in the writing that characterizes the
opening of "Royal Beatings," the first story in *Who Do You
Think You Are?*.

*Royal Beating*. That was Flo's promise. You are going to
get one Royal Beating.
     The word Royal lolled on Flo's tongue, took on trap-
pings. Rose had a need to picture things, to pursue
absurdities, that was stronger than the need to stay out
of trouble, and instead of taking this threat to heart she
pondered: how is a beating royal? She came up with a
tree-lined avenue, a crowd of formal spectators, some
white and black slaves. Someone knelt, and the blood
came leaping out like banners. (p. 1)

130

And Munro is at her most playful in the same story when Rose anatomizes a nonsense couplet that her imagination cannot leave alone — a dangerous business as her obsession with it leads to the royal beating she gets from her father:

*Two Vancouvers fried in snot!*
*Two pickled arseholes tied in a knot!*

Rose couldn't stop herself. She hummed it tenderly, tried saying the innocent words aloud, humming through the others. It was not just the words snot and arsehole that gave her pleasure, though of course they did. It was the pickling and tying and the unimaginable Vancouvers. She saw them in her mind shaped rather like octopuses, twitching in the pan. The tumble of reason; the spark and spit of craziness. (p. 12)

As a writer, Del's "cold appetite for details" (p. 46) enables her to see a rich mystery in the most ordinary accumulation of humdrum objects: "such a wealth of wreckage, a whole rich dark rotting mess of carpets, linoleum, parts of furniture, insides of machinery, nails, wire, tools, utensils" (p. 4). Just the mere listing of this miscellaneous rubbish has its attractions for Del, and *Lives of Girls and Women* often groups words together for the sheer pleasure of having them roll off the tongue. So, too, does *Who Do You Think You Are?* where, for instance, the names of Rose's friends at school (material for an endless narrative) are the Southern Ontario version of Milton's fallen angels:

Flo and Rose had switched roles. Now Rose was the one bringing stories home, Flo was the one who knew the names of the characters and was waiting to hear.
Horse Nicholson, Del Fairbridge, Runt Chesterton. Florence Dodie, Shirley Pickering, Ruby Carruthers. Flo waited daily for news of them. She called them Jokers. ("Half a Grapefruit," p. 40)

Behind this obsession with the evocative sonority of ordinary names is an attitude towards experience in contemporary writing which may be peculiarly Canadian. Although it does not appear in Margaret Atwood's catalogue of survival techniques for the Canadian literary imagination, one can well imagine how a contemporary Canadian writer, repelled by the crassness of modern-day North American commercial culture, might turn in compensation to a celebration of the small ceremonies — the phrase is the title of Carol Shields's first and, in my view, most successful novel — the small ceremonies of ordinary life. At all events, Munro, like Carol Shields, like David Adams Richards, like the mythicizing Margaret Atwood herself, wants to liberate us from a paralyzingly conventional way of looking at the ordinary world, a way that often snobbishly refuses to acknowledge the possibilities of beauty and poetry in mundane circumstance. In "Walker Brothers Cowboy," the opening story of her first collection, *Dance of the Happy Shades*, Munro transforms Woolworths into what it perhaps once truly was, an emporium of magical delights. It is a child's eye view of a plastic world:

> ...Woolworths so marvellous it has live birds singing in its fan-cooled corners and fish as tiny as fingernails, as bright as moons, swimming in its green tanks. (p. 4)

There is a similar response, though this time from an adult, to the bourgeois bathrooms of "The Shining Houses," a story in the same collection: in both cases, the tawdry has been made to yield up a small, authentic beauty. This process of transmutation can be seen at its most Wordsworthian at the close of "Walker Brothers Cowboy," where the unspoken significance of the father's visit to Nora, with its intimations of blighted lives, suffuses the daughter's consciousness as they drive home:

> So my father drives and my brother watches the road for rabbits and I feel my father's life flowing back from our car in the last of the afternoon, darkening and turning strange, like a landscape that has an enchantment on it, making it kindly, ordinary and familiar while you are looking at it, but changing it, once your back is turned, into something you will never know, with all kinds of weathers, and distances you cannot imagine. (p. 18)

Although Munro does not think of herself as a writer of ideas, it would be inadequate to restrict discussion of her use of words to her exploitation of this kind of hyperbolically heightened

Naturalism (exploring as it does, in any case, the landscape of the mind), especially as she herself has drawn attention to the element of Southern Gothicism in her books.¹ In *Lives of Girls and Women*, Del often tells us that she is enraptured not just by the imaginative possibilities of ordinary words but by words much more rich and strange. The language of the Bible, for instance, used to be her "secret pleasure — poetic flow of words, archaic expressions. *Said unto, tarried, Behold the bridegroom cometh*" (p. 157). Despite her affection for the ordinary, Munro is perfectly well aware of how stultifying it can be to the creative imagination to grow up in a small town in Ontario, and Del often has to retreat into an inner life that is sustained by the "richness of the words against the poverty of the place" (p. 100). During her times of profound alienation, books restore her: "I was happy in the Library. Walls of printed pages, evidence of so many created worlds — this was a comfort to me" (p. 119). When her romance with Garnet French founders, Del forces herself into a session of therapeutic reading: "I made myself understand what I was reading, and after some time I felt a mild, sensible gratitude for these printed words, these strange possibilities" (p. 242). The printed words' strange possibilities — sometimes difficult, remote, occult — take on a life of their own and offer up a different kind of reality from the uncomfortable one that Munro's heroines often have to suffer growing up in their Philistine environments. The marvellous scene at the climax of "Spelling," one of the most powerful stories in *Who Do You Think You Are?*, renders the sustaining power of words very movingly in its depiction of one of the most senile women in Flo's Old Folks' Home, "diapered, dark as a nut, with three tufts of hair like dandelion floss sprouting from her head" (*WDY*, p. 183), who only manages to retain some semblance of communication with the world around her by spelling words suggested to her by her visitors and nurses. Rose imagines the life those words might have for the old woman in the dark recesses of her mind:

> Then she was sitting waiting; waiting, in the middle of her sightless eventless day, till up from somewhere popped another word. She would encompass it, bend all her energy to master it. Rose wondered what the words were like, when she held them in her mind. Did they carry their usual meaning, or any meaning at all? Were

they like words in dreams or in the minds of young children, each one marvelous and distinct and alive as a new animal? This one limp and clear, like a jelly-fish, that one hard and mean and secretive, like a horned snail. They could be austere and comical as top hats, or smooth and lively and flattering as ribbons. A parade of private visitors, not over yet. (p. 184)

The elaborate playfulness involved in imagining words to be jellyfish, snails, top hats, and ribbons points to the emptiness of the rhetorical question, "Did they carry their usual meaning, or any meaning at all?" It is obvious that, in Rose's mind at least, the words that the old woman spells enable her to live beyond the privations of senility in a private, festive wonderland of the imagination, wishful thinking, no doubt. Still it is no wonder, given this description of the consolation of words, that the word that had popped into Rose's mind to ask the old woman to spell — the word "C-E-L-E-B-R-A-T-E" — should have been such an unexpectedly felicitous choice.

Words that offer the reader strange possibilities, evidence of so many created worlds, reflect the insidious attractiveness of non-conformity, the highest expression of which is often to be found in art. Frequently, Munro's stories dramatize the uncomfortable situations her heroines find themselves in when their love for the non-conforming word betrays a more general tolerant affection on their part for what others see as a threatening eccentricity. In "The Shining Houses," the protagonist, Mary, responds to the presence in her well-tended street of Mrs. Fullerton's decrepit house, the representative of all alien presences (including Mrs. Fullerton herself) among the shining houses of bourgeois respectability:

> ...these appeared every so often among the large new houses of Mimosa and Marigold and Heather Drive — dark, enclosed, expressing something like savagery in their disorder and the steep, unmatched angles of roofs and lean-tos; not possible on these streets, but there. (DHS, p. 24)

Mary's own nonconformity is not so strong or eccentric as to overcome the words of the owners of the other shining houses: "She could try all night and never find any words to stand up to

134

their words, which came at her now invincibly from all sides: *shack*, *eyesore*, *filthy*, *property*, *value*" (p.27). Unable to find the words, all she can do, as the last lines of the story tell us, is to stand aloof from the general condemnation of Mrs. Fullerton and bear silent witness to the world of the imagination: "There is nothing you can do at present but put your hands in your pockets and keep a disaffected heart" (p.29). I'm not quite sure what Mary would ever have been able to do or say, given her entrenched timidity, so I assume that the sentence's "at present," coupled with the switch to direct address, functions as some kind of choric comment on the possibility that the times may change for all of us. Certainly, keeping a disaffected heart for the present is about all that Del can do in *Lives of Girls and Women* in the face of her own monstrous presence (as she herself conceives it) among the "respectable" girls of Jubilee:

> Well-groomed girls frightened me to death. I didn't like to even go near them, for fear I would be smelly. I felt there was a radical difference, between them and me, as if we were made of different substances. (p.179)

This different substance from which Del is constituted finds all kinds of exotic expression in Munro's work, reflecting her own response to the extraordinary incidents and characters she experienced while growing up in Southwestern Ontario. At one point in an interview with Graeme Gibson, she remarks that "...the part of the country I come from is absolutely Gothic. You can't get it all down."[2] *Lives of Girls and Women*, for instance, begins abruptly with an extended portrait of Del's Uncle Benny, who is not her real uncle but whose social insubstantiality makes him loom much larger in Del's imagination and in Munro's than Del's real mother or father or Del herself, for that matter, though none of them can possibly be described as conventional. Uncle Benny "was the sort of man who becomes a steadfast eccentric almost before he is out of his teens" (p.2), and his conception of the world fascinates Del by its determined adherence to a fairy-tale absolutism in which the monstrous and grotesque supply the norm and the contingent:

> So lying alongside our world was Uncle Benny's world like a troubling distorted reflection, the same but never at all the same. In that world people could go down in

quicksand, be vanquished by ghosts or terrible ordinary cities; luck and wickedness were gigantic and unpredictable; nothing was deserved, anything might happen; defeats were met with crazy satisfaction. It was his triumph, that he couldn't know about, to make us see. (p. 25)

Significantly, Uncle Benny is associated with words. What Del likes best in all the debris littering his place are the newspapers piled on his porch with headlines unlike those to be found in the papers read by her mother and father: "FATHER FEEDS TWIN DAUGHTERS TO HOGS" or "VIRGIN RAPED ON CROSS BY CRAZED MONKS." Uncle Benny's newspapers teach Del the first lesson for any serious writer — an awareness of evil: "I was bloated and giddy with revelations of evil, of its versatility and grand invention and horrific playfulness" (p. 5). And Munro's work has enough of the eccentricity of evil to convince a recent critic, in a somewhat paranoid article, that her books are full of "idiots, senile old people, suicides, the fatally ill" with "the recurring image of the mother who is attacked by Parkinson's disease," victims all of a "society and life [seen] as cruel and deforming."[3] So much for fish bright as moons in fan-cooled corners.

Nonetheless, it is true that the writer-heroine in Munro's books responds, as the author herself does, not only to the hidden magic of the conventional — be it in words, bathrooms, or Woolworths — but to the threatening excitement of the bizarre and eccentric. In both cases, she (*she* especially) has to be on her guard against the scornful suspicion of all those around her — family, friends, neighbours — who are themselves, as it turns out, threatened by the writer's alien standards of taste and judgement. Sheer self-preservation demands not only a disaffected heart but a still tongue. In "Images," a story in Munro's first collection, the daughter conspires with her father to keep the outlandish truth away from her mother's fragile sensibility:

> Like the children in fairy stories who have seen their parents make pacts with terrifying strangers, who have discovered that our fears are based on nothing but the truth, but who come back fresh from marvellous escapes and take up their knives and forks, with humility and good manners, prepared to live happily ever after

— like them, dazed and powerful with secrets, I never said a word. (*DHS*, p. 43)

Never to say a word is necessary for an imagination that has "discovered that our fears are based on nothing but the truth" (necessary at least for the likes of Del, Rose, and most of Munro's other knowledgeable but desperately self-conscious heroines), especially when it becomes apparent that those who do not possess the artist's imagination have, nonetheless, some kind of dim awareness of a terrifying reality coexisting with the more comfortable one to which they daily cling. In "The Peace of Utrecht," the narrator can see its shadowy presence behind her old aunt's conventional pieties: "Even behind my aunt's soft familiar face there is another, more primitive old woman, capable of panic in some place her faith has never touched" (*DHS*, p. 208). The disturbing, alien presence of art is given comic and poignant expression in the title-story of *Dance of the Happy Shades*, where the annual, sacrificial trek to Miss Marsalles' musical party provides, on this particular occasion, not only the familiar discomfort of hypocritical ceremony (on the mothers' parts at least), but the added embarrassment of having to sit and listen "with a look of protest on their faces, a more profound anxiety than before, as if reminded of something that they had forgotten they had forgotten" to the radiant playing of a backward child in "an atmosphere in the room of some freakish inescapable dream" (p. 222). The moral is, however, inescapable, as the story's and the book's final paragraph makes clear:

> But then driving home, driving out of the hot red-brick streets and out of the city and leaving Miss Marsalles and her no longer possible parties behind, quite certainly forever, why is it that we are unable to say — as we must have expected to say — *Poor Miss Marsalles?* It is the Dance of the Happy Shades that prevents us, it is that one communiqué from the other country where she lives. (p. 224)

Communiqués from this other country, especially when they take the form of words, can be a source of profound irritation. "However I put it, the words create their space of silence, the delicate moment of exposure," writes the beleaguered heroine-writer of "The Office" (*DHS*, p.59), and in *Lives of Girls and Women*, Del records the effect her educated mother can have on those around her: "...just by using a word like *barbaric*, she could make a pool of silence, of consternation round her" (p.56). Even Munro's young heroines themselves have a distinctly ambivalent attitude towards the rich possibilities of the words they love, and they spend much of their upbringings in a futile yearning for the consolations of ignorance. In *Lives of Girls and Women*, Del cannot help but admire the empty, calm sophistication of her Uncle Bill's new wife: "I thought she was an idiot, and yet I frantically admired her, was grateful for every little colourless pebble of a word she dropped" (p.87). Del's love of archaic, biblical expressions "disgusts" Naomi, her closest friend, whose own instinctively outrageous behaviour withers as she grows older and more respectable. Her fate is not surprising in a community where "...reading books was something like chewing gum, a habit to be abandoned when the seriousness and satisfactions of adult life took over" (p.119). Yet Del herself frequently betrays her own cause, especially in her prudishly self-conscious, yet richly metaphorical, response to her mother's words. She tells us that her mother's old-fashioned, flowery language "made the roots of my teeth ache with shame," even though she knows full well that she "was not so different from my mother, but concealed it, knowing what dangers there were" (p.81). Her attitude towards her mother echoes that of the young girl in "Walker Brothers Cowboy": "I loathe even my name when she says it in public, in a voice so high, proud and ringing, deliberately different from the voice of any other mother on the street" (*DHS*, p.5). By the time of Munro's most recent collection of short stories, *The Moons of Jupiter*, the mothers have degenerated into the wordless, farcical figure who produces consternation around her by putting on a pair of her husband's trousers and standing on her head.

Fathers, mothers, friends, lovers at different times all find the word a fearful thing. Del's first satisfying love affair in *Lives of Girls and Women* ends in frustration and bitterness when Garnet French discovers that Del cannot see the world as he now does with the simplistic fanaticism of the convert to an unreasoning fundamentalism. His extreme simple-mindedness virtually divests life of language: "...the world I saw with Garnet was something not far from what I thought animals must see, the world without names." Words are obviously the last things that could heal a rift as complete as this one, "Nothing that could be said by us would bring us together; words were our enemies" (p.221); but words and the speculative imagination they advertize had always been Garnet's enemies, and the connection that Del speculatively makes between his attitude towards them and his feelings for her soon becomes irremediably substantive: "He hated people using big words, talking about things outside of their own lives. He hated people trying to tie things together. Since these had been great pastimes of mine, why did he not hate me?" (p.220). Garnet would no doubt have agreed with Rose's father in *Who Do You Think You Are?* in his assessment of the proper role of a woman: "...she should be naive intellectually, childlike, contemptuous of maps and long words and anything in books, full of charming jumbled notions, superstitions, traditional beliefs" ("Half a Grapefruit," p.45). In both cases, grown men are reverting to a childish, almost atavistic, conception of human relationships, like the children in "The Found Boat": "They thought of each other now hardly as names or people, but as echoing shrieks, reflections, all bold and white and loud and scandalous, and as fast as arrows" (*SIB*, p.110).

For the people of Jubilee or Hanratty (except for amiable eccentrics like Uncle Benny or less amiable ones like Del's mother), the enemy words signal a particularly despicable species of nonconformity, that of the intellectually pretentious. For Del's aunts in *Lives of Girls and Women*, "Pretensions were everywhere" and had to be neutralized in the ritual cruelty of a defensive mockery designed to reaffirm the superiority of the group over the individual. Hence the aunts delight in ridiculing what they consider to be the pretentious conversation of a local lawyer:

> After their marvellous courtesy to him I found this faintly chilling; it was a warning. *Didn't he think he was somebody!* That was their final condemnation, lightly said. *He thinks he's somebody. Don't they think they're somebody.* (p.37)

How much more neutralizing someone like Del or Rose needs, who "walked among them feeling bitterly superior and despondent" ("The Beggar Maid," *WDY*, p. 71). "We sweat for our pretensions" ("Half a Grapefruit," *WDY*, p. 39) admits Rose, after she has made the tactical error in the schoolroom of claiming that in her household she has a half-grapefruit for breakfast every morning. Just how much she has to sweat is indicated in the title-story, the last one in the collection, where Rose as a high-school student does not bother to write out a long poem to be learned by heart as she has already memorized it from the board. Miss Hattie, her teacher, insists that she turn her back to the board and recite the poem to the rest of the class, which she does without a mistake. Naturally enough, Rose expects some form of appreciation, "Astonishment, and compliments, and unaccustomed respect." Instead, in an unintentionally cruel adherence to a decorous uniformity, Miss Hattie punishes Rose for setting herself up above the others: "When Rose took the copy to her desk Miss Hattie said mildly enough but with finality, 'You can't go thinking you are better than other people just because you can learn poems. Who do you think you are?' " (p. 196).

Del's and Rose's furtive love affair with the intellect, in the largest sense of that word, suffers from all manner of self-induced petty treasons, compromises, breaches of promise. Their repeated backsliding in the face of their Philistine opposition, their recurring embarrassment over the words they profess to love, are indications of a larger distrust of language and art that makes itself felt throughout Munro's work and may perhaps be held fugitively by Munro herself. At times in her work, in the face of an "unsatisfactory, apologetic and persistent reality" ("The Peace of Utrecht," *DHS*, p. 197), the wealth of language seems not only an embarrassment but a positively wicked indulgence on the part of its sophisticated, superior practitioners. *Something I've Been Meaning to Tell You*, Munro's third collection of short stories, seems to me to be very chary of the written word, especially in its manifestations in metaphor. In the story "Memorial," for instance, words to Eileen seem offensive and fraudulent after the death of her mother:

> People die; they suffer, they die. Their mother had died of ordinary pneumonia, after all that craziness. Illness and accidents. They ought to be respected, not explained. Words are shameful. They ought to crumble in shame. (p. 221)

And yet the vivid condemnation of words here depends upon the contrast between the simple declarative sentences about the ordinariness of death and the sudden surge of metaphor and personification in "They ought to crumble in shame." The opening paragraph of another short story in this collection, "Forgiveness in Families," conveys this new, or renewed, suspicion of artistic arrangement by arranging words in the rough-hewn, repetitive syntax of the speaking voice:

> I've often thought, suppose I had to go to a psychiatrist, and he would want to know about my family background, naturally, so I would have to start telling him about my brother, and he wouldn't even wait till I was finished, would he, the psychiatrist, he'd commit me. (p. 93)

And, later in the story, there is a Joycean attempt to get some kind of hold over the precious ordinariness of being alive, its illustrious technique indicative of the artificiality of any undertaking that tries to cut through the pretensions of language to the unadorned reality of the experience:

> Then you're dying, Mother is dying, and it's just the same plastic chairs and plastic plants and ordinary day outside with people getting groceries and what you've had is all there is, and going to the Library, just a thing like that, coming back up the hill on the bus with books and a bag of grapes seems now worth wanting, O God doesn't it, you'd break your heart wanting back there. (p. 99)

Not surprisingly, perhaps, intellectuals in Munro's work — especially in *Something I've Been Meaning to Tell You* — come off badly. Being married to a writer and academic in "Material" involves the sacrifice of the wife to the dubious activity of the husband's manufacture of words. The estranged wife of the story generalizes — somewhat wildly — about the miserably slavish domestic routine that academics' wives must suffer for the sake of the word-mongering of their husbands: "...their husbands are such brilliant, such talented incapable men, who must be looked after for the sake of the words that will come from them" (p. 25). At the climax of the story, however, the narrator is forced to recognize that her ex-husband, inadequate human being though he may be, has transformed an incident in which originally, and in real life, he had played a contemptible part into an affecting piece of literature: "I was moved by Hugo's story; I was, I am, glad of it, and I am not moved by tricks. Or if I am, they have to be good tricks." As for the victim of the incident, Dotty, "She has passed into Art. It doesn't happen to everybody" (p. 43). There is a large difference between not being moved by tricks and being moved only by good tricks; the narrator's naïve or cynical qualification might well promote a sceptical response to the benefit conferred by literature upon poor Dotty. It's a scepticism about words that afflicts all of us at some time or other, including Munro herself, so it might be as well to close this essay by recalling that the not entirely successful grotesque ending of "Royal Beatings" strips Flo of all her precious vitality, all her good-humoured curiosity about the world's peculiarities, reducing her finally to a terrifying version of the animal state Del had discerned in Garnet French:

> After Rose put her in the Home, a couple of years earlier, she had stopped talking. She had removed herself, and spent most of her time sitting in a corner of her crib, looking crafty and disagreeable, not answering anybody, though she occasionally showed her feelings by biting a nurse. (*WDY*, p. 22)

Her refusal to speak the words that make her human comes at the end of the opening story of *Who Do You Think You Are?*, so that her articulate reappearances in the rest of the book are inevitably blighted by our knowledge of the fate that awaits her. The thought of Flo sitting silently for the rest of her days in the corner of her crib should be a sufficiently powerful advertisement for the importance of the serious, playful interest in words that, until *The Moons of Jupiter* at least, has been one of the key attractions of Munro's writing.

[1] See the interview with Graeme Gibson in *Eleven Canadian Novelists: Interviewed by Graeme Gibson* (Toronto: House of Anansi, 1973), p. 241.

[2] Gibson, p. 248.

[3] Rae McCarthy Macdonald, "A Madman Loose in the World: The Vision of Alice Munro," *Modern Fiction Studies*, 22 (Autumn 1976), 368.

# "Shameless, Marvellous, Shattering Absurdity": The Humour of Paradox in Alice Munro

### LORRAINE MCMULLEN

ALICE MUNRO writes in a tradition of Canadian humour which goes back to the eighteenth century, to Thomas Chandler Haliburton with his humour of situation, character, and language, and which continues through the nineteenth and early twentieth centuries, with such writers as E. W. Thomson with his eccentric characters and amusing incidents of the Ottawa Valley and Stephen Leacock with his sketches of small town life. Today, the humorous strain continues with writers like W. O. Mitchell, Sinclair Ross, Margaret Atwood, and Robert Kroetsch. Munro shares characteristics with all these contemporaries, like Mitchell creating bizarre figures and farcical situations, like Ross writing with a wry, understated humour, sharing with Margaret Atwood a penchant for destroying stereotypes and with Robert Kroetsch a preoccupation with paradox. Paradox in particular is to be expected in the literature of a country much of whose life, as Eli Mandel tell us, "suffers from a form of national schizophrenia."[1]

In an early Munro story, "An Ounce of Cure," the teenage protagonist says, "...I felt that I had had a glimpse of the shameless, marvellous, shattering absurdity with which the plots of life, though not of fiction, are improvised " (*DHS*, pp. 87–88). Munro is always aware of the coexistence in life of the shameless with the marvellous, and one of the ironies in her protagonist's words is that Munro's fiction contains, like life, "shameless, marvellous, shattering absurdity." Paradox is central to her work: her characters are always becoming aware of, and often trying to come to terms with, the paradoxical nature of the world and of humanity — the coexistence of the dull with the exciting, the grotesque with the commonplace, the prosaic with the romantic, the mundane with the marvellous — and the difficulty, if not the impossibility, of distinguishing the real and meaningful from the illusory and delusive, the constant and immutable from the transient and elusive, the true and genuine from the doubtful, the misleading, the fraudulent. Paradox, then, is a structural as well as a technical or linguistic attitude in Munro; though it is humorous at base, it goes beyond the superficially and conventionally comic toward a doubling of perspective.

Munro uses a variety of techniques to show that people and experience are made up of contraries and contradictions. Verbal humour, which, as *The New Encyclopaedia Britannica* reminds us, "requires two (or more) frames of reference whose collision gives rise to the comic effect,"[2] plays a significant part in Munro's revelation of the paradoxical nature of the world. Surprise, often an element of humour, is often an element of her stories, with the protagonist surprised by a twist in the plot or the reader by a startling metaphor. While the twist in the plot reveals the disorderly and the unexpected in life, the startling metaphor reveals what John Metcalf, in his interview with Munro, calls " 'the magic of the ordinary.' "[3] That everyday experience is at times incredible is one of the paradoxes often explored through language. Munro uses the paradoxes of language to reveal the paradoxes of life and the ambiguities of language to reveal the ambiguities of experience. She often lists several contradictory adjectives to convey the reaction to, or the effect of, an incident, or to convey the complex nature of the world. For Munro, as for Kroetsch, "Language, too, is paradoxical. On one hand, it's just everyday speech while on the other, it's an incredible contrivance."[4]

Munro's humour often takes the form of wit. As C. Hugh Holman defines it, "wit is primarily intellectual, the perception of similarities in seemingly dissimilar things...and is expressed in skillful phraseology, plays upon words, surprising contrasts, paradoxes, epigrams, comparisons, etc."[5] Delight arises from the yoking together of two ideas usually not considered related, from the paradox of a forced harmony of incongruities; of course, the more extreme the incongruity, the more successful the humour. The surprise of Munro's highly original similes and metaphors augments the humour of her comparisons between seemingly dissimilar things. To the adolescent Del Jordan, in *Lives of Girls and Women*, Mr. Chamberlain appears in her day-dream "featureless but powerful, humming away electrically like a blue fluorescent light" (p. 155); Naomi's mother, a nurse who collects gossip from her home cases, is "able to operate like an underwater vacuum tube, sucking up what nobody else could get at" (p. 146); Del's "need for love had gone underground, like a canny toothache" (p. 208); of encounters with her high-school boyfriend, Del says, "Our bodies fell against each other not unwillingly but joylessly, like sacks of wet sand" (p. 203). Later, in *Who Do You Think You Are?*, characters make startling comparisons even in serious or tragic situations, as when a fatal pulmonary embolism is made to seem slightly ridiculous. Rose quotes her mother: " 'I have a feeling that is so hard to describe. It's like a boiled egg in my chest, with the shell left on,' " adding that "she died before night, she had a blood clot on her lung" ("Royal Beatings," p. 2). In "Simon's Luck," "...the commotion of her heart turned from merriment to dismay, like the sound of a tower full of bells turned comically (but not for Rose) into a rusty foghorn," and "She had turned Simon into a peg on which her hopes were hung and she could never manage now to turn him back into himself" (p. 166). In "Marrakesh," the body of Dorothy's sunbathing granddaughter looks "as if it were a hieroglyph on her grass" (*SIB*, p. 166). Such analogies resonate with meaning, echoing in the reader's mind with a multitude of implications. They operate the more dramatically because of the narrative prose in which they are planted; the narrative goes on and the emotional effect of the imagery is borne along with it.

Munro uses paradox in much the same way that she uses startling metaphors and similes — to reveal the unusual, the complex, and the contradictory in events and the mixed and contradictory in emotions aroused by events. In "Marrakesh," two lovers appear to the protagonist "strange and familiar to her, both more and less than themselves" (p. 173). In "The Spanish Lady," the protagonist speaks of "a conviction, a delusion" and describes her reaction as a teenager to articles on popularity, "...any title with the word popularity in it could both chill and compel me" (*SIB*, p. 184). Both paradox and oxymoron are especially appropriate to *Live of Girls and Women*, in which Del's growing up is shown to be a time of emotional confusion, as she tries to sort out the genuine from the fraudulent and the illusory from the real. Munro describes Del's contradictory reactions and emotions: when she undresses for her boy-friend, she feels "absurd and dazzling" (p. 204); she finds his mother's suggestion that she use birth control "preposterous acceptance, indecent practicality" (p. 203); she views the Baptist Young People's meeting as "the last place in Jubilee, except possibly the whore-house, where I ever expected to be," and her lover as a "solid intrusion of the legendary into the real world" (p. 215). The child Del, reading Uncle Benny's sensational newspaper, says, "I was bloated and giddy with revelations of evil, of its versatility and grand invention and horrific playfulness." The contrast between her own home and the world reported in Uncle Benny's paper is one of the first polarities Del becomes aware of:

> Why was it that the plain back wall of home, the pale chipped brick, the cement platform outside the kitchen door, washtubs hanging on nails, the pump, the lilac bush with brown-spotted leaves, should make it seem doubtful that a woman would really send her husband's torso, wrapped in Christmas paper, by mail to his girl friend in South Carolina? (p. 5)

Munro juxtaposes details from these two opposing worlds, underlining a central aspect of her style, the use of surface details to reveal the essential, to find the marvellous in the mundane, the magical in the ordinary: "People's lives in Jubilee *as elsewhere*, were dull, simple, amazing and unfathomable—deep caves paved with kitchen linoleum" (p. 253, emphasis added). Even the sensational murder report, which for Del represents that strangely evil and fantastic world coexisting with her own safe and ordinary one, possesses its prosaic details; the grisly murder is made more real by the gift wrapping which links it to our ordinary world and its activities. In "Forgiveness in Families," a mother says of the behaviour of her eccentric son, "It's so terrible it's funny" (*SIB*, p. 96),[6] a comment which applies equally to many of Munro's bizarre characters and incidents.

The obverse, that magic exists in the ordinary, is equally present in Munro's work and is central to her view of life. "[D]ull, simple, amazing and unfathomable" applies to all of us and to our everyday existence. The protagonist of "Forgiveness in Families" discovers this as her mother lies critically ill:

> I sat outside Intensive Care in their slick little awful waiting room. They had red slippery chairs, cheap cover-ing, and a stand full of pebbles with green plastic leaves

growing up. I sat there hour after hour and read *The Reader's Digest*. The jokes. Thinking this is how it is, this is it, really, she's dying. Now, this moment, behind those doors, dying. Nothing stops or holds off for it the way you somehow and against all your sense believe it will. I thought about Mother's life, the part of it I knew. Going to work every day, first on the ferry then on the bus. Shopping at the old Red-and-White then at the new Safeway – new, fifteen years old! Going down to the Library one night a week, taking me with her, and we would come home on the bus with our load of books and a bag of grapes we bought at the Chinese place, for a treat. Wednesday afternoons too when my kids were small and I went over there to drink coffee and she rolled us cigarettes on that contraption she had. And I thought, all these things don't seem that much like life, when you're doing them, they're just what you do, how you fill up your days, and you think all the time something is going to crack open, and you'll find yourself, *then* you'll find yourself, in life. It's not even that you particularly want this to happen, this cracking open, you're comfortable enough the way things are, but you do expect it. Then you're dying, Mother is dying, and it's just the same plastic chairs and plastic plants and ordinary day outside with people getting groceries and what you've had is all there is, and going to the Library, just a thing like that, coming back up the hill on the bus with books and a bag of grapes seems now worth wanting, O God doesn't it, you'd break your heart wanting back there. (pp. 98–99)

What Munro seeks to do is to make us see the wonderful and the delightful in everyday existence and realize its value, rather than waiting out our lives for the extraordinary, unaware that it is everywhere around us. In the description of the waiting room, it is such mundane details as plastic chairs and plastic plants that encapsulate the experience. "... [T]he texture is the thing that I've got to have,"[7] Munro told Metcalf, and she captures texture through seemingly trivial details.

Munro's works contain obvious forms of humour as well. She can achieve comic effects through bizarre and farcical situations, as in "An Ounce of Cure," a broadly humorous story, which Munro refers to as "the work of a beginning writer."[8] The story begins with the protagonist's brief statement, "My parents didn't drink" (*DHS*, p. 75) and goes on to describe her first experience with alcohol. In a fit of depression over the ending of a high-school romance, she drinks quantities of whiskey at a house where she is baby-sitting. At the unexpected result — she is violently ill — she phones her best friend, who rushes to her rescue, accompanied by three more teenagers. The scene when the parents return unexpectedly early is told with the flair of the professional comedian. The sitter's friends have cleaned up the mess, washed her clothes, and plied her with coffee, in the meantime switching on the record-player and turning the incident into a party. The parents return to loud music, dancing, and a sitter clad in her slip and reeking of alcohol: "and there — oh, delicious moment in a well-organized farce! — there stood the Berrymans, Mr. and Mrs., with expressions on their faces as appropriate to the occasion as any old-fashioned director of farces could wish" (p. 84). The narrator, recalling the scene, comments: "But the development of events on that Saturday night — that fascinated me; I felt that I had had a glimpse of the shameless, marvellous, shattering absurdity with which the plots of life, though not of fiction, are improvised" (pp. 87–88). The word "absurd" appears frequently in Munro's works.

The comedy in this story resides in disparity. The reliable young baby-sitter, the daughter of temperance parents, is discovered drunk and half-dressed, entertaining noisy friends. The reader is aware of the girl's innocence, while the couple assume the worst. Irony is added to comedy of situation. The situation itself is perceived in two self-consistent but incompatible frames of reference, that of the Berrymans and that of the baby-sitter. While humour often consists in unmasking — revealing someone as different from what she appeared to be — in this instance, the unmasking works two ways: the girl is not what she is supposedly unmasked to be — frivolous, irresponsible, of questionable morals — but is what she appeared to be, virtuous and serious. The element of surprise in the early return of the parents adds to the humour. The girl is both innocent and ignorant. As her mother points out: " '...ignorance, or innocence if you like, is not always such a fine thing as people think and I am not sure it may not be dangerous for a girl like you' " (p. 76). A further

149

source of amusement is the reader's feeling of superiority in contrast to the fifteen-year-old protagonist.

In *Lives of Girls and Women*, Del Jordan is involved in a similar comic scene. The adolescent Del takes off her clothes in Jerry Storey's bedroom to satisfy his curiosity, only to have his mother return unexpectedly. Unlike the baby-sitter, Del escapes down the back stairs to hide naked and shivering in the cellar while Jerry chats with his mother in the kitchen just above her. Added to her farcical situation is her recollection of Mrs. Storey's claim to broadmindedness, her advanced view that virginity is a thing of the past. Judging from Jerry's reaction to his mother's unexpected return, Del assumes that reality would throw Mrs. Storey's advanced ideas into reverse. To add to the irony, the situation, like the earlier one, is not what it appears to be. Once again, appearance undercuts reality. Munro gives us a double version of illusion versus reality: Del and Jerry are not as guilty as appearances would suggest, nor is Mrs. Storey as advanced as her stated views would suggest.

Another kind of comic scene Munro sets up is exemplified in a later story, "The Beggar Maid." Here Munro portrays a conflict of social values in a scene contrasting the values of Rose's lower-class family with those of her upper-middle-class fiancé, Patrick. Patrick's meeting with Flo, Rose's stepmother, is "just as bad as she [Rose] thought it would be." Munro selects details which show Flo's vulgarity: "The table was spread with a plastic cloth, they ate under the tube of fluorescent light. The centerpiece was new and especially for the occasion. A plastic swan, lime green in color, with slits in the wings, in which were stuck folded, colored paper napkins" (*WDY*, p. 86). During dinner, Flo adds to the vulgarity with macabre stories of suicides in the country area in which she grew up. Later, Patrick consoles Rose, " 'Of course that's not your real mother.... Your real parents can't have been like that' " (p. 87). For maximum effect, Munro juxtaposes this scene with Rose's visit to Patrick's well-bred family, an episode which has its own humour.

Disharmony as a basis for humour is nowhere better demonstrated than in Munro's grotesques. A penchant for grotesques is one of the characteristics that link Munro with Eudora Welty, Flannery O'Connor, and other Southern, regional writers she admires.[9] While there is an element of the grotesque in everyone, our craving for superiority inclines us to delight in the incongruity of others. As Henri Bergson tells us in *Laughter: An Essay on the Meaning of the Comic*, laughter defends society by ridiculing the deviant. Through such characters as Uncle Benny, Becky Tyde, and Franny McGill, Munro portrays the fantastic and yet, in keeping with her characteristic view, shows that these eccentrics are, in some ways, not far removed from our own reality, that, in fact, they form part of the "real world."

Uncle Benny, "the sort of man who becomes a steadfast eccentric almost before he is out of his teens" (*LGW*, p. 2), is only one of several bizarre characters on Flats Road. With his stray animals, his turtles, his house stuffed with bits and pieces of machines and furniture, and his sensational newspapers, Benny provides for the child Del a totally different world from that of her parents. And yet Benny and his world are believable. His antics — advertising for a wife, driving in Toronto even though he can't turn left — have a familiar ring; they are consistent with stories all of us have heard. Del realizes later that Benny's different world is not really so different from her own. "So lying alongside our world," she concludes,

> was Uncle Benny's world like a troubling distorted reflection, the same but never all the same. In that world people could go down in quicksand, be vanquished by ghosts or terribly ordinary cities; luck and wickedness were gigantic and unpredictable; nothing was deserved, anything might happen; defeats were met with crazy satisfaction. It was his triumph, that he couldn't know about, to make us see. (p. 25)

Like Uncle Benny's world, Munro's bizarre characters are "troubling distorted reflection[s]" of ourselves, and the unpredictability of a world in which anything might happen is echoed in these eccentrics as in the farcical situations Munro so effectively portrays.

An early story, "Day of the Butterfly," goes back to the cruel laughter of childhood to reveal that eccentricity is often in the eye of the beholder. Helen recalls her grade six class-mate, Myra Sayla, the dark-haired, dark-eyed daughter of a fruit-store operator, who because of her difference in appearance and background is perceived by her class-mates as eccentric. When Helen happens to engage Myra in the inconsequential conversation of her age, a friendship develops. Myra becomes real, takes on humanity by becoming known. Helen recalls: "It was queer to think that Myra, too, read the comics, or that she did anything at all, apart from her role at the school" (*DHS*, p. 105). The eccentric must be kept remote, and stories must be built around her, or she joins the family of humanity, becomes a person who must be treated with compassion, understanding, and respect. Many of Munro's bizarre characters, by revealing their human side, remind us of the coexistence within each of us of the eccentric and the fantastic along with the conventional and the expected. Bizarre characters, our "troubling distorted reflections," become another avenue by which Munro reveals life's paradoxes, through which she develops a major theme of her work — the coexistence of contradictory elements within the individual and within the world. To see the familiar in the absurd and the absurd in the familiar is characteristic of the double vision of the humorist.

Munro's vision darkens in her later works. Her bizarre characters become less eccentric than grotesque, not loveable reminders of our own weaknesses but pathetic victims of our brutality. In "Executioners," from *Something I've Been Meaning to Tell You*, Munro gives us a picture of the unpleasantly different. Stump Troy, a local bootlegger who had lost his legs in a mill accident, gets involved in a feud and dies helplessly in his house in a fire obviously set by his enemies. In the same story, another character shows us how a deformity can be used to advantage. The family maid, Robina, whose arm had been amputated following a childhood accident, always wore long sleeves. "But," says the narrator,

> it seemed to me this was not for shame; it was to increase the mystery, and importance. Sometimes on the road young children would trail after her, calling, "Robina, Robina, show us your arm!" Their calls were wistful, and full of respect. She would let them go on for a bit before she shooed them away, like chickens. She was chief of those people I have mentioned, who can turn disabilities into something enviable, mockery into tributes. I never thought of that arm except as something she had chosen, a sign of perversity and power. (p. 144)

Later, as part of the darker vision, we see that the disabilities which mark the grotesque's difference are ridiculed and exploited by the "normal." In "Privilege," this attitude is all too apparent in the treatment of Franny McGill. The infant Franny, it was said, had been smashed against the wall by her drunken father as a baby, or she had fallen out of a cutter and been kicked by a horse. "Her face had got the worst of it. Her nose was crooked, making every breath she took a long, dismal-sounding snuffle. Her teeth were badly bunched together, so that she could not close her mouth and never could contain her quantities of spit." A caricature. Abused by her family and by her school-mates, Franny goes on to further, endless abuse: "She would get pregnant, be taken away, come back and get pregnant again, be taken away, come back, get pregnant, be taken away again. There would be talk of getting her sterilized, getting the Lions Club to pay for it, there would be talk of shutting her up, when she died suddenly of pneumonia, solving the problem" (*WDY*, p.26). Our society is unmasked in Munro's ironic account of our attitude to disabilities like Franny's. Plans for "getting her sterilized" courtesy of a business-men's club, or for "shutting her up," are the closest society comes to helping her; there is no suggestion of the responsibility or the guilt of those who abuse her, merely the bleak, terse, final statement, "...she died suddenly of pneumonia, solving the problem." The irony here is much blacker than in Munro's earlier works.

Franny becomes a foil in Munro's onslaught on feminine myth and stereotype:

> Later on Rose would think of Franny when she came across the figure of an idiotic, saintly whore, in a book or a movie. Men who made books and movies seemed to have a fondness for this figure, though Rose noticed they would clean her up. They cheated, she thought, when they left out the breathing and the spit and the teeth; they were refusing to take into account the aphrodisiac prickles of disgust, in their hurry to reward themselves with the notion of a soothing blankness, undifferentiating welcome. (p.26)

A second grotesque figure in *Who Do You Think You Are?* shows herself, like Robina, more able to cope with the world. Becky Tyde was "a big-headed loud-voiced dwarf, with a mascot's sexless swagger, a red velvet tam, a twisted neck that forced her to hold her head on one side, always looking up and sideways. She wore little polished high-heeled shoes, real lady's shoes. Rose watched her shoes, being scared of the rest of her, of her laugh and her neck" ("Royal Beatings," p. 6). The cause of Becky's deformity was polio, not so sensational as Franny's accident, but her background has its sensational elements: her father had kept her shut up after her illness because "He didn't want people gloating" and was said to have beaten her and to have fathered on her a child that was "disposed of." As a result of this last rumour, he was horsewhipped by several young men, "in the interest of public morality" (p. 7), and died shortly thereafter. Becky, now living with her brother, has "after her long seclusion started on a career of public sociability and display" (p. 9). Becky's two sides reflect the duality that Munro is so often concerned to reveal: "Present people could not be fitted into the past. Becky herself, town oddity and public pet, harmless and malicious, could never match the butcher's prisoner, the cripple daughter, a white streak at the window: mute, beaten, impregnated" (p. 8).

A third bizarre character in *Who Do You Think You Are?* reminds us again of the thin line between the eccentric and the conventional. Milton Homer shouts at dogs, trees, and telephone poles and marches in all town parades. As Rose perceives him, he lacks social inhibition. "Whatever it is that ordinary people lose when they are drunk, Milton Homer never had..." ("Who Do You Think You Are?", p. 194). Munro shows us, through Homer, as through other bizarre characters, that the difference between grotesque and "ordinary people" is a quantitative one. While distorting reality, they nevertheless mirror it; by exaggerating certain aspects of humanity, they make us more aware of our own frailties and eccentricities.

That everyone contains contradictory impulses and plays various roles is an aspect of Munro's world which she sometimes states, sometimes dramatically reveals. In "Marrakesh," Viola, according to her sister, "was a great one for the smile to the face and the knife in the back" (*SIB*, p. 159). In "Executioners," the child Helena realizes, when Robina's younger siblings accept her as their leader, that "This was magic, it was intoxication" and that "With them I was not who I was" (*SIB*, p. 146). In "The Ottawa Valley," the narrator recalls her mother's awareness of life's polarities:

My mother always mentioned that her. [a cousin's] husband was an alcoholic, immediately after she had stated that she held an important job with the city's leading law firm. The two things were seen to balance each other, to be tied together in some inevitable and foreboding way. In the same way my mother would say of a family we knew that they had everything money could buy but their only son was an epileptic, or that the parents of the only person from our town who had become moderately famous, a pianist named Mary Renwick, had said that they would give all their daughter's fame for a pair of baby hands. *A pair of baby hands?* Luck was not without its shadow, in her universe. (*SIB*, pp. 227–28)

In "The Beggar Maid," Rose sees opposing ways of life in the contrast between her family's house and that of the retired English professor with whom she boards when she attends college:

What Dr. Henshawe's house and Flo's house did best, in Rose's opinion, was discredit each other. In Dr. Henshawe's charming rooms there was always for Rose the raw knowledge of home, an indigestible lump, and at home, now, her sense of order and modulation elsewhere exposed such embarrassing sad poverty, in people who never thought themselves poor. (*WDY*, p. 67)

One aspect of reality is illuminated by awareness of its opposite.
Munro shows people struggling with their contradictory impulses and emotions. Rose, engaged to Patrick, thinks "It was a miracle; it was a mistake. It was what she dreamed of; it was not what she wanted" (*WDY*, p. 77), in a reaction similar to that of her almost lover, Clifford, who says to his wife, "'It's absolutely true I've wanted out ever since I got in. And it's also true that I wanted in, and I wanted to stay in. I wanted to be married to you and I want to be married to you and I couldn't stand being married to you and I can't stand being married to you. It's a static contradiction'" ("Mischief," pp. 27–28). Rose expresses her ambivalent feelings about Patrick in contradictory metaphors as

she recalls her impulse to return to him after abruptly breaking their engagement:

> Then she had a compelling picture of herself. She was running softly into Patrick's carrel, she was throwing her arms around him from behind, she was giving everything back to him. Would he take it from her, would he still want it? She saw them laughing and crying, explaining, forgiving. *I love you, I do love you, it's all right, I was terrible, I didn't mean it, I was just crazy, I love you, it's all right.* This was a violent temptation for her; it was barely resistable. She had an impulse to hurl herself. Whether it was off a cliff or into a warm bed of welcoming grass and flowers, she really could not tell. It was not resistable, after all. She did it. ("The Beggar Maid," p. 94)

Here dream merges into reality as Rose does exactly what she had pictured herself doing.

Munro's characters often possess the duality they observe in the world around them. When Rose returns to her home town and meets a school-mate with whom she had felt a special kinship, she realizes the opposition between his inner and outer reality:

> All the time she talked, she was wondering what he wanted her to say. He did want something. But he would not make any move to get it. Her first impression of him, as boyishly shy and ingratiating, had to change. That was his surface. Underneath he was self-sufficient, designed to living in bafflement, perhaps proud. She wished that he would speak to her from that level, and she thought he wished it, too, but they were prevented. ("Who Do You Think You Are?", p. 205)

Del's mother exemplifies this duality, which Munro sees as inherent in all of us. While ridiculing the Presbyterian Church for comparing the local dance-hall to Sodom and Gomorrah, she feels the same way about the dance-hall. While publicly campaigning for birth control, she considers it unnecessary to discuss the topic with her daughter, convinced that "sex was something no woman — no *intelligent* woman — would ever submit to unless she had to" *(LGW*, p.203). Del describes her mother's contradictions with irony:

> She was on the side of poor people everywhere, on the side of Negroes and Jews and Chinese and women, but she could not bear drunkenness, no, and she could not bear sexual looseness, dirty language, haphazard lives, contented ignorance; and so she had to exclude the Flats Road people from the really oppressed and deprived people, the real poor whom she still loved. (p.8)

Del describes her mother's divisions with appropriate metaphor: "Inside that self we knew, which might at times appear blurred a bit, or sidetracked, she kept her younger selves strenuous and hopeful; scenes from the past were liable to pop up any time, like lantern slides, against the cluttered fabric of the present." Aware that we must somehow integrate opposites, Del's mother says of an acquaintance, "What good is it if you read Plato and never clean your toilet?" (p.74). Unlike other mothers in the town, she diverges from the traditional maternal role to take on such unusual activities as selling encyclopedias door-to-door and writing letters to newspapers espousing feminist causes. Her mother's unconventional behaviour is responsible for much of Del's ambivalence and contradictory emotions. She recalls, "I felt the weight of my mother's eccentricities, of something absurd and embarrassing about her....I did want to repudiate her ....At the same time I wanted to shield her" (p.64). Through her portrayal of Del's ambivalent attitude to her mother, who is consistently out of step with the small town, Munro undermines the conventional view of the mother-daughter relationship in many of its aspects.

Munro's protagonists are often self-deprecatory. Del says of herself and her high-school boy-friend, "... we found that the way to survive the situation was to make fun of it. Parody, self-mockery, were our salvation" (p.197). While self-deprecation is especially appropriate to the child and teen-age Del and, later, Rose, it is sometimes used effectively with adult narrators as well. By allowing the audience to feel superior, the narrator's self-deprecating humour arouses sympathy as well as laughter. Munro's protagonists often exhibit a wry irony. In "Forgiveness in Families," the protagonist reports of her scapegrace brother:

" 'That's a deep one, your brother, she [her mother] used to say, he's got some surprises in store for us.' She was right, he had"; of his involvement in a school cheating-ring she says, "One of the janitors was letting him back in the classroom after school because he said he was working on a special project. So he was, in his own way. Mother said he did it to make himself popular, because he had asthma and couldn't take part in sports" (*SIB*, p. 94).

As part of her revelation of the disparity between illusion and reality, Munro explodes several myths. In *Lives of Girls and Women*, for example, she thoroughly discredits the concept of sex as romantic and glamorous. In her portrayal of Mr. Chamberlain's exhibitionist *tour de force* as seen through the eyes of the adolescent Del, she comically explodes the myth of the power and importance of the male organ. Central to this scene are Del's lack of reaction to, and her lack of appreciation of, what Chamberlain views as " 'Quite a sight' " (p. 171). Her first thought when Chamberlain exposes himself is, "Not at all like marble David's" (p. 169). Her description is at variance with Chamberlain's pride of ownership, "Raw and blunt, ugly-coloured as a wound, it looked to me vulnerable, playful and naïve, like some strong snouted animal whose grotesque simple looks are some sort of guarantee of good will," as her non-involvement is at variance with his expectations, "It did not seem to have anything to do with me" (pp. 169–70).

Del's earlier exalted view of nature, "I had been looking at trees, fields, landscape with a secret strong exaltation. In some moods, some days, I could feel for a clump of grass, a rail fence, a stone-pile, such pure unbounded emotion as I used to hope for, and have inklings of, in connection with God" (p. 188), is juxtaposed with her view as she drives with Chamberlain through the summer countryside:

> ...I saw that the whole of nature became debased, maddeningly erotic. It was just now the richest, greenest time of year; ditches sprouted coarse daisies, toadflax, buttercups, hollows were full of nameless faintly golden bushes and the gleam of high creeks. I saw all this as a vast arrangement of hiding places, ploughed fields beyond rearing up like shameless mattresses. Little paths, opening in the bushes, crushed places in the grass, where no doubt a cow had lain, seemed to me specif-

ically, urgently inviting as certain words or pressures. (pp. 168–69)

Del's reaction to Chamberlain's remark, " 'Hope we don't meet your Mama, driving along here,' " might well be, "I did not think it possible. My mother inhabited a different layer of reality from the one I had got into now" (p. 169).

Not long after her outing with Chamberlain, Del is kissed by a young man she has met at a dance. Her description of this experience further undercuts the romantic view of sex: "He bent over and pressed his face against mine and stuffed his tongue, which seemed enormous, wet, cold, crumpled, like a dishrag, into my mouth" (p. 190).

Del's description of her first experience of sexual intercourse, while it lacks the grossness of preceding sexual incidents, is clearly anti-romantic. Again, her thoughts point to the comic disparity between reality and romantic expectations: "I had always thought that our eventual union would have some sort of special pause before it, a ceremonial beginning, like a curtain going up on the last act of a play. But there was nothing of the kind" (p. 227). The theatrical simile is in keeping with Del's tendency to play-act and her difficulty in sorting out the real and the unreal. The purely mechanical difficulties she relates — standing in the garden, conscious of her buckle being shoved into her stomach and of the pain in the arches of her feet, holding up her lover's pants for fear of being seen, and finally crashing into the flower bed — negates any idea of an ecstatic or mystical experience. The magic moment is overwhelmed by practical details. The earth doesn't move.

Another area of ritual which Munro satirizes is that surrounding courtship and marriage. Through the contrasting attitudes and behaviour of Del and her friend Naomi, she exposes the comic — indeed, the ridiculous — element in the views of young women of what is important for them. In her description of the school, which points up the difference between Naomi's new world, when she transfers to a business course, and the world she used to share with Del in the college entrance courses, Munro again uses surface details to sharpen the contrast:

...Suddenly freed from Latin, Physics, Algebra, she mounted to the third floor of the school where under the sloping roof typewriters clacked all day and the walls were hung with framed maxims preparing one for life in the business world. *Time and Energy are my Capital; if I squander them, I shall get no Other.* The effect, after the downstairs classrooms with their blackboards covered with foreign words and abstract formulae, their murky pictures of battles and shipwrecks and heady but decent mythological adventures, was that of coming into cool ordinary light, the real and busy world. (p. 178)

Del views with ambivalence the role which young women were expected to play in a Canadian town of the 1950s, while Naomi embraces it with enthusiasm. When Naomi moves from her typing course to an office job, Del says, "I felt that she had moved as far beyond me, in what I vaguely and worriedly supposed to be the real world, as I in all sorts of remote and useless and special knowledge, taught in schools, had moved beyond her" (p. 195). Munro satirizes the rituals most teenage girls unthinkingly accepted: "I was amazed and intimidated by her as her boring and preoccupied new self. It seemed as if she had got miles ahead of me. Where she was going I did not want to go, but it looked as if *she* wanted to; things were progressing for her. Could the same be said for me?" (p. 182); "What was this masquerade she was going in for now, with her nail polish, her pastel sweater?" (p. 179). It seems to Del that this world of Naomi and her office friends is the one she ought to fit into, bored though she is by the conversations about washing hair and sweaters, and by the social aspect, which consists of shopping for silver and linen and attending wedding and baby showers. Of Naomi's friends in the workaday world Del observes, "They were tolerant of what most people in town would think of as moral lapses in each other, but quite intolerant of departures in dress and hair style, and people not cutting the crusts off sandwiches, at showers" (p. 182).

Del makes an unenthusiastic attempt to adapt to aspects of Naomi's new life-style, especially her new stress on grooming, observing "Love is not for the undepilated" (p. 180). Munro gives a satirical picture of Del as she walks with Naomi to the Gay-la Dance Hall:

We walked out the highway on a Friday night, in our flowered, full-skirted dresses. I had done my best; I had

160

washed, shaved, deodorized, done up my hair. I wore a crinoline, harsh and scratchy on the thighs, and a long-line brassiere that was supposed to compress my waist but which actually pinched my midriff and left a little bulge beneath that I had to tighten my plastic belt over. I had the belt pulled in to twenty-five inches, and was sweating underneath it. I had slapped beige makeup like paint over my throat and face; my mouth was as red, and nearly as thickly painted, as an icing-flower on a cake. I wore sandals, which collected the gravel of the roadside. Naomi was in high heels. It was June by this time, the air warm, soft, whining and trembling with bugs, the sky like a peach skin behind the black pines, the world rewarding enough, if only it had not been necessary to go to dances. (p.186)

Munro underlines the artificiality of the episode, in this instance, by contrasting the artificiality of the girls' appearance with the beauty of the natural world.

Del, like the author, rejects Naomi's world: "What was a normal life?" Del asks herself.

It was the life of the girls in the Creamery office, it was showers, linen and pots and pans and silverware, that complicated feminine order; then, turning it over, it was the life of the Gay-la Dance Hall, driving drunk at night along the black roads, listening to men's jokes, putting up with and warily fighting with men and getting hold of them, getting hold — One side of that life could not exist without the other, and by undertaking and getting used to them both a girl was putting herself on the road to marriage. There was no other way. And I was not going to be able to do it. No. Better Charlotte Brontë. (p.194)

Munro is a satirist for whom disorder, chance happenings and meetings, and the bizarre characters who reveal us to ourselves are all parts of an absurd yet real world. Irony is at the core of Munro's view of humanity and events, a view she expresses with wit and humour, mixing paradoxes, startling comparisons, and unexpectedly incisive details with farcical scenes and eccentric or contradictory personalities. In her use of comic devices, Munro goes beyond the clever and the humorous. Her careful and accurate structuring of situations and juxtaposition of incidents reveal the coexistence of the bizarre with the ordinary, the genuine with the fraudulent, the immutable with the transient. Her ironically perceived characters, whether appearing to us as outlandish or ordinary, reveal to us our own contradictory impulses and ambivalent feelings, and through their weaknesses and vulnerability remind us of our own weaknesses, our own vulnerability. Challenging myths and sweeping away stereotypes, Munro induces us to recognize, with her, the "shameless, marvellous, shattering absurdity" around and within us.

NOTES

[1] Eli Mandel, *Contexts of Canadian Criticism: A Collection of Critical Essays*, Patterns of Literary Criticism, No. 9 (Toronto: Univ. of Toronto Press, 1971), p. 3.

[2] Arthur Koestler, "Humour and Wit," *The New Encyclopaedia Britannica*, 1980 ed.

[3] John Metcalf, "A Conversation with Alice Munro," *Journal of Canadian Fiction*, 1, No. 4 (Fall 1972), 58.

[4] V.S., "Studhorse Poet Works in Reverse," *The Globe and Mail*, 29 May 1981, p. 16.

[5] C. Hugh Holman, *A Handbook of Literature*, 4th ed. (Indianapolis: Bobbs Merrill, 1980), p. 467.

[6] See also Helen Hoy, " 'Dull, Simple, Amazing, and Unfathomable': Paradox and Double Vision in Alice Munro's Fiction," *Studies in Canadian Literature*, 5, No. 1 (Spring 1980), 100–15, for a detailed exploration of Munro's use of verbal paradox.

[7] Metcalf, p. 56.

[8] Metcalf, p. 58.

[9] See J.R. (Tim) Struthers, "Alice Munro and the American South," *Canadian Review of American Studies*, 6 (Fall 1975), 196–204; rpt. (revised) in *The Canadian Novel: Here and Now*, ed. John Moss (Toronto: NC, 1978), pp. 121–33, for a study of Munro and Southern writers.

# The Structure of Style
## in Alice Munro's Fiction

GERALD NOONAN

OF STYLE IT HAS BEEN JUSTLY SAID: "Here we leave solid ground."[1] The intricacies of Alice Munro's style in her first four volumes of fiction corroborate this dictum and emphasize as well the wisdom of a corollary statement: "Style has no...separate entity." That, too, has been justly said:

> Young writers often suppose that style is a garnish for the meat of prose, a sauce by which a dull dish is made palatable. Style has no such separate entity; it is non-detachable, unfilterable. The beginner should approach style warily, realizing that it is himself he is approaching, no other; and he should begin by turning resolutely away from all devices that are popularly believed to indicate style — all mannerisms, tricks, adornments. The approach to style is by way of plainness, simplicity, orderliness, sincerity.[2]

In this essay, accordingly, the analysis of Munro's style is not separate but is inextricably related with content and structure. To keep all the components in closer focus, it may help to declare at this point the general thesis that Munro's vision of reality and her methods of art in depicting it (i.e., her "content" and "style" and "structure") grow progressively, if not steadily, more complicated and paradoxical in the course of her work: *Dance of the Happy Shades*, *Lives of Girls and Women*, *Something I've Been Meaning to Tell You*, and *Who Do You Think You Are?*

In the beginning, Munro's focus seems to be on fact, on stripping away "a kind of mental cellophane" ("The Peace of Utrecht," *DHS*, p. 193) that preserves in our memories the fantasies of childhood. As we soon discover, however, even "The facts are not to be reconciled" ("Dance of the Happy Shades," *DHS*,

p. 223). There is about real life a paradoxical, contradictory quality which pits one verity against another; the result, in style, we call oxymoron — a device that complicates the analysis by, ultimately, producing more concealing cellophane. The problem is that the verbal artistry of oxymoron, or perhaps our ease in labelling it, all too readily leaves the impression that paradox is, for Munro, a terminal vision.[3] On the contrary, her later work repeatedly presents the view that paradox is not a planing above the common level of life — it *is* the common level; it is reality. What's more, the "tricks and trap doors" of art ("Tell Me Yes or No," *SIB*, p. 124), by its conventions and traditional transgressions upon belief, contribute to the masking of real life. Thus, in *Who Do You Think You Are?*, the confrontation of art and life is dominant and deliberate, shaping the structure and stratagems of the stories. Every story is framed in retrospection, and the narrator uses the distancing to counter some conventional expectation — which is triggered by the initial part of the fiction — with what does actually "happen" later. In these accounts, the later "happenings" cannot be entirely dismissed as just more fiction since the actuality of what occurs later often abolishes, in effect, the plot conflicts of the earlier parts of the story.

As a prime example, consider the story "Mischief" in the main part of which Rose's extramarital affair with Clifford is not consummated despite, or because of, episodes of anxiety, guilt, and deception of hotel clerks, waitresses, and taxi-drivers, as well as spouses. After the story's leap forward in time, Rose has divorced Patrick; Clifford and Jocelyn, his wife, have become wealthy and are living in Toronto. In the concluding event, as a kind of desultory aftermath of a party, Clifford does at last make love to Rose "rather quickly on the nubbly hooked rug. Jocelyn seemed to hover above them making comforting noises of assent." The consummation so fervently wished for earlier in the story is now an incident witnessed by Jocelyn and is not important enough to disrupt social patterns. Rose does reflect on Clifford and Jocelyn's "selfishness, obtuseness, and moral degeneracy" but eventually decides "to go on being friends...because she needed such friends occasionally, at that stage of her life" (*WDY*, p. 132).

In the account of this advance to jadedness, the reader may almost forget that the chief conflict in the felt experience, the major part of the story — the effort of Clifford and Rose to couple without Jocelyn's knowledge — is rendered absolutely pointless by the witnessed adultery among assenting adults. To be sure, as Munro reminds us elsewhere, all the history presented is fiction; still, wholesale destruction of the early and orthodox plot conflict — set forth in the accepted manner of psychological realism — by the brief finale is a startling stratagem. The contradiction is embedded in the story's structure, not in any array of oxymorons. The structure, by transposing the intently dramatic into something almost commonplace, shows how life contradicts the expectations of art.

Munro's increasing distrust of art becomes evident in a comparative assessment of earlier stories. In "An Ounce of Cure," from the initial volume, the last sentence implies some achievement in therapy: "I am a grown-up woman now; let him [her unrequited high-school love] unbury his own catastrophes" (p. 88). In "The Ottawa Valley," however, at the end of the third volume, the conventions of art are interfering with full therapy:

> If I had been making a proper story out of this.... That would have done.... The problem, the only problem, is my mother. And she is the one of course that I am trying to get; it is to reach her that this whole journey has been undertaken. With what purpose? To mark her off, to describe, to illumine, to celebrate, to *get rid* of, her; and it did not work.... I could go on, and on, applying what skills I have, using what tricks I know, and it would always be the same. (p. 246)

At first, the precocious Del in *Lives of Girls and Women* believes her made-up novel is true — "not real but true" (p. 248). Later, she recognizes it as a "mysterious and as it turned out unreliable structure" (p. 251) and undergoes an apprenticeship of fact — "I would try to make lists." She knows, however, that "The hope of accuracy we bring to such tasks is crazy, heartbreaking" because the task she sets herself is a stasis in which "every last thing, every layer of speech and thought, stroke of light... [would be] held still and held together — radiant, everlasting" (p. 253). Del's ambition nurtures an illusion of art which by two volumes later is despaired of by another Munro narrator. Rose, at the end of *Who Do You Think You Are?*, reflects on the ineffable division between herself and a childhood friend, Ralph Gillespie: "...there was always something further, a tone, a depth, a light, that she couldn't get and wouldn't get" ("Who Do You Think You Are?," p.205), even though "...she felt his life, close, closer than the lives of men she'd loved, one slot over from her own" (p.206).

Ultimately, then, the artist, instead of holding up life — "every last thing, every layer... stroke of light" — radiant and everlasting, admits that there is "a tone, a depth, a light" that is beyond art, that "There seemed to be feelings which could only be spoken of in translation" ("Who Do You Think You Are?", p.205). The confessed limits of art, and the professed complexities of life, make it seem as if the narrator is taking the reader into her confidence. If feelings can "only be spoken of in translation," if "not speaking of them" may be "the right course to take" ("Who Do You Think You Are?," p.206), the narrator and reader share the same slot, peering out at the untranslatable realities of life.

A very early example of this unity in puzzlement of narrator and reader occurs in "Sunday Afternoon" where both, it seems to me, come to realize at the same time the vague, untranslatable unease. Alva is not sure, nor am I, of the precise degree of wrongfulness in the Gannett life-style — the drinks on Sunday afternoon, the radishes cut like roses, "a look of being made of entirely synthetic and superior substances" (DHS, p.163), an island up north all their own. The physical contact between Alva and Mrs. Gannett's cousin, the unexpected kissing, makes things "not so unreal" (p.170). The reader is told: "She saw it differently now...." The reader may see it differently now, also, but both the reader and Alva are still confronted by a "mysterious" feeling, nonetheless, as the story ends: "But things always came together; there was something she would not explore yet — a tender spot, a new and still mysterious humiliation" (p.171).

In this world of untranslatable things, the collision of fact, as in oxymoron, is ubiquitous, but the ultimate purpose is to challenge art's ability to present real life, and that challenge is embedded primarily in structure. The structure of "Simon's Luck," a later story, specifies how the philosophy of Munro's narrator has changed from that of Del at the end of Lives of Girls and Women. Far from desiring to convey everything as "radiant, everlasting," Rose wants to avoid "the dazzling alteration" which she sees as stemming both from "the celebration and shock of love" and from "the disappointment, the losses, the dissolution" of love. In either case, Rose thinks: "...you were robbed of something — a private balance spring, a little dry kernel of probity" (*WDY*, p. 170). Rose proceeds to the coast and creates a new life for herself there, with probity. Eventually, she hears the "preposterous" news of Simon's death while she is on a break from the filming of a preposterous TV drama. The juxtaposition of the "real life" news with the unreal TV drama provides the story's challenging and paradoxical assessment of art's scope.

Viewers of the TV drama, Rose reflects, are protected "from predictable disasters, also from those shifts of emphasis that throw the story line open to question, the disarrangements which demand new judgments and solutions, and throw the windows open on inappropriate unforgettable scenery" (pp. 172–73). In real life, however, such "disarrangements" exist: "Simon's dying struck Rose as that kind of disarrangement. It was preposterous, it was unfair, that such a chunk of information should have been left out, and that Rose even at this late date could have thought herself the only person who could seriously lack power" (p. 173).

The "chunk of information" was, of course, left out of the story itself earlier, and Rose, therefore, felt that she had been deserted, exploited. The revelation of Simon's death at that point, as an explanation of his failure to call again, would have been perhaps too melodramatic, too pat. More certainly, *had* the death been revealed earlier, there would be no story, not this one at any rate. Thus, although the narrative may seem direct and artless in the smaller components of style — few oxymorons, for example, occur in this story — the overall structure poses a number of interrelated paradoxes about fiction and reality, which culminate in an artfully oblique puzzle.

Munro's use of a plainer style, and more complex structure, may be analogous to Rose's preference as stated in her time of crisis in "Simon's Luck": "...she so much wanted, required, everything to be there for her, thick and plain as ice-cream dishes." The use of oxymoron, however, the coupling in phrase of paradoxical fact, "removes the world for you" as love does "going well...[or] going badly," and either way you are "robbed of something...[the] little dry kernel of probity" (p. 170).

In Munro's fourth volume of fiction, the probity is an adherence to the complications of life that are beyond the conventions of art. To keep her eye steadily on the dry kernel of reality, not

the things "she had been running from, any more than the opposite of those things" ("Simon's Luck," *WDY*, p. 170), Rose, the
narrator in all ten stories, keeps her distance from most events.
Her reflective commentary from a later time unifies the book and
keeps reminding the reader that in this art as in life "the story line
[is] open to question, the disarrangements [exist] which demand
new judgments and solutions" (pp. 172–73). The distancing is
maintained naturally enough since the stories take place within
the mind of the narrator more than did the stories in the earlier
volumes. Further, as a result of the distancing and the within-the-
mind focus, the passages of specific detail are fewer, replaced by
description more consciously remembered by Rose, more con-
iously illustrative — detail observed in retrospection as well as
in immediacy.

Munro's sense of life as paradox is not softened by the shift in
technique; paradox is presented more directly. In "Providence"
when Patrick, the estranged husband, spends time with the snap-
shot album, Rose silently declares the photos of her earlier life
"true lies" (*WDY*, p. 133). Previously, Rose has found that neither
things nor the ideas in them gain constancy: "Those things aren't
going to help her.... Pots can show malice, the patterns of linoleum can leer up at you, treachery is the other side of dailiness"
("Royal Beatings," p. 16).

The "mental cellophane" attacked in *Dance of the Happy
Shades* is still there: "When Rose told people these things, in later
years.... She had to swear they were true" ("Privilege," *WDY*,
p. 27). And when needed, specific detail is used to strip off the
cellophane:

> ...Men who make books and movies ["of an idiotic,
> saintly whore"]...cheated...when they left out the
> breathing ["a long, dismal-sounding snuffle"] and the
> spit ["constantly running"] and the teeth ["badly
> bunched together, so that she could not close her
> mouth"]; they were refusing to take into account the
> aphrodisiac prickles of disgust....(*WDY*, p. 26)

It is significant that this cellophane in the later book has to do
with the greater outside world, the "men who make books and
movies." In *Dance of the Happy Shades*, Munro is concerned
with fantasies more personally circumscribed. The narrator in

"The Peace of Utrecht" describes her own and her sister's reminiscence of childhood as "that version of our childhood which is safely preserved in anecdote, as in a kind of mental cellophane" (p. 193).

Munro's style in these early stories of *Dance of the Happy Shades* relies mainly upon the careful evidence of facts to puncture the cellophane. Her selection of factual detail takes the reader more surely into the reality behind the mental cellophane and evokes the past, and present, in a way that the reader cannot dismiss as mere emotion and illusion because the emotion and illusion are inherent in the facts. A corollary of this strategy, the effect of the stories, is that our child-selves, and our current selves, contrary to our fantasies, do not "emerge beyond recognition incorrigible and gay" (p. 193); instead, the past and present are seen as corrigible — correctable — and sad. And part of the sadness stems from the very awareness that correctable as human activity may be, the contrariness, the mysteriousness of human existence invariably prevents any imposition of the rational as corrective. It's as if, says a later narrator in "The Spanish Lady," "As if we were all wound up a long time ago and were spinning out of control, whirring, making noises, but at a touch could stop, and see each other for the first time, harmless and still" (*SIB*, pp. 190–91). At a touch, the uncontrollable spinning *could* stop but it doesn't in real life. Further, Munro's narrator consistently doubts the ability of art to stop and convey the true nature of life. As "The Spanish Lady" narrator concludes: "This [the 'could stop' concept of the previous quotation] is a message; I really believe it is; but I don't see how I can deliver it" (p. 191).

Not surprisingly, then, the delivery of music's "message," in "Dance of the Happy Shades" — the performance on the piano by the gangly girl from the school for the retarded — is the outstanding event at Miss Marsalles' annual music-class gathering.

> What she plays is not familiar. It is something fragile,
> courtly and gay, that carries with it the freedom of a
> great unemotional happiness. And all that this girl does
> — but this is something you would not think could ever
> be done — is to play it so that this can be felt, all this can
> be felt, even in Miss Marsalles' living-room on Bala
> Street on a preposterous afternoon. (*DHS*, p. 222)

Present in the quotation are three major elements of Munro's work. First, there is the contradictory essence of life, the combined positive and negative as it exists in the perceiving mind, something positive in "fragile, courtly and gay," but something negative, too, in the "unemotional happiness." Second, there is the rare triumph of art, at first hearing at least, doing "something you would not think could ever be done." Third, there is the banal reality in which rests both the essence of life and the triumph of art: "...all this can be felt, even in Miss Marsalles' living-room on Bala Street on a preposterous afternoon." And in this particular story, the enduring presence of the banal overrides the brief breakthrough of art:

> For the moment she is finished it is plain that she is just the same as before, a girl from Greenhill School. Yet the music was not imaginary. The facts are not to be reconciled. And so after a few minutes the performance begins to seem, in spite of its innocence, like a trick....
> (p. 223)

As a general rule, that is the distinctive quality of Munro's early style — "...the facts are not to be reconciled." (Later, it is the events which are not to be reconciled, the "disarrangements" of real life.) Her descriptive adjectives are often contradictory, oxymoronic. Further, the specific detail she uses evokes such precise connotation that the irreconcilable is readily acknowledged. For example, to express the incongruity of the retarded children amid the socially pretending suburbanites in "Dance of the Happy Shades," the narrator allows herself a couple of guesses which pinpoint alternate but irreconcilable milieus with striking clarity: "It must seem at first that there has been some mistake.... Is it the wrong house, are they really on their way to the doctor for shots, or to Vacation Bible Classes?" (p. 220).

Often, the detail that Munro uses throughout a story builds up, unperceived, the mental cellophane or texture of the situation which the author wishes the narrator and reader to share. The "twist" of the story that then punctures the wrapping occurs in one of three main ways: (1) something happens, as in the pianist's performance of "Dance of the Happy Shades," to symbolize the chief aspect of the tale; (2) a contradictory point, concealed within the course of the story, is unveiled at the end in order to demonstrate for both narrator and reader that the seemingly broad sweep of reality theretofore was, indeed, after all, mental cellophane; (3) a reminder is given at the end that the account is shaped by the demands of fiction and that the way of reality is not at all the way of art.

In *Who Do You Think You Are?*, the device of distancing enables the narrator to combine all three methods in the course of her reflection. In "Dance of the Happy Shades," however, the story of Miss Marsalles' piano party is contained within present time, and the playing of the surprisingly gifted retarded girl works as an objective correlative assessing the attitudes and values of the Rosedale compatriots to a nicety. Despite her "undeniable" high level of talent, the girl, to them, is just "a girl from Greenhill School." As for Miss Marsalles, despite her obvious value as a music teacher who has developed the talents of generations, her status, in the eyes of her former Rosedale students, has declined along with the value of her progressively shoddier residence and addresses;

> *In the old days*...the address was in Rosedale; that was where it had always been. (p. 213)

> Now...an even smaller place...on Bala Street. (Bala Street, where is that?) (p. 211)

Within themselves, the ex-Rosedale matrons contain conflict and ambiguity in that despite their materialistic, socially conscious outlook, they are reluctant to condemn on that basis — "...this aspect of Miss Marsalles' life had passed into that region of painful subjects which it is crude and unmannerly [and self-doubting?] to discuss" (p. 216). Miss Marsalles' life of the old days represents the traditions and the trappings of old Rosedale, where the current generation of mothers, now removed with their families to the suburbs, had their upbringing. The downward slide of Miss Marsalles suggests to them the decay of the values they once held dear, values they would like now to think were worthwhile and thriving still in suburbia. The ambiguity, then, engendered by the retarded girl's advanced music matches nicely several other layers of ambiguity: that which the mothers feel about Miss Marsalles, their Rosedale heritage (which they affirm), the value of art (which they affirm more theoretically),

171

and the necessity of certain levels of material comfort (upon which they conspire to be silent).

Munro's second stratagem, the contradictory point unveiled at the end of a story, is used in "Postcard" to startle both narrator and reader into a new realization. The relationships throughout between the narrator, Helen, a department store clerk, and Clare MacQuarrie, the aging bachelor from one of the town's leading families, has been as factual and as uncomplicated as the postcards that Clare is constrained to send home from his annual winter trip to Florida. There is a no-nonsense directness, too, to Clare's marriage — to someone else in Florida — and his return to town with a bride. Helen's loud midnight protest in front of the MacQuarrie house is quite direct, as well. After she has been calmed and driven home by the town constable, Helen thinks, in the story's final sentence, of her lost lover: "... what I'll never understand is why, right now, seeing Clare MacQuarrie as an unexplaining man, I felt for the first time that I wanted to reach out my hands and *touch* him" (p. 146). We realize only at that point how the lack of tenderness, the non-expression of feeling, has been the cause of the failure in the relationship, a cause that Helen has continually condoned. Thus, the story's neglect of that aspect until the end is consistent with the reality.

The third stratagem, the interplay of life and art, is exemplified at the close of both "The Office" and "An Ounce of Cure." In both instances, the endings remind the reader that the narrator's first-person account is something of a deliberate catharsis. The landlord of "The Office" is summed up at the end as a bizarre and prejudiced busybody, and the narrator comments in the final sentence: "I arrange words, and think it is my right to be rid of him" (*DHS*, p. 74). In "An Ounce of Cure," the "splendidly unexpected" result of the narrator's first encounter with alcohol is her fascination with "*the way things happened,*" "the shameless, marvellous, shattering absurdity with which the plots of life, though not of fiction, are improvised" (*DHS*, pp. 87–88). And again, in the final sentence, there is the reminder of catharsis: "I am a grown-up woman now; let him unbury his own catastrophes" (p. 88).

Although *Lives of Girls and Women* is the only one of Munro's books to be labelled a novel, the beginning chapters strike me as being accounts, rather than fragments of a continuing novel, and for that reason, perhaps, the details cited in descriptions seem more documentary than selected. The adjectives that describe Uncle Benny, for example, in the initial segment, "The Flats Road," are consistent, not undercut with oxymoron: "All his movements seemed slowed down, ceremonious and regretful" (p. 23). A similar consistency characterizes the narrator's realization at the end of Uncle Benny's account: "So lying alongside our world was Uncle Benny's world like a troubling distorted reflection, the same but never at all the same" (p. 25). The vision of juxtaposed realities in later works — Ralph Gillespie's "one slot over" — is more complex, less striated. The worlds are more intermeshed.

Elsewhere in *Lives of Girls and Women*, as well, the description though vivid is comparatively free of the paradoxical: Mr. Boyce, the United Church organist, is "short, with a soft moustache, eyes round and wet-looking, like sucked caramels" (p. 121); the country women who come to the revival meeting are "in loose print dresses, running shoes on their feet, arms bare, big and rosy as hams, holding quilt-wrapped babies" (p. 209). (The decor here of print dresses, running shoes, hams, and quilts is consistent, a departure from earlier juxtapositions of things and ideas startlingly at odds.) The image by which Del remembers her first real lover, Garnet French, is particularly striking, but again without the oxymoronic: "All weekend the thought of him stayed in my mind like a circus net spread underneath whatever I had to think about at the moment. I was constantly letting go and tumbling into it" (p. 214). The style in *Lives of Girls and Women* is consistent with the content inasmuch as the world-view expressed is, like Uncle Benny's alternative, comparatively stable and knowable. The interplay of past and present in Del's mother's mind, for example, is fairly clear-cut: "Inside that self we knew, which might at times appear blurred a bit, or side-tracked, she kept her younger selves strenuous and hopeful; scenes from the past were liable to pop up any time, like lantern slides, against the cluttered fabric of the present" (p. 74). Del herself is more sensitive than her mother to the snide criticism her mother's activities evoke from townspeople who accept the status quo: "I myself was not so different from my mother, but concealed it, knowing what dangers there were" (p. 81).

If we consider the broader issue of the development in Munro's first four books, Del's greater consciousness of self and of others in *Lives of Girls and Women* may be seen as the beginning of a more inward-scouring awareness which culminates in the complex, mysterious, and precarious grasp of reality that is conveyed in *Who Do You Think You Are?*. In *Lives of Girls and Women*, however, Del's perception of the complexities of art and life does not go beyond some "surprise" at how "the whole mysterious and as it turned out unreliable structure" of her carefully thought out, but unwritten, novel had arisen from "a few poor facts, and everything that was not told." Del reflects further: "It is a shock, when you have dealt so cunningly, powerfully, with reality, to come back and find it still there.... And what happened, I asked myself.... Such questions persist, in spite of novels" (p. 251).

Munro's third volume provides a quantum leap in the search for the answer to such questions, the search for an expressed reality. In *Something I've Been Meaning to Tell You*, the focus is on "connections that cannot be investigated, but have to be relied on." The "connections" in the stories provide "messages" which go beyond "the facts" and allow us to believe "Without any proof" ("Winter Wind," p. 201). The stories are about the difficulties of playing roles, of finding one's "real self"; a common ingredient is the lack of empirical evidence upon which the mind can base objective understanding, and, thus, there is a concomitant decline in the manipulation of fact. The narrator, as a manipulator in fiction, however, encounters the same lack of certainty, empiricism, the same amorphous no-man's-land where possible invention challenges belief. In "Winter Wind," the narrator reflects:

> But that only takes care of the facts. I have said other things. I have said that my grandmother would choose a certain kind of love. I have implied that she would be stubbornly, secretly, destructively romantic. Nothing she ever said to me, or in my hearing, would bear this out. Yet I have not invented it, I really believe it. Without any proof I believe it, and so I must believe that we get messages another way, that we have connections that cannot be investigated, but have to be relied on. (p. 201)

There is a strong similarity between this narrator and the character, Et, in the volume's first story. Et makes up the report of Blaikie Noble's second runaway marriage: "She never knew where she got the inspiration to say what she said, where it came from. She had not planned it at all, yet it came so easily, believably" ("Something I've Been Meaning To Tell You," p. 21). Et questions herself, as the narrator does later: "...what did she mean to do about this story when Blaikie got back?...She did not know what she wanted. Only to throw things into confusion, for she believed then that somebody had to, before it was too late" (p. 22). Et's notion, presumably, is that throwing things into confusion is preferable to the passive unawareness of her brother-in-law, Arthur. She doesn't quite articulate the concept but sometimes has it "on the tip of her tongue to say to Arthur, 'There's something I've been meaning to tell you.' She didn't believe she was going to let him die without knowing. He shouldn't be allowed." The ending of the story suggests that this state of unknowing, non-telling, is common in what is supposed to be the closest relationships: "But Et let it go, day to day. She and Arthur still played rummy and kept up a bit of garden, along with raspberry canes. If they had been married, people would have said they were very happy" (p. 23). The "confusion" that Et prefers, instinctively, to passive unknowing acceptance is similar to what the narrator in "Winter Wind" perceives as characteristic of her grandmother's life, a confused quality for which, when it has gone from her life, the grandmother weeps: "She knew and did not understand...how it could have been different or how she herself, once so baffled and struggling, had become another old woman whom people deceived and placated and were anxious to get away from" (p. 206). The "baffled and struggling" life-style that the grandmother prefers and the "confusion" that Et prefers are related to the constant difficulty — an accepted aspect, it is implied, of normal lives — in distinguishing the real from the fanciful. In "Memorial," the character Eileen, "with her fruitful background of reading, her nimble habit of analysis...can later explain and arrange it for herself. Not knowing, never knowing, if that is not all literary, fanciful" (p. 224). In the final story of the volume, "The Ottawa Valley," the narrator is also trying to go beyond the literary to achieve more satisfactory "explanations" and "arrangements" of facts about her mother.

Other stories in the volume are of particular interest in the way they reach specifically toward the same terminal, the mystery of real life and the inadequacy of art to solve it. The narrator in "Material" reflects that "What holds anybody in a man or a woman may be something…flimsy…some half-fraudulent mystery" (p. 27). And though her first reaction to ex-husband Hugo's story is that it is "an act of magic…Lovely tricks, honest tricks" (p. 43), she later objects to the philosophy that decides in advance "what to do about everything…run across in this world, what attitude to take, how to ignore or use things" (pp. 43–44). Her congratulatory letter to Hugo involuntarily becomes something else: *This is not enough, Hugo. You think it is, but it isn't. You are mistaken, Hugo"* (p. 44).

In "Tell Me Yes or No," the transformation in the recollection of a past lover occurs even after his reported death. The narrator, through mistaken identity, is given a packet of love letters sent to her lover by another woman. The narrator realizes that there were depths in her illicit lover, depths of fantasy or manipulation, that she had not dreamed of before. That is the case even though their time together had a solid, factual base. "The thing we old pros know about, in these fantasies," the narrator reflects, "is the importance of detail, solidity…" (p. 109). At the end of the story, when it is clear that she had no solid understanding of the man, the narrator admits to using the stratagems of fiction to come to some acceptance of the affair: "I invented you, as far as my purposes go. I invented loving you and I invented your death. I have my tricks and my trap doors, too. I don't understand their workings at the present moment, but I have to be careful, I won't speak against them" (p. 124). Again, the mysterious workings of the human heart, the "half-fraudulent mystery," is paralleled by the half-fraudulent artifices of literature. In the course of Munro's canon of short stories, a similar development occurs: the early importance of "detail and solidity" is overmastered by the "tricks" and "trap doors" of fiction.

Puzzlement and transformation also dominate in "Forgiveness in Families," a story wherein the hippie and one time "loonie" son, Cam, a brother of the narrator, receives a heartfelt tolerance from their mother, which the more orthodox and responsible daughter concludes "is a mystery to me, how it comes or how it lasts" (p. 105). A descriptive passage in the story indicates how "things" in Munro's world are transformed by the emotion of an event. The narrator's mother is in an intensive care ward, and the daughter waits in the hospital's "slick little awful waiting room. They had red slippery chairs, cheap covering, and a stand full of pebbles with green plastic leaves growing up. I sat there hour after hour and read *The Reader's Digest*. The jokes. Thinking this is how it is, this is it, really, she's dying" (pp. 98–99). She thinks of the details of her mother's existence and her own as a child:

> And I thought, all these things don't seem that much like life, when you're doing them, they're just what you do, how you fill up your days, and you think all the time something is going to crack open, and you'll find yourself, *then* you'll find yourself, in life.... Then you're dying. Mother is dying, and it's just the same plastic chairs and plastic plants and ordinary day outside with people getting groceries and what you've had is all there is...O God...you'd break your heart wanting back there. (p. 99)

The things, "what you've had," remain stable; the ideas in Munro's things do not — they transform things under the pressure of emotion in surprising, mysterious ways.

As noted previously about the later story, "Simon's Luck," the narrator deliberately wishes to avoid this kind of "dazzling alteration," preferring the "dry kernel of probity." Again, for the narrator in "The Spanish Lady," the "real reality" is the major concern. The sharp point of Hugh's unfaithfulness is its attack upon reality: *"It is terrible when you find out that your idea of reality is not the real reality"* (*SIB*, p. 176). At the end of her reflective train journey to Vancouver, the narrator is shocked into a new "message" by the sudden death of one of the old men on a slum bench on Hastings Street: "What we say and feel no longer rings true, it is slightly beside the point. As if we were all wound up a long time ago and were spinning out of control, whirring, making noises, but at a touch could stop, and see each other for the first time, harmless and still" (pp. 190–91). In the next sentence, the story ends with a confession of art's inadequacy to convey the "out of control" quality of life: "This is a message; I really believe it is; but I don't see how I can deliver it" (p. 191). The uncontrollable mystery of life and of art dominates the content and the method of all thirteen stories in the volume.

In *Who Do You Think You Are?*, the structure of the stories, as was indicated earlier, juxtaposes the complexities of life and of art. In these stories, too, Rose's distant vantage point serves to undercut the intensity of the usual psychological reality created by fiction. The title-story is thus particularly pertinent as a conclusion for the collection. Ralph Gillespie, a class-mate of Rose's, is portrayed as he was in early school-days, and as he is in later life, a war veteran and Legion member. In her adult reunion with Ralph, Rose feels that the distancing of the intervening years counters the remembrances of childhood rapport:

> ...there was always something further, a tone, a depth, a light, that she couldn't get and wouldn't get.

> All the time she talked, she was wondering what he wanted her to say. He did want something. But he would not make any move to get it. (p. 205)

> There seemed to be feelings which could only be spoken of in translation; perhaps they could only be acted on in translation; not speaking of them and not acting on them is the right course to take because translation is dubious. Dangerous, as well. (pp. 205–06)

Upon the news of Ralph's accidental death, Rose can say little "about herself and Ralph Gillespie, except that she felt his life, close, closer than the lives of men she'd loved, one slot over from her own" (p. 206).

Those last words of the book indicate the extent of reality, the "one slot over," that Munro's distancing, her strategy of fiction, now aims for. They indicate, as well, the extent of reality which cannot be achieved. The best that can be hoped for is a realization by writer and reader that the life or truth depicted is just "one slot over" from one's own. It is as if there exists a personal delusion, a cocoon of egotism, that prevents us from ever recognizing ourselves totally or objectively, in art or in life — the very kind of personal immunity intimated in the title phrase, "Who do you think you are?". The individual always has a sense of self larger and different than appears in another's perception. There will always be "something further, a tone, a depth, a light" lost in translation.

In Munro's ultimate art of "disarrangement," then, the solid, detailed texture of style is muted lest the surface of the objects, the immediacy of them, be misinterpreted as the whole of reality.

The distancing of the narrator helps emphasize a more honest view of life, free of the illusions of art, free of the illusions of total understanding and total communication, illusions that the glitter of verbal paradox helped earlier to sustain. In her first four volumes of fiction, the process of Munro's style is from detail and verbal paradox to the paradox of event and structure, the real complications of life which, in turn, complicate art.

NOTES

[1] William Strunk, Jr. and E. B. White, *The Elements of Style* (New York: Macmillan, 1959), p. 52.
[2] Strunk and White, p. 55.
[3] A recent article (Helen Hoy, " 'Dull, Simple, Amazing and Unfathomable': Paradox and Double Vision in Alice Munro's Fiction," *Studies in Canadian Literature*, 5 [Spring 1980], 100–15) supplies a thoroughgoing overview of Munro oxymorons. In some instances I would dispute what is oxymoronic and what is normal. To take the first three citations by Hoy: Munro's phrase "ironic and serious at the same time" does not strike me as being "incompatible" with description of a love affair; the phrase "mottoes of godliness and honor and flaming bigotry" is not noticeably paradoxical applied, say, to the reality of several troubled regions in the world today; and the concept of "special, useless knowledge" (p. 100) is surely more familiar than oxymoronic in any academic grove except one's own.
    My ultimate reservation is that a focus upon the oxymoron is of little assistance in interpretation of the later stories. I believe that Hoy, to remain consistent in her pursuit of the oxymoron, must execute some procrustean foreshortening of the later works. One sentence, in particular, in which the scars show is "The exploration of the prosaic and the marvellous runs through Munro's fiction, is developed most extensively in *Lives of Girls and Women*, and becomes more complex and ambiguous in *Who Do You Think You Are?*" (p. 108). Use of the oxymoron may be most extensive in *Lives of Girls and Women*, but if "exploration" of the discordant opposites is "developed most" there, the later work could hardly be "more complex and ambiguous." My argument is that in the later work structure dominates and supplies a complexity and ambiguity undreamt of in *Lives of Girls and Women*.
    Similarly, when John Moss, in his Introduction to *The Canadian Novel: Here and Now* (Toronto: NC, 1978), generalizes about

Munro's "heightened realism...making the truth so palpably self-evident that the reader, the critic, is hard pressed to discover arguments to be pursued or explanations to be given, and yet is enthralled with the complexities her writing evokes" (pp. 8–9), I submit that greater attention to Munro's structure and the art-that-repels-art is the beginning of elucidation — though I agree with Moss that Munro remains a "most enigmatic writer" (p. 8).

# Who Do You Think You Are?:
## Alice Munro's Art of Disarrangement

LAWRENCE MATHEWS

Later on Rose would think of Franny when she came across the figure of an idiotic, saintly whore, in a book or a movie. Men who made books and movies seemed to have a fondness for this figure, though Rose noticed they would clean her up. They cheated, she thought, when they left out the breathing and the spit and the teeth; they were refusing to take into account the aphrodisiac prickles of disgust, in their hurry to reward themselves with the notion of a soothing blankness, undifferentiating welcome. (p. 26)

THIS PASSAGE, a few pages into "Privilege," the second story in *Who Do You Think You Are?*, is jarring. The flow of the narrative has been disrupted by what looks like gratuitous feminist pamphleteering. In fact, it is difficult not to read this passage as an attack on Robertson Davies for his presentation of Anna Dempster in *The Deptford Trilogy*. The reader can be forgiven for wondering whether Alice Munro is nervous about Davies' literary intrusion into her Southwestern Ontario bailiwick. As a comment on *Fifth Business*, the passage is singularly beside the point; Davies is clearly not interested in the sort of realism which Rose demands. More important, the passage's function in "Privilege" remains unclear: in this story, we hear nothing more on the subject of male illusions about women.

But this passage does introduce an idea which is reiterated again and again as we follow Rose through the ten stories of *Who Do You Think You Are?*: literature, and, for that matter, art in general, have nothing useful to say to her. What they do say is either irrelevant or downright untrue, as in the case of the unnamed books and movies about idiotic, saintly whores. This point is made so insistently that its presence can hardly be accidental. In "Half A Grapefruit," for example, Rose finds that the English literature she reads in high school speaks of a world to which she does not belong. Katherine Mansfield's story, "The Garden Party," makes her angry:

> There were poor people in that story. They lived along the lane at the bottom of the garden. They were viewed with compassion.... She could not really understand what she was angry about, but it had something to do with the fact that she was sure Katherine Mansfield was never obliged to look at stained underwear; her relatives might be cruel and frivolous but their accents would be agreeable; her compassion was floating on clouds of good fortune, deplored by herself, no doubt, but *despised* by Rose. (p. 48)

In "The Beggar Maid," Rose realizes that the painting of "King Cophetua and the Beggar Maid" provides a false image of her relationship with Patrick. She cannot identify with the Beggar Maid's "milky surrender," her "helplessness and gratitude"; on the other hand, she knows that Patrick is completely unlike King Cophetua, who, Rose imagines, "could make a puddle of her, with his fierce desire" (p. 77). But Patrick believes that Rose *is* like the Beggar Maid, and, in agreeing to marry him, she is in a sense agreeing to play the Beggar Maid's role. The result is, of course, disastrous. In "Mischief," Rose's ill-fated tryst with Clifford at Powell River coincides with a concert whose heavily Romantic programme (Glinka, Tchaikovsky, Beethoven, Smetana, Rossini) mocks her aspirations to enjoy a passionate affair. Clifford will not fulfil her desire to be "loved, not in a dutiful, husbandly way but crazily, adulterously" (p. 124); he dismisses the idea as " 'mischief' " (p. 122). The Romanticism of the music finds no echo in Rose's life.

Such examples can be multiplied almost endlessly. In "Simon's Luck," there is a young woman who is writing a paper on the suicide of female artists — "She mentioned Diane Arbus, Virginia Woolf, Sylvia Plath, Anne Sexton, Christiane Pflug" (p. 157) — but Rose has no desire to emulate these women: survival is what interests her, and, in the end, it is Simon who dies. In "Spelling," Rose is a member of the chorus in a television production of *The*

*Trojan Women*, a play in which female suffering is raised to tragic dignity; in the same story, Flo slides pathetically into senility. In "Half A Grapefruit," *Macbeth* is irrelevant to the world of West Hanratty (p. 49); in "The Beggar Maid," Patrick is misleadingly reminded of Rose by the title of *The White Goddess* (p. 78); in "Mischief," Rose is baffled by a "symbolic" play (p. 106); and in "Providence," Rose's daughter, Anna, likes two television programmes, "Family Court" and "The Brady Bunch," neither of which reflects the life they are actually leading (p. 140). In all of these stories, art — if that term might be defined broadly enough to include "The Brady Bunch" — bears no direct relation to reality, at least to the reality of Rose's life. Patrick is not a king; her "love" for Clifford is not to be consummated in some dream world conjured up by the *Pastoral*; female artists who commit suicide have nothing to say to Rose — instead they excite the prurient interest of a woman who is herself "emaciated, bloodless, obsessed" (p. 157). And so on.

But the most explicit outbust against art comes at the end of "Simon's Luck." Rose is acting in a television series; a scene involving a girl who seems to be about to commit suicide is being shot:

> The girl didn't throw herself into the sea. They didn't have things like that happening in the series. Such things always threatened to happen but they didn't happen, except now and then to peripheral and unappealing characters. People watching trusted that they would be protected from predictable disasters, also from those shifts of emphasis that throw the story line open to question, the disarrangements which demand new judgments and solutions, and throw the windows open on inappropriate unforgettable scenery. (pp. 172–73)

Out of context, this passage looks even more quixotic than the apparent attack on Robertson Davies in "Privilege": a philippic against the conventions of prime-time television! But the next paragraph reveals that Rose has interpreted her own experience according to similar conventions:

> Simon's dying struck Rose as that kind of disarrangement. It was preposterous, it was unfair, that such a

chunk of information should have been left out, and that Rose even at this late date could have thought herself the only person who could seriously lack power. (p. 173)

Art not only bears false witness to life, but we tend (or at least Rose does) to impose equally mendacious aesthetic patterns upon our own experience. She is disconcerted by the "chunk of information" which shatters the neat pattern she has imposed upon her relationship with Simon. Rose's life has many such "disarrangements which demand new judgments and solutions," and art has nothing useful to teach her about how to cope with them.

Distrust of aesthetic pattern is not an entirely new motif in Munro's work. In this respect, the most obvious forerunner of *Who Do You Think You Are?* is "Material," a story in *Something I've Been Meaning to Tell You.* But in "Material" the emphasis is, as Bronwen Wallace has pointed out, on the contrast between the way men (whether artists or not) order their experience by means of their perverse expertise in knowing "how to ignore or use things" (p. 44) and the way women do *not* do this, but rather see their experience in terms of "scraps and oddments" (p. 43), imposing no pattern, and thereby avoiding the comforting self-deceit to which men — if the narrator is to be believed — are inevitably subject.[1] In *Who Do You Think You Are?*, however, gender is no longer an issue. One of Rose's problems is precisely that she *does* continually succumb to the temptation to see her experience as ordered and must continually re-learn the lesson of "Material": it is, as the narrator of the story writes, *"not enough"* (p. 44) to regard the chaos of experience as though it existed only to provide raw material for our fantasies of order.

Two questions, then. How does Munro herself deal with the problem of imposing an artistic form upon the raw material of Rose's experience? And what value does she expect these stories to have for her readers, whose experience is presumably as subject to "disarrangement" as Rose's?

The answer I should like to propose to the first question is that Munro supplies the reader with the missing "chunk of information," so that the stories in *Who Do You Think You Are?* do not give us merely an aesthetically successful ordering of Rose's experience. They also give us the information we need to be able to perceive that the aesthetic pattern is possibly, and often

184

probably, "false," in the sense that it does not provide a adequate rendering of the full truth of that experience. Nor does the missing "chunk" allow us to devise a new, definitive pattern which yields the story's "real meaning." Instead, the presence of the new information raises questions about the validity of any pattern we might find in the story. It is not that our narrative expectations are reversed: they are neither reversed nor fulfilled. Each story arouses the need to interpret Rose's experience but does not satisfy that need.

Munro uses two principal means of conveying the new "chunks of information." One is the use of the epilogue (in almost every story); the other is the use of characters, situations, and anecdotes which are not necessary to the development of the main strand of the narrative, but which seem to bear some thematic relation to it. Examples include Franny McGill in "Privilege"; the stories Flo tells in "Half a Grapefruit"; the anecdote of the undertaker at the beginning of "Wild Swans"; Dr. Henshawe, whose career represents a road Rose chooses not to take, in "The Beggar Maid"; the stories Simon tells Rose about his past in "Simon's Luck"; and the old woman whose pastime furnishes the title for "Spelling." These "chunks of information" and those provided by the epilogues all raise unanswerable questions about the meaning of Rose's experience. In order to demonstrate this point, I should like to look more closely at the technique of "disarrangement" as it is used in "Royal Beatings" and "Mischief."

If Munro had chosen not to include the epilogue to "Royal Beatings," the story would still have all of the qualities for which her work is usually praised. The effect of the epilogue is to cause us to question the validity of Rose's perception of the past, as it has been delivered by the narrative. The anecdote of the horse-whipping of Becky Tyde's father by three men, including one named Hat Nettleton, has been inserted early in the story, apparently to say something about the psychology of cruelty which permeates the culture of Hanratty and environs, and this explains, in part, the psychology of the "royal beatings" which Rose receives at home. The horsewhipping, carried out by the "Three useless young men" at the instigation of "more influential and respectful men in town" (p.7) was, ironically, a kind of revenge for the beatings the misshapen Becky was said to have suffered at the hands of her father. Perhaps this leads the reader ɔ look for further parallels between Becky and Rose, but Nettleton is soon forgotten. The epilogue, however, thrusts him back into the limelight. "Years later, many years later" (p. 20), Rose happens to hear a radio interview with Nettleton on the occasion of his hundred-and-second birthday. The interview reproduces the clichés of the genre so faithfully that Rose first thinks it is a scene from a play. Nettleton, at the interviewer's prodding, delivers what is expected of him: *"We worked and we was glad to get it....Didn't have no T.V.,"* and so on (p. 21). Rose, naturally enough, is struck by what she takes to be the falseness of the picture of Nettleton which the interview has given: "Horsewhipper into centenarian....Oldest resident. Oldest horsewhipper. Living link with our past" (p. 22).

The reappearance of Hat Nettleton changes our understanding of the story. For Rose, of course, what he does in the interview is tantamount to denying his true identity, since, as far as she is concerned, the most important fact about him has been concealed. But in fact what he says is determined largely by the demands of the interviewer. As far as we know, he tells no lies, and he is hardly going to volunteer information about the horsewhipping, even if he does remember it. That Nettleton's version of his past so blatantly diverges from Rose's memory of it raises the question of the accuracy of Rose's account of her own past. Is her understanding of it as selectively based and misleading as that of the centenarian horsewhipper?

A sentence in the opening pages speaks unobtrusively to this issue:

> This was, of course, in the days before the war, days of what would later be legendary poverty, from which Rose would remember mostly low-down things — serious-looking anthills and wooden steps, and a cloudy, interesting, problematical light on the world. (p. 5)

What Rose understands of the physical world is determined by her vantage point within it. Is it fair to make a parallel statement about her perception of human nature? Are the "royal beatings" the moral equivalent of the "low-down things" that she sees — not the whole truth (or even a metaphor for the whole truth) about her childhood, but the only *part* of the truth that she is equipped to perceive? And has her desire to interpret her childhood in terms of "legendary poverty" led her to omit, to fals

There is other evidence to suggest that this may be the ca.
Rose, listening to Flo's stories, gets the sense that "Present tim
and past, the shady melodramatic past of Flo's stories, were quite
separate..." (p.8), and Rose's imagination is stimulated by
the thought of Flo's exotic and mysterious early life, "crowded
and legendary, with Barbara Allen and Becky Tyde's father and
all kinds of old outrages and sorrows jumbled up together in it"
(p.10). Yet every time a situation in the story is coloured by
someone's imagination, a more convincing, "realistic" account is
presented along with it. Thus, Rose likes the phrase "royal
beatings" because it conjures up the image of an "occasion both
savage and splendid"; but she recognizes that "In real life they
didn't approach such dignity..." (p.1). Flo enjoys recounting
the legend about Becky Tyde's illegitimate child: " 'Disposed of,'
Flo said. 'They used to say go and get your lamb chops at Tyde's,
get them nice and tender!' " But she adds "regretfully" that " 'It
was all lies in all probability' " (p.7). The old men who congre-
gate in front of the store believe that the star in the western sky is
"an airship hovering over Bay City, Michigan...lit by ten
thousand electric light bulbs"; Rose's father "ruthlessly" demol-
ishes this myth by pointing out that the "airship" is really the
planet Venus (p.20). Perhaps the relation between Rose's
memory of the events of her childhood and the "truth" of those
events parallels the relation between the imaginary airship and
the real planet.

The prominence given to Hat Nettleton's account of the past
certainly stimulates the reader to speculate along these lines. The
irony of the epilogue seems to lack the sort of "point" we might
expect it to have. Neither differences nor similarities between
Rose and Nettleton are emphasized. Perhaps Rose, unlike Nettleton (insofar as she understands Nettleton), has a view of her
past experience which is unromanticized, "balanced," "objective." Perhaps, on the other hand, she has, unwittingly, under-
gone a transformation as dramatic as Nettleton's ("horsewhipper
to centenarian"), and perhaps this has affected her view of the
past. Certainly the question has been raised. In the epilogue, we
have one of "those shifts of emphasis that throw the story-line
open to question" (p.172).

The first story in the volume, then, alerts us to the possibility
that any pattern that Rose perceives in her life (and that we

.eive through her) is suspect. Every story raises pertinent but
answerable questions about the "real" meaning of her experi-
nce (as opposed to the ostensible meaning towards which the
story-line has been leading us). "Mischief" provides a particularly convenient example of Munro's technique here because
Rose's response and the reader's are clearly distinguished. As in
"Simon's Luck," Rose comes to realize, at the end of the story,
that yet another narrative has suffered "disarrangement." The
reader can easily assimilate Rose's disorientation to his/her own
pattern, but then *that* pattern is disrupted, too.

Rose's unconsummated affair with Clifford in the early fifties
has ended badly. We enter the epilogue, set at some point in the
seventies, prepared to dislike him. It is something of a surprise to
find that we are meant to despise his wife Jocelyn, as well, but the
evidence is overwhelming. We listen to the banal trendiness of
her speech — " 'What is happening now...is that Clifford is
wide open' " — and the point is underlined immediately: "Was
Jocelyn's talk a parody, was she being sarcastic? No. She was
not" ("Mischief," p. 127). As for Clifford, there is "Something
obscene about his skinniness and sweet, hard smile" (p. 129).
To complete the unattractive family portrait, both husband and
wife have, with success, become unabashedly materialistic.

At the end of the story, Rose and Clifford finally consummate
their affair, with Jocelyn, ironically, an approving onlooker.
Rose's feelings about this are complex: "curious, disbelieving,
hardly willing, slightly aroused and, at some level she was too
sluggish to reach for, appalled and sad." In the morning, she
decides that their friendship is at an end:

> She was angry at Clifford and Jocelyn. She felt that they
> had made a fool of her, cheated her, shown her a glaring
> lack, that otherwise she would not have been aware of.
> She resolved never to see them again and to write them a
> letter in which she would comment on their selfishness,
> obtuseness, and moral degeneracy. (p. 132)

At this stage, the reader does not share Rose's sense of disarrangement; rather, he/she feels entitled to ruminate compla-
cently about Rose's moral education. At last, Munro seems to be
telling us, Rose has learned the lesson that she should have
learned twenty years in the past. Certain people *are* selfish,

obtuse, and morally degenerate, and it is best to avoid th.
   But the story's last sentence changes all that: "Sometime la.
she decided to go on being friends with Clifford and Jocelyn.
because she needed such friends occasionally, at that stage of her
life" (p. 132). What does this tell us about Rose? Are we to
deplore her for needing Clifford and Jocelyn, or should we
applaud her for having the maturity to recognize that she does
need them? And what, exactly, does she need them *for*? This
sentence gives us the "chunk of information" which disarranges
our pattern and demands "new judgments and solutions,"
although it does not give us the basis for arriving at them.
   Certainly our suspicions are aroused to the point that we want
to re-examine Rose's behaviour in the epilogue. The unholy —
and carefully chosen — trinity of "selfishness, obtuseness, and
moral degeneracy" takes on new significance. There is something
intrinsically selfish about Rose's notion of her friendship with
Clifford and Jocelyn. Whether *they* need *her* is apparently not a
question which interests Rose, and the fact that she needs them
(only) "at *that* stage of her life" (emphasis added) suggests a sort
of consumerism with respect to personal relationships: last year's
model can, without qualms, be cast aside. As for obtuseness and
moral degeneracy, Rose remains ironically unaware of the similarities between her moral attitudes and those of Clifford and
Jocelyn, similarities emphasized at one level by her participation
in the previous evening's sexual activity.
   The story of Rose's "love" for Clifford lends itself to this sort
of analysis as well. Selfishness: it is Clifford, not Rose, who
thinks of the undesirable consequences for others that their affair
would have — "It was being away from home for a month that
had made him see everything differently. Jocelyn. The children.
The damage" (p. 122). Obtuseness: Rose ignores the signals
warning of Clifford's withdrawal from her — his failure to write,
the "businesslike" phone call from Prince George (p. 116). Moral
degeneracy: it hardly makes sense to say that Clifford is more
"degenerate" than Rose; it is true that he betrays her, but Rose is
willing to betray Patrick by having the affair in the first place. No
doubt the evidence for the prosecution here is far from conclusive. But the point is that it is not until the last sentence of the
story that one would even think of making the case.
   What Munro gives us in *Who Do You Think You Are?*, then, is
an art which is based on the disruption of pattern, an art which

ns rooted in scepticism about, even hostility towards, the
nd of "truth" which most literature claims to deliver. What
alue can be ascribed to this kind of fiction, which seeks to
perform the literary equivalent of proving a negative? A clear, if
implicit, answer to this question is provided by the last story in
the volume, "Who Do You Think You Are?".

This story is partly about Rose's relationship with a high-
school class-mate named Ralph Gillespie, partly her reminiscence of a town eccentric with the archly literary name of Milton
Homer: "Whatever it is that ordinary people lose when they are
drunk, Milton Homer never had, or might have chosen not to
have — and this is what interests Rose — at some point early in
life." It is tempting to write Milton Homer off as yet another of
Munro's regional grotesques, and yet there is evidence that he is
meant to be more than that. "Milton" and "Homer," taken
together, suggest literary profundity and universality, and the
fact that, for whoever named him, "...there was probably no
thought of linking together the names of two great poets,"
underlines for the reader that Munro has very deliberately done
just that. In writing about this man, she seems to be saying, she is
dealing not merely with Hanratty's mild equivalent of the village
idiot, but with the basic stuff of human nature, the same *materia
poetica* that Homer and Milton used.

Ralph Gillespie is the primary artist figure in the story. It is he
who first alerts Rose to the possibility that Milton Homer can be
related to a tradition of literary art when he shows her that he has
changed the title of a poem in his high-school English book: "He
had stroked out the word *Chapman's*... and inked in the word
*Milton*, so that the title now read: *On First Looking into Milton
Homer*" (p.194). Later, Ralph develops a Milton Homer imitation, the means by which he achieves social acceptance: "He was
so successful that Rose was amazed, and so was everybody else.
From that time on Ralph began to do imitations..." (p.200).
After high school, he joins the navy. Years later, Rose hears from
Flo that he has returned to Hanratty. His attempt to get a job at
the Legion fails, Flo says, because of " 'the way he carries on,' "
a phrase that refers primarily to his imitations:

> "...half the time he's imitating somebody that the
> newer people that's come to town, they don't even know
> who the person was, they just think it's Ralph being

idiotic....Ralph don't know when to stop. He Milton Homer'd himself right out of a job." (p. 202)

Ralph is an artist who does present an unambiguous "truth" about his subject. He has found a way to translate reality (Milton Homer and the others) into the artistic form of his mimicry. Those in his audience who know Milton Homer can appreciate the way in which he does this, but for the others, the "newer people," the line between art and reality blurs, and Ralph, for them, himself becomes the subject-matter. In the same way, one might suggest, regional writers may come to be understood as doing no more than embodying the spirit of their regions, or feminist writers as having significance only in their "representative" quality. (It is easy to see why these possibilities might perturb Munro.) It is not that these kinds of writing are without value: Ralph does a very *good* Milton Homer. But the form he has chosen has severe restrictions — like Hat Nettleton's radio interview, like Rose's half-hour television programme, like the well-made short story which makes a clear thematic "point" about its protagonist. The problem is that each of these forms requires that too much be omitted. Ralph, for example, has no way of rendering Milton Homer's *inner* experience, although the possibility of his having chosen to be the way he is, "is what interests Rose."

For Rose, too, is an artist figure in this story. The central focus of the narrative is on her attempt to understand Ralph and her feelings for him. The "disarrangement" in "Who Do You Think You Are?" is caused by the way Ralph's version of Milton Homer parallels (or does not parallel) Rose's version of Ralph. To what extent, the story leads us to ask, does Rose's account constitute a parody of the "real" Ralph, and to what extent is it an accurate reflection of his true being?

Rose's artistic task is, of course, much more difficult than Ralph's, since she is interested in what lies behind the social facade:

Her first impression of him, as boyishly shy and ingratiating, had to change. That was his surface. Underneath he was self-sufficient, resigned to living in bafflement, perhaps proud. She wished that he would speak to her from that level, and she thought he wished it, too, but they were prevented.

this scene, Rose meets Ralph for the first time in many years, but their encounter is characteristic of all their shared experience: Rose's perception of his inner self remains intuitive, unverified, and unexpressed, even to Ralph himself. Deciding not to reach out to him in this way, Rose observes that "There seemed to be feelings which could only be spoken of in translation..." (p. 205). Perhaps, then, her perception of Ralph is false or inadequate, and perhaps what truth there is in it cannot be articulated accurately.

Unlike Ralph's version of Milton Homer, her version of Ralph depends on the interpretation of that which cannot be defined in any "objective" way: attitudes, feelings, moral and psychological phenomena whose true nature can only be guessed at, however educated Rose's guess may be. Where Ralph's Milton Homer is recognizably a precise rendering of the surface, or public Milton Homer, Rose's ambitiously conceived Ralph is a multidimensional being, the hypothetical nature of whom Rose is herself only too well aware. Ralph tells us nothing of Milton Homer's internal reality; Rose tells us nothing verifiable about Ralph. The two approaches comment critically on each other, and neither is fully satisfactory. But Rose's way is superior, in the sense that it addresses that most deeply felt, if unfulfillable, of human needs: to know completely the person whose life is lived "one slot over" (p. 206) from one's own.

In *Who Do You Think You Are?*, Munro successfully keeps these two approaches in balance. Surface detail is — as always in her work — brilliantly realized, and it may seem that a world which is, in one sense, so vividly accessible to the reader should easily yield its meaning to him as well. And the critic who wishes to prove that Munro, too, does a good Milton Homer, will find much that can be confidently labelled "regional" or "feminist." But the art of disarrangement reminds us that any significant truth that literature delivers is a partial and provisional one. Rose's thoughts on her own acting ability make the point concisely: "...there was always something further, a tone, a depth, a light, that she couldn't get and wouldn't get" (p. 205). The context here, it is important to note, is not one of despair. Similarly, the consciousness that there is "always something further" permeates these stories, but far from providing a reason for Munro to abandon her art, it has given her the impetus to create more of it.

The value of the art of disarrangement, it might be said, lies in its continual commentary on its own tentativeness, in the face of life's complexity and mystery. It is not that the artist should abandon her attempt to render experience fully and accurately, anymore than Rose should stop trying to make sense of Ralph Gillespie. The point is, rather, that one should proceed warily, in humility, even, in a sense, quixotically. Munro's engagement in this endeavour, in full awareness of its difficulties, points to what will prove to be of enduring interest in her work.

NOTE

[1] Bronwen Wallace, "Women's Lives: Alice Munro," in *The Human Elements: Critical Essays*, ed. David Helwig (Ottawa: Oberon, 1978), p. 61.